THE POLITICS OF
LITERARY EXPRESSION

Contributions in Afro-American and African Studies
Series Adviser: Hollis R. Lynch

THE POLITICS OF LITERARY EXPRESSION

A Study of Major Black Writers

DONALD B. GIBSON

Contributions in Afro-American
and African Studies, Number 63

GREENWOOD PRESS
Westport, Connecticut • London, England

Library of Congress Cataloging in Publication Data

Gibson, Donald B
  The politics of literary expression.

  (Contributions in Afro-American and African
studies ; no. 63 ISSN 0069-9624)
  Bibliography: p.
  Includes index.
  1. American fiction—Afro-American authors—
History and criticism. 2. American fiction—
20th century—History and criticism. 3. Afro-
American authors—Political and social views.
4. Politics in literature. 5. Social problems
in literature. I. Title. II. Series.
PS374.N4G48   813'.009'896073   80-27284
ISBN 0-313-21271-6 (lib. bdg.)

Library of Congress Catalog Card Number: 80-27284
ISBN: 0-313-21271-6
ISSN: 0069-9624

First published in 1981

Greenwood Press
A division of Congressional Information Service, Inc.
88 Post Road West, Westport, Connecticut 06881

Printed in the United States of America

10 9 8 7 6 5 4 3 2 1

Copyright Acknowledgments

The author and publisher are grateful for permission to reprint from the following works.

Jean Toomer, *Cane* (New York: Boni and Liveright, 1923), copyright 1923 by Boni & Liveright, copyright renewed 1951 by Jean Toomer. Reprinted by permission of Liveright Publishing Corporation.

Ralph Ellison, *Invisible Man* (New York: Random House, 1952), copyright 1952 by Ralph Ellison. Reprinted by permission of Random House, Inc., and William Morris Agency, Inc., on behalf of author.

Specified material from pp. 106, 113 and 185 in *Uncle Tom's Children* by Richard Wright. Copyright 1938 by Richard Wright; renewed 1966 by Ellen Wright. Reprinted by permission of Harper & Row, Publishers, Inc.

Charles Chesnutt, *The Marrow of Tradition* (Ann Arbor: University of Michigan Press, 1969), copyright 1969 by the University of Michigan. Reprinted by permission of The University of Michigan Press.

For
David Marcus
and
Douglas Myers

Contents

I don't really care that much about art. I'm interested in life, and only in art in so far as it enables me to express what I feel about life.

—*Ben Shahn*

Preface

THIS BOOK IS WRITTEN from the assumption that writing is always and without exception value laden, that authors cannot write anything without expressing what they consider socially worthwhile and desirable. This is no less true of creative literature than of history, sociology, economics, and even science. In their expression of social value, writers always imply by the hundreds of creative choices they make that a particular way of thinking, acting, or believing is better than other ways of thinking, acting, or believing. The literary critics' job, then, is to describe and evaluate the value system informing literary works, and they do this by means of analysis of its social dimension. In so doing they will make explicit what is implicit in varying degrees in literature, the value system inherent in it that seeks to influence individuals and the society at large. Such value systems are antecedent to literature and are in kind incapable of distinction from the values that underlie law and social policy. Hence creative literature, in its expression of social value, is a political instrument. This is what I mean by the politics of literature.

I have dealt with the formal aspects of the works under considera- tion here only when their forms are directly related to their expression of value. I have not considered the aesthetic dimension of these works either. I do not consider that dimension unimportant, but I leave that to others in their own critical contexts.

I wish to thank Professor Hyatt H. Waggoner (who when he reads this text will think either that he is my Frankenstein or I his) for more than I can say here. I would also like to thank Professor Milton R. Stern for the many conversations we have had, however brief and uncompleted, about what literature is and what literary criticism should be. For support during various phases of this project, I wish to express great appreciation to the National Endowment for the Humanities, to the American Council of Learned Societies, to the Rutgers University Faculty Academic Study Program, and to the Rutgers University Foundation. I want also to thank the staffs of the libraries of the University of Iowa, Rutgers University, Princeton University, and Harvard University. Finally, for her invaluable aid in completing the final stages of this manuscript, I wish to thank Patricia Pratt.

THE POLITICS OF
LITERARY EXPRESSION

Introduction: Preface
to a Social Theory
of Literature

IF A STRAND of agreement has been clear among black critics and writers, it has been to the effect that a significant problem is involved when formalistic[1] methods of criticism are applied to the literature of black writers.[2] The reasons for this have to do in part with the theoretical base on which formalism rests and the resulting incompatibility when formalistic methods are used to deal with a literature based on entirely different assumptions. The relation between formalism and various modes of philosophical idealism is apparent in the values and beliefs of a great number of its early proponents and their later adherents. A number of the early formalists adopted religious beliefs wholly compatible with the assumptions underlying formalism.[3] Others, who were not necessarily practicing Catholics or Anglo-Catholics, subscribed to philosophical schemes not incompatible with specifically religious ones.

All formalists are not necessarily Christian, but a necessary relation exists between formalism and modes of thought not entirely naturalistic in orientation.[4] More particularly, however—and in order to avoid the argument about whether a critic may with consistency be a philosophical naturalist and a formalist—

the formalist, insofar as he or she emphasizes formalism, lifts the work of literature out of history and time in valuing those aspects of a work not subject (or at least seemingly so) to temporal limitation.[5]

Herein lies the rub. Most black writers of the past and of the present write with an eye to the social situation of the time in which they are writing. With few exceptions, black writers have produced literature that reflects their situations as social beings existing within a particular historical framework and subject to the pressures of a special nature resulting therefrom. This is true even of black writers most committed to the same assumptions underlying formalism. I cite as examples Robert Hayden and Melvin Tolson. Black writers, in the body of their work if not in its particulars always, seem unwilling to ignore the realities of race in American society. But even those who have deemphasized social matters and given a good deal of attention to form have not found their way to the hearts of formalists, even writers who like Tolson and Hayden have managed form very well. Of course those who have been quite expressive of social concern have been least acceptable to critics of a formalist persuasion, and this is in part because their work has been said to confine itself to the historical moment.[6]

In other ways formalism is a perspective inimical to the analysis and evaluation of the work of black writers. Formalists tend to be conservative. They tend to believe that reality is located somewhere outside the sphere of history and time and that individuals can do nothing to change that reality; or they believe that truth and reality exist inherent within institutions that represent the collective wisdom of humankind and hence should not be tampered with.[7] They tend to believe that institutions have divine sanction and should not be changed, or, if they are to be altered, they should assume earlier forms. Such an orientation allows for the possibility of literature's assuming a mode of existence beyond the historical, in the one case, or beyond the limitations of a particular historical period, in the other. In any case such beliefs theoretically may allow literature to exist apart from the social necessities or conditions of a particular time.[8] Such considerations have been responsible for the denigration of any literature that focuses on social issues. If social literature is not entirely denigrated by formalists, then its social character is diminished or destroyed by emphasis on its formal character. The conception that true literary value exists outside the limitations of time is also responsible for the charge most frequently leveled against the writing of black authors that it is parochial and incapable of withstanding the test of time.

The conservatism of formalists is not limited to literary matters. Formalists who are consistent in their thinking are likely to espouse political conservatism too.[9] Hence, when confronted with material by black writers that criticizes social institutions and in varying degrees suggests the necessity for change, formalist critics, reacting to values contrary to their principles, will respond negatively. If they do respond negatively on this score, they will perhaps take exception to the implication of literature by most black writers that present social reality takes precedence over conceptions locating essential reality elsewhere. The relation between political conservatism and racism becomes apparent here.[10] The formalist critic, ostensibly in the process of making literary assessments and analyses, is likely to be making judgments that have no relation whatsoever to literature as such.[11]

My point so far has been to amplify the argument that many black critics have made against formalist criticism. I find myself, however, uncomfortable with the argument as it now stands, a discomfort reflected in my conscious avoidance of the term *new critic*. Just as hardly anyone these days will lay claim to being a new critic, probably few will claim to be pure formalists. This consideration does not negate the argument. Most critics are probably eclectic, but the influence of formalism has been so astoundingly great that it, despite having lost its virginity through liaison with other perspectives, is alive, well, and thriving. Its influence exists in the work of any critic who either consciously believes that literary works are entities in and of themselves or treats them as such. The influence of formalism exists in any critical practice that does not carry the critic through the work to considerations beyond it. Hence mythological or psychological criticism may, though ostensibly something else entirely, carry on it the stamp of formalism.[12] Any scheme whose application implies acceptance of the notion that literature has a nature and character exclusively its own—no matter what the intention of the practitioner—suggests an underlying assumption that literature has some mode of existence peculiar to itself and consistent with the nature of things.[13]

The influence of formalism can also be seen in the widespread practice of clever, subjective interpretation of literary works.[14] Such interpretations may exist under the aegis of any critical scheme, but it was formalism that opened the way for the excesses of subjective interpretation. Formalism's emphasis on symbolic reading invites subjective interpretation that transmutes a work's social referent into idea and out of the realm of sociohistorical reality much in the same way that Don Quixote in his madness transformed windmills into giants and flocks of sheep into armies.[15] Formalism's insistence on the existence of some level of reality beyond the natural encourages attempts at intuitional discovery of or reference to that reality.[16]

Largely because of the influence of formalism, we are likely to prefer certain kinds of literary works to others. We tend to prefer the complex to the simple (though there is no justification for such preference beyond taste); we prefer the symbolic to the realistic; the indirect expression to the direct—paradox, irony, and ambiguity to simple statement.[17] Critics have tended to prefer these kinds of works, not because the simple, the realistic, the direct give us nothing to do (because they are open and unrequiring of explication), but because they reflect in their existence the idea that reality is confined to the physical world, that reality is no more than the facts made available to us by experience.

One need not be a formalist as such to practice criticism much in the way that a formalist would. The techniques of formalist analysis have been widely taught for at least twenty-five years, and I suspect that many have forgotten or never known what the sources of those techniques are or what their application means. In any case those techniques and modes of analysis have been so deeply ingrained that the fact that no one wants to be called a new critic does not answer the problem. Perhaps identification with the term is so meaningless because we are all new critics, and proclaiming oneself one is like inviting people to feel one's pulse.[18]

The salient point is not necessarily that the literature of black writers is anathema to formalism but rather that any critical scheme either sharing the basic assumptions of formalism or greatly influenced by its prejudice will not be compatible with the literature of black writers. Failure to recognize this has led to a lot of irrelevant commentary on the literature of black writers. For example, any analysis of Wright's *Native Son* as a symbolic construct—despite the clear and obvious fact that the book does indeed contain symbols—seriously misses the point.[19] Missing the point, however, is not the least of the problems of such an analysis. More important, it does utmost violence to the meaning of the novel, for it transmutes it into something entirely different from what it is. It recreates the novel, shifting its center of focus from a specific sociohistorical context to a realm removed from time and history, a distortion of the highest magnitude. Such a distortion results from a theoretical bias of such kind as to prompt the questions leading to the analysis of the novel as a symbolic construct, a bias clearly antithetical to the orientation of the novelist.

What I have said so far should suggest that the critics of literature by black writers are not free to apply whatever critical scheme they find at hand unless the critics intend to do violence to the material. When I say they are not free, I mean they are not free if their motives are positive ones. They are not free if they respect the literature with which they are dealing and if they want to discuss it in a meaningful way. All critical schemes have their basis in values antecedent to literary considerations, and critics need to know the implications of the critical frame of reference from which they proceed. Otherwise they may betray the very values they express in the concern itself with the literature of black writers. They must avoid distorting the work of black writers, translating it into terms so obviously distant from reality. I am not addressing myself to the critics who do not like black people or what they write and who use the literature to express their racism. I am talking instead to the critics who mean well by their criticism.

What then should a critical scheme look like that would be capable of including a literature explicitly social in character? In general terms I will delineate the broad outlines of such a theory, pointing to the direction it might take. My explanation is not intended to be definitive, since I could hardly present a full-scale critical theory in this context, nor have I worked out all the problems it involves.

My theory begins with the assumption that the universe is naturalistic in character; that is, all phenomena that occur in the universe and of which we have knowledge can be explained by reference to natural causation. Any forces, values, truths, realities existing outside the natural context are beyond the human capacity to know or apprehend them. This describes a kind of functional agnosticism and may, I believe, be assumed despite one's personal religious beliefs. Despite the problems this assumption might raise, I present it as a given and pass on in order not to be mired here.[20]

The implication of my theory is that any phenomenon of a social character is entirely social and historical in origin and character, that all values have their origins in history and have no sanction beyond their historical context. In relation to literature this means that literary value is a function of social value, that literary values are grounded in time, in history, and that values of a metaphysical character attributed to literature are extraneous and immaterial.[21] The mode of existence of a literary work is not problematical.[22] Its existence is no different from that of any other natural phenomenon. But what then about the mode of existence of a literary work within the context of tradition? Does the high evaluation of a work of literature over the years lend to that work a character and status beyond the historical moment? Does the test of time point to some essential character or nature which a work possesses that causes it to exist beyond its time? Does the work possess an inherent quality that defies the exigencies of time insofar as it lasts from generation to generation? Again the answer is no. From my perspective, every work is a product of culture and as such bears a certain relation to culture. Whatever allows the existence of a classic literary work is within the cultural context, which claims its own classics, and is not in the work itself. Otherwise I should think that all cultures would share the same classics. A classic exists in relation to the needs of a particular culture and will remain a classic only as long as it fulfills those needs. The discovered classic was not a classic before it was discovered and named such. If *Moby Dick* had to await the twentieth century to be recognized as an American classic, it is because the nineteenth and the early twentieth centuries did not need *Moby Dick*, not because contemporary Americans are more perceptive, sensitive, and knowledgeable about literature than were their forebears.

It has been said that the function of literature follows from its nature. Wellek and Warren in *Theory of Literature* say that the function of a work of literature is to be true to the claims of its own nature.[23] I have already implied that literature has no nature; it has character that allows us to distinguish it from other phenomena, but it has no nature any more than a tree has a nature. Trees were something else before they became trees and in the evolutionary process are probably becoming something else. Trees have characteristics and character but not an essential nature. So do works of literature.[24]

If literature has no nature but has instead character, then what is its function?[25] If we conceive of literature as having its roots in society and culture, then we might assume that its function must in some way be social and cultural, and if this is so, then literature must serve a function not different in kind from that served by other widespread cultural phenomena. If it is related to cultural need, then it is unlikely that its function is merely to bring pleasure, amusement, or joy. That can be done in less expensive ways. Pleasure, amusement, and joy may be produced by literature, but those are not its primary functions.[26] Any cultural phenomenon that involves as great an expenditure of time, energy, and money as the pursuit of literature in all its phases must be for something other than amusement. The resources of the society that go into literature, its teaching, criticism, publication, and distribution, are great whether literature is broadly defined (as simply creative or imaginative in character) or narrowly defined (as belles lettres).

The question of the function of literature is the same question as, What does literature do for the culture? If we were to ask the question about children's literature, the answer might be more convincing than about literature for adults. Literature, however, generally does essentially the same thing: It sustains currently existing values and standards of the society; it keeps the social fabric intact. To a considerably lesser extent (and I cannot emphasize "considerably" enough), it may even criticize those standards and values as a means of allowing some possibility of change. Even so, the end is the same: to sustain and legitimate the institutions of the society; to render harmonious the relation between the majority of people and the social structure.

What then are the implications in regard to the practical criticism of literature by black writers? First, such an orientation as this eliminates the bias against black writers inherent in critical schemes that locate literary values beyond the temporal. Critics who use this approach deal with the literature in regard to its relation to social values. They ask what values of a social character the writer intends through his or her writing to support. They ask how the writer stands in regard to social institutions, what his or her social values and politics are, and whether the writer professes values that would tend to support or to challenge those values responsible for oppression within that society. They ask whether the writer is reactionary or liberal, conservative or radical in orientation, for they assume that the writer wants to convince a reading public that some things are good and others bad.[27] Such questions do not indicate a simplistic attempt at categorizing writers, for no two writers stand exactly in the same place, and the differences among them are as the color variation in the spectrum.

Since this approach emphasizes idea, it is not averse to definition of the writer's message.[28] On the one hand, it does not eliminate the work that intentionally has a message, and on the other, it assumes that all works have a message, whether implicit or explicit. The poet MacLeish has said, "A poem must not mean, but be"; I would say, "A poem cannot be without meaning."[29] The large proportion of literature by black writers carries a relatively explicit message about the society and about the black person's position in the society. Because of this, and because the message is often about oppression, literature by black writers has been denigrated as parochial—not universal in character. The approach outlined here does away with the notion of universality as a literary value, since the concept itself is expressive of a prospective that values distance from the particularities of social existence. The point is made by reference to the inclination on the part of many critics to universalize the materials of black writers, to remove them from their particular social contexts, and hence to make them acceptable, palatable. The tendency is seen in the critical commentary on *Invisible Man*, which has emphasized its protagonist as representing the plight of "twentieth-century Western man" or such.[30]

The interest in message proposed here has ramifications in relation to the form-content problem. Had R. P. Blackmur spoken about a hypothetical novel from the perspective suggested here, he would have said (instead of saying that Wright paid attention to everything in *Native Son* except the writing) that our hypothetical writer paid attention to all the problems of writing and none of the problems of race.[31] The point is that here we would emphasize the primacy of content over form. That does not say that form is not significant; such a position is untenable. It does say, however, that the critic will be concerned with form only insofar as that issue relates to the expression of value and obviously not as an issue in itself. A clear relation between form and value emerges when we consider social involvement: The greater the writer's commitment to the idea that literature is its own end, the greater his or her concern for the formal aspect of writing. Conversely, the greater the writer's social commitment, the less attention he or she is likely to give to matters of form.[32] Consequently considerations of form are significant, for a writer's social values are often expressed by his or her handling of form. Again this is not a simple matter: The question is never whether a writer gives attention to form but the extent to which the writer's effort is directed toward perfection of form. The complexity comes in describing accurately the relative value that a writer places on form in relation to the character of the content of his or her writing. Hence the intent is not to establish simple categories.

The question of content brings to mind the tremendous extent to which critics of all persuasions have given attention to content. The fact that some works seem acceptable on the basis of their content and others do not leads one to believe that, in the work of critics ostensibly given to considerations of form, cards are being passed beneath the table or at best being dealt from the bottom of the deck. Some content seems more acceptable than other content. Eliot's commentary about his conversion seems more acceptable than Wright's commentary about the character of his early life. The point is that, for good or ill, the relevance or irrelevance of content is likely to be determined by the extent to which that content supports the basic assumptions of the critic about what is important in life.[33]

Such a consideration seems to bear on the question of literary aesthetics. I do not believe that a distinction exists between aesthetic values and other values. Ostensible judgments of value made on an aesthetic basis always express values unrelated to the objects of their attention. Although in relatively few instances do critics make judgments of literary worth on an explicitly aesthetic basis (outside of reviews perhaps), such judgments are constantly made implicitly.

In regard to evaluative judgments, the implications of this perspective are clear. A literary work needs to be judged in relation to the comment it makes about the society. A work that might be beautiful in form, in the manner of expression, in the character of its figures of speech, must be adjudged negatively if its message is reactionary. There can be no good poems about the necessity of gas chambers or the value of authoritarian political organization.[34] Of course, even critics who might accept the basic premises outlined here might disagree, but since the appeal to absolute authority is precluded by those premises, such a limitation is implicit. Again the question is not simple, for specific determinations have not been made as to the character of the social commentary that a work makes. Simply stated, it should not be contradictory to the basic assumptions and it should be progressive in kind.

In writing about the literature of black writers the critic may ask, in addition to the questions suggested above, any number of questions designed to reveal the social orientation of the writer. What attitudes does the writer reveal about social class, race, religion, politics, women, economics, individualism? What does the writer have to say about authority—where it exists, who exercises it, what the response of the individual to it should be, what are its origins and justifications? These are only some of the questions that might be asked, but these alone in their ramifications indicate countless other questions of a more specific nature.

I have intended to describe a theoretical scheme that will not by definition exclude the great concerns of the majority of black writers. It assumes that any particular black writer or black person may be anything insofar as his or her attitudes and values are concerned and further that the social and political reality of blackness supersedes other considerations. Just as literature is the expression of value that has as its end to influence attitudes and thus to justify or modify behavior, so does the act of criticism. Just as the creative act is a social act, so is the critical act, and critics express attitudes and values in the act of criticizing as do historians, sociologists, economists, or physicists in the act of performing their professional activities.[35] The criticism of literature is a social and ultimately a political act, the criticism of literature by black writers no more or less so. My advocacy finally is for a theoretical basis for a practical criticism—not one essentially black in character but one that certainly does not exclude or denigrate black writers and social writers in general. This seems to me the proper direction, for the main difficulty of criticism has been that it quite openly has neglected black writers. The causes of that neglect are not separable from the causes of racism and other forms of oppression in our society.

The following essays intend to exemplify what criticism may look like if based on the preceding assumptions. I hope the scheme outlined is broad enough to admit of a wide variety of approaches to literature, not only of black writers but to literature as a whole. The essays are not definitive in any sense. Much more needs to be said not only about these five writers but about many other writers as well, about theory, about literary history, and about theory of literary history. I hope this book will move others to work along at least in the general, if not specific, direction pointed to here.

NOTES

1. Although it might be difficult to find a pure formalist, a point made in greater detail below, I will define in ideal terms what is usually meant

by the word. The best simple definition is that given by René Wellek and Austin Warren in *Theory of Literature*, 2d ed. (New York: Harcourt, Brace, and World, 1955), p. 231: "Modern critics limiting themselves to aesthetic criticism are commonly called 'formalists'—sometimes by themselves, sometimes (pejoratively) by others. As we shall use it here, it names the aesthetic structure of a literary work—that which makes it literature."

2. See Addison Gayle, Jr., *The Way of the New World* (Garden City, N.Y.: Anchor Books, Doubleday, 1976), pp. ix-xii.

3. For example, Allen Tate, Cleanth Brooks, and Austin Warren. The idea of critical heresy, not new in the twentieth century, was so prevalent because of its implication that certain acts of criticism were analogous to deviations from religious orthodoxy. The term *heresy* itself has strictly religious denotation. I find it incredible that literary critics in the twentieth century would find heretics among their number.

4. The basis for one's assumptions about what art or literature essentially is lies antecedent to considerations of aesthetics. Certain assumptions about the nature of things preclude the formalist's conclusion that art has a "nature," for such a conclusion lends to art an ontological dimension, a status beyond the natural. If, therefore, the formalist describes the mode of existence of a literary work of art, that mode is of necessity philosophically idealistic. Wellek and Warren, *Theory of Literature*, wrestle mightily with this problem in their chapter "The Mode of Existence of a Literary Work of Art," only to beg the question by asserting that literature has "a special ontological status" (p. 144), but they do not seem to realize that their whole argument applies not only to poetry but to any written language. According to the argument, "Kilroy was here" has the same ontological status as Keats's "Ode."

5. Two examples will suffice to make the point. First, "Art imposes some kind of framework which takes the statement of the work [of art] out of the world of reality." Wellek and Warren, *Theory of Literature*, p. 13. Second, "Allen Tate, speaking of the 'Cantos,' writes that Ezra Pound's 'powerful juxtapositions of the ancient, the Renaissance, and the modern worlds reduce all three elements to an unhistorical miscellany, timeless and without origin.' " Joseph Frank, "Spatial Form in Modern Literature," *Sewanee Review* 60: (Spring, summer, and autumn 1945). Reprinted in its entirety in Mark Schoerer, Josephine Miles, and Gordon McKinzie, *Criticism: The Foundations of Modern Literary Judgment* (New York: Harcourt, Brace and World, 1948), p. 392.

6. For a detailed discussion of this point, see Hoyt Fuller, "Towards a Black Aesthetic," in *The Black Aesthetic*, ed. Addison Gayle, Jr. (Garden City, N.Y.: Anchor Books, Doubleday, 1972), pp. 3-6.

7. The classic statement of such conservatism is T. S. Eliot's comment in his introduction to *For Lancelot Andrews* (London: Faber and Grier, 1928), p. ix: "The general point of view may be described as classicist in literature, royalist in politics, and Anglo-Catholic in religion."

8. A case in point is John Steinbeck's *The Grapes of Wrath*. Nothing is wrong per se in discussing its structure or symbolism, but any study that does not grow out of the critic's basic awareness of the novel's historicity, its implications regarding contemporary social and economic policy, cannot but distort the novel's clear meaning. The opposite perspective is taken by Howard Levant, *The Novels of John Steinbeck* (Columbia: University of Missouri Press, 1974), p. 93, who says, "Continuing sales and critical discussions suggest that *The Grapes of Wrath* has outlived its directly reportorial ties to the historical past; that it can be considered as an aesthetic object, a good or bad novel per se. In that light, the important consideration is the relative harmony of its structure and materials."

9. Allen Tate, John Crowe Ransom, Robert Penn Warren, and Donald Davidson are among the most prominent of the apologists for formalism in the 1920s and later. *I'll Take My Stand* proudly asserts the politically reactionary stance of these literary men. A reissue of the book, edited by Virginia Rock and Louis D. Rubin (New York: Harper and Brothers, 1962), contains biographical sketches of the twelve contributors to the volume. In the sketch on Donald Davidson, Virginia Rock writes, "A nirvana of objectivity makes no appeal to Davidson; he stands firm against 'progress' reduced to statistical measure, against an acceptance of determinism by social 'forces,' against racial integration. In 1954 he became chairman of the Tennessee Federation for Constitutional Government, opposing desegregation on the principle of states' rights" (p. 365).

10. See n. 9.

11. This is based on the assumption that values exist in a system and must of necessity exist in relation to each other. We strive constantly to reconcile contradictory values yet may concurrently hold and support values that are contradictory. For the most part, though, value schemes are consistent. This means that it is possible to hold literary values not in accord with one's political, social, and philosophical values, but it is more likely that literary values will accord with other values.

12. It has not been the least bit unusual in recent times to use psychology or mythology in the explication of texts. If the critic's use of psychology or mythology has as its end to treat the text as an independent entity, a discrete phenomenon, then I would say that such a critical exercise carries the stamp of formalism.

13. Although Wellek and Warren, *Theory of Literature*, distinguish

between their sense of how a work of literary art exists and the phenomenologists' perspective, which assumes "an eternal, not-temporal order of 'essences,' " (p. 145), vestiges of such an assumption remain in their thinking. When, for example, they speak of a work of art having "a special ontological status" (p. 144), when they identify the nature of literature with its structure by stating, "The use of a thing—its habitual or most expert or proper use—must be that use to which its nature (or its structure) designs it" (p. 228), one cannot but infer that literature, properly viewed, is, in essence, consistent with the nature of things.

14. There are literally hundreds and hundreds of examples of such criticism, so many that citing any particular one seems hardly necessary to make the point. Any reader who does not recall instances may refer to any issue of the *Explicator*.

15. Cleanth Brooks, while not making exactly the same point I do here, complains about the excesses of imaginative exercise that formalism has fostered: "The symbol-mongering that I speak of is a grotesque parody of anything like an adequate 'close reading.' It magnifies details quite irresponsibly; it feverishly prospects for possible symbolic meanings and then forces them beyond the needs of the story." Brooks, *A Shaping Joy: Studies in the Writer's Craft* (London: Methuen and Co., 1971), p. 144.

16. If we are dealing with the unknown and the unverifiable when we study literature, then we may feel free to create arbitrary constructs explicating it. At best, such constructs are logically consistent and make some real difference in how the work is read.

17. The point is apparent in a great deal of criticism. The theoretical point is made by W. K. Wimsatt, Jr.: "Every good poem is a complex poem and may be demonstrated so by rhetorical analysis. And further it is only in virtue of its complexity that it has artistic unity. Without complexity it could have the unity of a cobblestone but not that of a typewriter." Wimsatt, "The Structure of the 'Concrete Universal' in Literature," *PMLA* 62: 275.

18. The publication of Wellek and Warren's *Understanding Poetry* (New York: Henry Holt and Co., 1939) was indeed a landmark in establishing the direction of criticism and the character of that criticism for years to come. Prior to its publication, critics were talking to one another, and that conversation obviously had an effect on teaching. But with *Understanding Poetry* the influence of formalism was exerted directly on the undergraduate population of students taking English courses. That textbook is probably the most influential literature text ever to come into existence.

19. A good example is Robert Bone's discussion of Wright's novel: "Book III, therefore the novel, suffers from a major structural flaw,

flowing from the fact that Wright has failed to digest Communism artistically. The Communist party is simply not strong enough as a symbol of relatedness." Bone, *The Negro Novel in America* (New Haven: Yale University Press, 1958), p. 150. Such a comment is as relevant to the meaning of the text as the color of the dust jacket.

20. The proposition is not to be argued since it, as well as other propositions of its kind, is incapable of logical proof or demonstration.

21. Probably few in our time would argue explicitly for the metaphysical character of literature. We are far too worldly for that. The argument (or assumption) is frequently made obliquely, however, whenever reference is made to timelessness. (See n. 5.) The assumption underlies Eliot's reference to "monuments of literature" in "Tradition and the Individual Talent," *Selected Essays of T. S. Eliot* (New York: Harcourt Brace and Co., 1950), p. 5.

22. The argument put forth by Wellek and Warren, in "The Mode of Existence of a Literary Work of Art," *Theory of Literature*, with its description of a poem as "a system of norms of ideal concepts" and likening it to a system of language, is indeed impressive. One cannot help but feel, however, that the intention of the argument is to lend metaphysical status to the structures of works of art. For this reason they say, finally, that the work of literary art has "a special ontological status," thus having it both ways. Underlying their argument is the assumption that literature has a unique quality that differentiates it absolutely from other phenomena.

23. Ibid., p. 26.

24. Wellek and Warren, in ibid., identify "nature" with "structure." The point is ably made by E. D. Hirsch: "In one respect aesthetic criticism has been distortive. By claiming to be intrinsic to the nature of literature, it implies that the nature of literature is aesthetic. But, in fact, literature has no independent essence, aesthetic or otherwise. . . . Aesthetic categories are intrinsic to aesthetic *inquiries*, but not to the nature of literary works." Hirsch, "Some Aims of Criticism: The Literary Study of Literature," in Frank Brady, John Palmer, and Martin Price, eds., *Literary Theory and Structure* (New Haven: Yale University Press, 1973), p. 52.

25. The assumption here is that the function of literature follows from the conception of what it is.

26. Conceptions of what literature is fall within the Horatian categories of *dulce* or *utile*, being one or the other or a combination of the two, with the emphasis being more or less on one or the other. But these are not mutually exclusive categories. In culture even joy, amusement, or pleasure has a function in relation to the sustaining of the coherence of the whole.

27. "When we talk about people's politics, we really talk about their ways of seeing the meanings of human experience. We are really talking about deep attitudes and visions, often unspoken and even unformulated, concerning the nature of human possibility and, therefore, the nature and possibility and desirability of liberation and, therefore again, the nature and function of the state, the very concept of government. It is the underlying visions that I refer to when I say that *Billy Budd* is a political fiction and when I refer to politics as universal in human affairs." Milton R. Stern, ed., introduction to Herman Melville, *Billy Budd* (Indianapolis: Bobbs-Merrill, 1975), p. xx.

28. Cleanth Brooks has had a great deal to say about literature and communication. See, for example, Brooks, "The Heresy of Paraphrase," in *The Well-Wrought Urn* (New York: Harcourt, Brace and Co., 1947). Elsewhere Brooks has commented on the same problem: "[I. A.] Richards, no more than Tate or Ransom, would accept the dilemma which the Marxist critic offers: that of propaganda art on the one hand and the Ivory Tower on the other. For him, a poem is not a more or less true statement in metrical garb, but an organization of experience, and it is in terms of what may be called its psychological structure—the resolution, inter-animation, and balancing of impulses—that all the more valuable effects of poetry must be described. He has expressed this more simply and emphatically in the statement that 'it is never what a poem says that matters, but what it is.' " Brooks, *Modern Poetry and the Tradition* (Chapel Hill: University of North Carolina Press, 1939), pp. 47-48.

29. Compare Stern, introduction to *Billy Budd*, p. xix: "I will go so far as to say that in its deepest concerns almost all serious literature is political."

30. An example is William J. Schafer, "*Invisible Man*: Somebody's Protest Novel," in John Hersey, ed., *Ralph Ellison: A Collection of Critical Essays* (Englewood Cliffs, N.J.: Prentice-Hall, 1974), p. 126: "The problem of identity and existence that Ellison poses transcends the issues of social justice and equity; it is not a question of 'the Negro problem' or 'race issues.' "

31. "*Native Son* is one of those books in which everything is taken with seriousness except the writing." R. P. Blackmur, *Language As Gesture* (London: George Allen and Unwin, 1954), p. 413.

32. I am sure this generalization does not hold in some cases, but I believe it stands up as a generalization. It should not suggest that writers want either to write a poem or to deliver a message. Both motives are always operative when an author writes. The question is one of degree: To what extent does the writer wish to produce a beautiful object; to what extent does he or she wish to write a letter to the world?

33. Only pure phenomenologists would insist that it is possible to deal with a work of art without reference to our values as critics. See Wellek and Warren, *Theory of Literature*, pp. 144-45. C. S. Lewis comments on the relation between the values of the critic and those expressed in the work of literature: "[Shelley's] *Epipsychidion* raises in an acute form a problem with which Mr. Eliot has been much occupied: I mean the problem of the relation between our judgment on a poem as critics, and our judgments as men on the ethics, metaphysics, or theology presupposed or expressed in the poem. For my part, I do not believe that the poetic value of the poem is identical with the philosophic; but I think they can differ only to a limited extent, so that every poem whose prosaic or intellectual basis is silly, shallow, perverse, or illiberal, or even radically erroneous, is in some degree crippled by that fact. I am thus obliged to rate Epipsychidion rather low, because I consider the thought implied in it a dangerous delusion." Lewis, *Rehabilitations* (Cambridge: Oxford University Press, 1939), pp. 26-27.

34. One's response to this particular question probably rests on the necessity of logical consistency in that if prior assumptions require that the work of art be distant from the observer or critic, that the work of art is an entity standing more or less independently, then one responds to the question in a predictable way. The converse is also true.

When Coleridge suggested in "Occasion of the Lyrical Ballads" the desirability (not necessity) of "that willing suspension of disbelief, which constitutes poetic faith," he meant something different from what Cleanth Brooks means when he says "that in 'reading well' we are willing to allow our various interests as human beings to become subordinated to the total experience." Brooks, *Well-Wrought Urn*, p. 253.

35. "Literature and criticism are social functions. . . . The critic and scholar will increasingly realize that he is socially engaged in all his activities." Walter Sutton, *Modern American Criticism* (Englewood Cliffs, N.J.: Prentice-Hall, 1963), p. 289.

1

Richard Wright:
The Politics
of a Lone Marxian

FEW AMERICAN WRITERS have been as consistently political in mood and outlook as Richard Wright. Throughout the 1930s many writers were politically oriented, but most of them changed their politics with the changing of the time, some reversing their leftist leanings entirely and becoming political reactionaries of the worst sort. Wright is not among these. His politics changed over the course of the years and his fiction reflects that change, but unlike some others, he did not alter a number of his basic social ideas and values. Wright never strayed so far from his early thoughts about literature as to repudiate the spirit of the values reflected there. More specifically, Wright believed in the 1930s that literature should have social ends. This idea never changed. In no work throughout his career is the social dimension neglected: From beginning to end, Wright remained a social critic.

In his 1937 essay "Blueprint for Negro Writing" Wright describes what he sees as the nature and function of literature, indicating his belief that literature by black writers (and by implication all writers) should have definite and specific ends beyond itself:[1]

This chapter is a revised version of the author's address at the University of Iowa's Institute for Afro-American Culture, July 1971.

> Every short story, novel, poem, and play should carry
> within its lines, implied or explicit, a sense of the oppres-
> sion of the Negro people, the danger of war, of fascism,
> of the threatened destruction of culture and civilization;
> and, too, the faith and necessity to build a new world.[2]

In the beginning of the essay, Wright speaks of the necessity for
black writers to define their task in relation to the working class,
standing "shoulder to shoulder with Negro workers in mood and
outlook." The character of the essay as a whole indicates clearly
Wright's belief that literature should serve a social function, should
take its place in political struggle toward the achievement of progressive ends. This position seems, to say the least, somewhat
doctrinaire.

At the same time, however, Wright, in a careful attempt in his
blueprint to avoid the narrowness of critics and writers of similar
persuasion, found it wise to admit and deal with certain problematical aspects of his position. He had, for example, to deal with
aesthetic considerations, with writing as a craft,[3] with the problem
of literature as propaganda.[4] He admits, in short, the relevance of
the position of those who see literature as an end in itself, who
agree with Wellek and Warren in *Theory of Literature* that the
function of literature is to be true to the claims of its own nature.[5]
In discussing the role of nationalism in the work of black writers,
Wright admits at once the necessity and the limitations of nationalism, saying that black writers must accept nationalism only to
transcend it.[6] In regard to Marxism as a frame of reference from
which to write, he says that though it has the capacity to "unify
the writer's personality, organize his emotions, and buttress him
with a tense and obdurate will to change the world," it is "yet, for
the writer . . . but the starting point."[7] The quality of mind apparent here, a quality that allowed Wright to deal with elements
antithetical to his professed beliefs, is operative in his fiction. In his
first three long works, *Lawd Today*, *Uncle Tom's Children*, and
Native Son, he puts forth a certain political vision. In each case
elements antithetical to his vision obtrude, elements inconsistent
with his apparent political vision. After these works Wright vacil-

lates, leaning more and more toward the expression and embracing of those obtrusive elements, of values primarily private and subjective in nature (as opposed to social, political, and objective), until finally his emphasis is the opposite from that with which he began.[8] As the one waxes, the other wanes. His most private, subjective expression comes finally during the course of his fiction-writing career to be in diametrically opposite relation to the social and political.

We may say, in consequence, that in certain ways Wright remains true to the conception of writing set forth in "Blueprint for Negro Writing," and in certain ways he does not. Wright is careful in all of his fiction to set a social framework and to indicate a relation between the situation of the individual and the social context in which the individual functions. The social dimension is always present and its impingement clear. However, within this framework, Wright's work becomes increasingly personal and subjective during the course of his career. Early in his career and before he left the Communist party, this subjective quality was in part probably responsible for the doubts the party had about Wright's reliability.[9] The party was right in that from the beginning, elements of Wright's fiction were inimical to the party's political aims. If "Blueprint for Negro Writing" was not suspect in the same way *Native Son* was among party members, it should have been, for even in that early piece Wright's resistance to any definitive, all-inclusive system, his skepticism and unwillingness ever to give himself over entirely to any system of values outside his own, should have been apparent.[10] It is clearly apparent in Wright's first extended fictional work, *Lawd Today*.

Lawd Today describes two worlds: the world as it appears to the central character, Jake, and the world as it is from the perspective of the author.[11] The novel's framework describes the system of institutions responsible for the character and situation of Jake. It contains a perspective considerably broader than his, a perspective of which he is only dimly aware and has no understanding. The broader view is the author's, and the interplay between the two views produces a not overly subtle irony. The action takes place during the course of a single day, February 12, Abraham Lincoln's birthday. The reader is intended to see the disparity between the ideals associated with this national holiday and the actuality of the lives of Jake and his associates. They do not live in squalor—Jake eats well, dresses well, is personally clean, and has a good job—but the quality of their lives as described gives the impression of sordidness and poverty. For example, his friend Slim suffers from tuberculosis, and Bob carries a venereal disease.

Jake is shown to be victimized by the government, by others in the ghetto, and by his own ignorance and naive notions about life and the world. He also suffers from his irascibility, irresponsibility, and immaturity. The implication is that all of these qualities are related, that Jake's character and temperament are the result in part of the influence on him of forces beyond his control. Despite this, however, Wright lacks sympathy almost entirely, to the extent of despising Jake. The only time Wright seems not to judge Jake harshly is during the times Jake is victimized by racism or thinks consciously of racial oppression. At such times Wright seems to view Jake as a black victim, his case representative of all black victimization. For the most part, however, as when his wife slashes him in self-defense at the end of the book or when he is robbed at the blind pig, we are likely to feel that Jake merely gets his just deserts.

This element of the novel, its tone, contrasts sharply with the ostensible intention of the novel. Had *Lawd Today* been written by a white, it would be seen at once as the most blatantly racist of novels. (The description in the novel of Jake dressing to go out is an example.) At the same time, the reader is intended to recognize the rampant racism encountered by black people, the inequities of capitalism and its relation to racism, the effects of these forces on the lives of the particular individuals, and the disparity between American ideals and actuality. Hence *Lawd Today* is radical in its attack on American social institutions but conservative in its rather traditional sense of manners and morality, the standard by which its characters are judged personally. This same paradox seems present in most of Wright's subsequent fiction, although it takes different forms. Wright the social and political man and Wright the person, the discrete, particular human individual, were often not one and the same.

In *Uncle Tom's Children*, Wright's first published book, both stances are apparent.[12] Considered in its entirety, the book obviously was written by an author whose primary concerns are social in character. Each of the stories centers around social problems; the resolution of each plot points markedly toward social issues. The significant factor, however, has to do with the nature of the values implicit within each story, for although all are socially oriented, they differ in the specific degree to which they intend to advocate a political ideology, the value of a political response. The first three stories invite a sympathetic emotional response and moral judgment only; the other two urge concerted, aggressive action against social oppression. The first three are not ideologically based, except in the broadest sense; the others are written from the vantage point of Marxist ideology. In the one case Wright created from his own personal, particular values and vision; in the other, his views are more in line with a particular political framework.

Although written during the time Wright was most committed to the Communist party, *Uncle Tom's Children* gives every evidence of his unwillingness (or perhaps his inability) to function within the confines of a doctrinaire Marxism. "Big Boy Leaves Home" is by no means Marxist, despite the popular tendencies among naive reactionaries to equate racial protest and communism. Group action takes place, but it is defensive in character, has only the survival of the protagonist as its end, and is not undertaken in relation to class interests. The survival of the protagonist is largely dependent on his own individual capacities, and the culmination of the story does not imply a specifically and intentionally political orientation. The story is, of course, political in implication in its assessment of social institutions and their role in the creation of the conflict. A similar interpretation may be made of "Down by the Riverside," although that story is explicitly critical of the role of the military institution in enforcing and sustaining oppression. Still the focus is upon the fate of a particular individual; its despair and the sense of hopelessness it conveys are hardly suggestive of the possibility of humans exerting influence on their destinies. On the other hand, these stories are not unlike many Marxist-oriented stories that have as their end the revelation of conditions calling for social change. It is in this area that they may be seen as reflecting a

Marxist perspective, but the revelation of atrocious social conditions, of course, is not limited to Marxist writing.

Although I think it a terribly mistaken reading, one critic has interpreted "Big Boy Leaves Home" as symbolically reminiscent of the myth of the garden of Eden, its theme being "a familiar one in American literature: the initiation of a youth into violence and his escape from it. Big Boy, indeed, may be considered a kind of postpubescent black Huck Finn who must light out for the territory . . . in order to achieve his freedom."[13] This reading is mistaken because it blunts the story's clear emphasis on a particular geographical location and historical time, relegating its deeper meaning, its most significant meaning, to a far broader category (the experience of "Western man") than that to which it clearly belongs. There simply is no "garden" in the story, as the critic says; the snake in the story does not tempt the woman, and the woman does not tempt Big Boy, at least from no perspective other than the white woman's fiancé's.

The reading of the story as about adolescent development can be supported more easily because the character is indeed between childhood and adulthood, and the plot shows him at the beginning of his assumption of adult perogatives, chief among which is his final independence from parental authority and social dictate. Big Boy is indeed forced to grow up very quickly, but he is physically and emotionally equipped to do so. The title of the story also points toward this analysis. What, then, is the emphasis of the story: character or social situation? Indeed the progression of the stories reveals an increasing interest and focus on the social and a diminishing focus on individual character, but even in the most doctrinaire stories, the role of the specific character within the social environment is not neglected. Had Wright been more doctrinaire, his fiction more committed to political ideology, the emphasis on the delineation of individual character would have been yet slighter.

"Down by the Riverside" yields the same conclusion, its title finally becoming, in relation to the plot's outcome, slightly ironic. The title comes from the black spiritual:

> I'm going to lay down my sword and shield,

> Down by the riverside,
> Down by the riverside.
>
> I'm going to lay down my sword and shield,
> Down by the riverside.
> Ain't gone study war no more.

The irony resides in the fact that the passivity advocated by the spiritual has no place in the world described in the story. The time dictates the need indeed to "study war," and the attempt on the part of the central character, Mann, to live honestly and justly has as its outcome his involvement in circumstances that mean certain death for him.[14] Juxtaposed against the futility of Mann's situation, a situation imposed upon him by no fault of his own beyond his doing what any man might to preserve and protect his family, is his supreme will exerted at the conclusion of the story not to save himself, for that is impossible, but to choose the time of his own death, a heroic though futile action. The tone of the story indicates the author's respect for that action's meaningfulness; yet the context leads, in relation to the title, to a slight irony. I attribute the disparity to Wright's sympathetic expression of a perspective inconsistent with his professed politics. Were the theme of the story that a man alone has little chance (as in Hemingway's *To Have and Have Not*), I doubt that Wright would have been as strongly supportive of, insistent on, the heroism of Mann's death. I also doubt that Wright would have suggested, as the story does, that Mann's fate is analogous to "man's." His death is indeed not meaningless if the story's social meaning is attended to, for his death shows the unmitigated inhumanity of oppression.[15] In any case "Down by the Riverside" is not in any strict sense the expression of a Marxist position. Wright's personal experience either contravenes the necessity of ideological expression or at best minimizes its importance.

In "Long Black Song" the tension between Wright the public author, the ideologue, the writer of social protest, and Wright the private author, the purveyor of privately held beliefs, ideas, and symbols comes to the fore in a clearer, more explicitly bifurcated way than anywhere else. The story is divided into two sections, the first belonging to Sarah and the second to Silas, her husband. In a sense Sarah dominates the whole narrative in that it is all perceived from her vantage point, but the values implicit in the story belonging to Sarah are by no means negated by those belonging to Silas. The story is finally paradoxical, for Wright refuses to judge the two sets of values and does not come to a conclusion, even a qualified one.

The first section of "Long Black Song" constitutes the most highly symbolic writing of Wright's published fiction, and most interestingly, and expectedly, its symbolic character is basic to and inseparable from the system of values it articulates. Sarah, reminiscent of several of Jean Toomer's characters in *Cane* (the whole story, for that matter, is more typical of Toomer than of Wright), is a dreamer, a person whose imaginative life is more real than her actual life, whose most vital energies are channeled into fantasy, whose feelings are dominant and whose sexuality is not completely constrained by legal or rational considerations.[16] A creature of unfulfilled longings, she is unsatisfied emotionally and sexually with her practical, pragmatic husband, and with the character and quality of her life. Her imagination and tendency to fantasize are so strong as to overcome her knowledge that social distinctions have real existence, her desire being to see and to deal with reality as though it were all one, all phases of it unified and synthesized— hence her willing seduction by the traveling clock salesman unites past and present, the salesman and Tom (her lover prior to marrying Silas), her unfulfilled longings, her expression of these through sexual intercourse.[17] Racial and social distinctions, all practical considerations, finally disappear under the pressure of her imagination, and through the imposition on actuality of imagination she seeks the fulfillment of long-standing hopes and desires. Prior to the arrival at the farm of the salesman she recalls her youth:

> Never in all her life had she been so much alone as she was now. Days were never so long as these days; and nights were never so empty as these nights. . . . Yes, there had been all her life the long hope of white bright days and the deep desire of dark black nights and then

> Silas had gone. . . . There had been laughter and eating
> and singing and the long gladness of green cornfields in
> summer. There had been cooking and sewing and
> sweeping and the deep dream of sleeping grey skies in
> winter. Always it had been like that and she had been
> happy. But no more. The happiness of those days and
> nights, of those green cornfields and grey skies had
> started to go from her when Tom had gone to war. His
> leaving had left an empty black hole in her heart, a
> black hole that Silas had come in and filled. But not
> quite.[18]

Later, at the moment of her sexual climax, the point is made
through parallels of language that the experience of sexual relations
with the salesman is a synthesizing experience, drawing together a
whole complex of feeling and emotions, concentrating them in one
moment and altering the character of her present life and its
circumstances:

> A liquid metal covered her and she rode on the curve of
> white bright days and dark black nights and the surge of
> the long gladness of summer and the ebb of the deep
> dream of sleep in winter till a high red wave of hotness
> drowned her in a deluge of silver and blue and boiled
> her blood and blistered her flesh. [P. 113]

The clock, the only symbol of consequence in any of the stories
in *Uncle Tom's Children*, and for that matter one of the very few
symbols in all of Wright's fiction, is reflective of the character of
the cluster of values held by and represented by Sarah. The clock is
broken and Sarah's child bangs on it. Sarah tells the salesman that
she and Silas do not have a clock, do not need a clock; they know
when to get up and go to bed by the rising and setting of the sun.
"We just don' need no time, Mistah." The point is that Sarah,
given as she is to the blurring or nonrecognition of distinctions,
does not wish to impose on her life the differentiations occasioned
by the fact of mechanical time. It is consistent with her character
that she should live in a timeless realm, timeless as the imagination

is unconstrained by time. The merging of past and present in her mind is indicative of her resistance to time insofar as time is a means for rationally ordering experience by segmenting it. The symbol, therefore, relates to her character and her character alone and does not mean, as Kinnamon says, the "Blacks need no clock, for their lives are close to the pulse of the earth itself, unlike whites whose mechanical, rational civilization is sterile and artificial."[19] Surely Kinnamon should know that Wright would hold no such stereotyped thought; that Silas, having ordered his life in much the same manner as the "successful" white farmers around him, holds no such conception of time; and that Southern, rural white life is not exactly an expression of "mechanical, rational civilization."

Unlike Sarah, Silas holds a system of values completely rational, orderly, and pragmatic. No dreamer, he; Silas sings no long black song or any song at all. Silas knows very well the rules and customs governing interaction between black and white, and he knows the extent to which he will conform to those rules and the circumstances under which he will not. He is indeed moved through anger to act as he does in response to his knowledge of Sarah's infidelity, but a certain cold and rational basis for his response indicates that it stems from a rigid, unyielding code of conduct. The tone of the sections describing Silas's responses creates sympathy for him on the part of the reader. When, for example, he speaks the lines beginning, "The white folks ain never gimme a chance!" the reader is not invited to qualify the speech through his knowledge of the actual circumstances surrounding the relation between Sarah and the salesman. The reader is, in fact, invited to agree with Silas that he has been betrayed by his own blood. This constitutes a problem, however, for we as readers know that Silas's perspective is totally different from Sarah's. Sarah's intention was simply to fulfill the needs of her own personality, and from her perspective the salesman (who looks like "a little boy selling clocks") was not white but might have been anyone. She tends to overlook or minimize racial difference; "Silas hates white folks." Since Wright presents both perspectives in such a way that we are not invited to judge either character negatively for his and her actions, what conclusions may we reach regarding the meaning of the story?

First, the conclusion does not lie within the story; that is, the story does not allow us to judge one character right and the other wrong, limited, or injudicious. The great temptation is to apply our own standards of morality or logic, and hence to conclude that Sarah broke faith with Silas or, perhaps, more charitably, she, in following the dictates of her psyche, is responsible for the death and destruction that follow. We might look critically at Silas and say that he, in following the pattern of his white neighbors and trying to be like them, is attempting to be something which by nature he is not. That line, however, is simply racist. Or we might say that Silas is limited in his desire to acquire more than he needs for subsistence; that he is too narrow in his view of morality and in his sense of his wife's responsibilities; or that he is too practical and pragmatic to fulfill the emotional needs of his wife. None of these interpretations, as tempting as they might be to one wishing to reconcile Wright's ostensible political views at the time with his fiction, is supported by the story.

The fact is that in the story Wright presents two perspectives, each a viable and defensible position in terms of its presentation. One perspective is personal and private, belonging to the particular past of the character herself; the other is social and stems primarily from Silas's condition as a black man in a particular place. One might wish, depending on one's own value scheme, that Wright had used the story to point out the luxury and irresponsibility of the individual's fulfillment of needs exclusive of social considerations. As it is, however, Wright simply presents the problem: Sarah's needs are legitimate, and her intentions are not dishonorable; Silas's reactions also are legitimate and honorable, and they stem inexorably from his personality in conjunction with his social and historical situation. Must one subjugate personal need, want, and desire to larger social ends? Do larger social considerations dictate the need for the subjugation of the personal and individual? The story does not say. Wright simply presents the conflict, and in the terms of the story it is not resolved as it would well have been had Wright been either more personally or ideologically committed in the writing of this story.

"Fire and Cloud" and "Bright and Morning Star" are both

more closely oriented toward and consonant with Wright's professed Marxism, although neither reflects the stance of the true
believer, the uncritical follower. These stories express Wright's
conviction that the Communist party was inept in its attempt to
deal with black people. Wright believed that it was simply not
enough to approach black people en masse with theoretical Marxism;
rather, the party needed to work through existing black institutions,
thereby taking into account the realities of life in black commu-
nities.[20] Wright's view that the abstract principles of Marxism are
meaningful only in relation to specific social and historical situations and in relation to specific experience is articulated in both
stories.

"Fire and Cloud" makes considerably more sense examined
from this perspective. Otherwise Wright's atypical attitude toward
religion, especially Christianity, seems strangely incongruent. We
might expect, had Wright's thinking been more doctrinaire, that
Reverend Taylor would finally arrive at the point of losing faith
or at least having his faith shaken by the realization of the distance between his religious ideals and the practical situation faced
by the poor in the town. At the conclusion of the story, however,
Reverend Taylor is at least as devoutly religious as he was at the
beginning, and the reader is not invited to assess Taylor's continued Christian commitment in any but the most positive light.
The story, indeed, could well be read as advocating a more militant and socially active Christianity, a theme hardly on the face of it
compatible with Marxism. Even Reverend Taylor's new awareness
of the necessity for collective effort is consistent with the idea of
Christian brotherhood. Edward Margolies's observation that
"Taylor's socialist vision is couched in Biblical allusions, but
remains, nonetheless, true to form," misses the point.[21] Reverend
Taylor never arrives at a "socialist" vision. Rather he has come to
see that his otherworldly view of Christianity will not serve in
dealing with the world. His faith is as strong at the end of the story
as at the beginning; yet Wright not only sympathizes with his
Christian view but presents it in such a way as to seem convincing
to the reader. Kinnamon writes that Reverend Taylor "does not

give up God entirely," but the story suggests that he does not give up God at all. It is Wright, not Taylor, who is the Marxist. Taylor's militance has strong biblical precedent, especially in Exodus (to which there are so many parallels, including, of course, the title of the story), as well as in the history of the Christian church. If what I have said so far is indeed the case, then what in the story prevents its being read as Christian and anti-Marxist?

"Fire and Cloud" is finally more Marxist than Christian because the Christian elements of the story are subsumed within a larger context; hence the story involves Christianity but is about something larger. This is made manifest by Wright's expression of social and political values through the conflict of the story (plot and delineation of character as well). The most narrow conflict is within Reverend Taylor. The second level of personal conflict is between Reverend Taylor and Deacon Smith. The third personal level of the conflict is between Reverend Taylor and the municipal officials, the mayor, the chief of police, and head of the anti-Communist "Industrial Squad." On the broadest level, the conflict is between good and evil, the forces of authoritarianism, inhumanism, and reaction versus progressive humanitarianism. On a lower level the conflict is between black and white, but ultimately this is shown to be not the real issue. The characters in the story support either reaction or progressivism, and they are judged in relation to which side they support. Reverend Taylor's decision to support the march and his change from a conciliatory to a more militant and aggressive attitude are all viewed from a framework presented in the story as broader than his religious perspective. Therefore the resolution alone of the story's conflicts is a victory for progressivism and not for Christianity per se, for another Christian might well have made choices different from those made by Reverend Taylor. The joining together of Christian and Communist is strategic, not ideological. Wright indicates in the story the personal reality to Reverend Taylor of his Christian commitment and in effect says that the culture and history of the man cannot be ignored and that progressive aims can be achieved by working through existing and deeply rooted institutions.

In "Bright and Morning Star" a corollary point is made. Aunt Sue, the central character of the story, reflects Wright's notion that simple presentation of Marxist ideology to a peasantry is not enough because old habits of social knowledge and response are not easily discarded. She knows that her old Christian training is incompatible with her newly adopted Marxism, but she is unable to avoid singing spirituals from time to time, and without consciously intending it she seeks to synthesize her past and present perspectives. She understands Marxism by analogy to her Christian faith:

> And day by day her sons had ripped from her startled eyes her old vision, and image by image had given her a new one, different, but great and strong enough to fling her into the light of another grace. The wrongs and sufferings of black men had taken the place of Him nailed to the Cross; the meager beginnings of the Party had become another Resurrection; and the hate of those who would destroy her new faith had quickened in her a hunger to feel how deeply her new strength went. [P. 185]

This is good educational psychology, for clearly we learn by analogizing new experiences to old knowledge. Aunt Sue's suspiciousness of whites is a masterly touch on Wright's part. In her discussion with Johnny-Boy about who has informed on the group, she says, relying on her suspicion of whites bred from a lifetime of experience, "You can't trust every white man yuh meet." Johnny-Boy's ideological stance requires that he make no distinction whatsoever between white and black workers, all being of one class —the exploited. Wright might have chosen to make the "correct" ideological point, but instead he makes the point that comes out of his experience: Racial experience does in fact make a difference; it is of significance. Aunt Sue is right, and her acceptance and recognition of the reality of her past allows her a certain awareness not available to her son. In handling the materials of the tale, Johnny-Boy instructs the party (which may or may not have been pleased, were the message perceived), showing that the ends of the party are served through Aunt Sue's reliance on a traditional response bred from her pre-Marxist experience. The party might well have been pleased by her devotion to the cause, but in indicating that devotion, Wright could not help but assert his personal criticism of the party's stance in relation to black people, an impertinence at best (from the party's point of view) and a basic criticism of doctrinaire Marxism at worst. Aunt Sue, as devoted as she is to the party, is motivated far more personally than ideologically.

Hence, considered in its entirety, *Uncle Tom's Children* is in style, subject, and theme leftist but by no means Marxist in any thoroughgoing sense.[22] Where Wright's achievement is not based on Marxist ideology, it is because he did not find it possible to suspend his own private sense of reality or his critical faculties, a quality of personality largely responsible for the course of his fiction from beginning to end. The elements of the book that are not Marxist, that stem from his personal experience, his own private view of the way things are, are the seeds of his later inclinations toward existentialism and further proof that his existentialism is native and not an attempt on his part to graft European experience onto his own.[23]

Wright's second (though first published) novel, *Native Son*, is more explicitly political than both *Lawd Today* and *Uncle Tom's Children* in its direct and open attack on the shortcomings of the institutions of our society. It attacks an exploitative economic system, a judicial system geared to support the bigotry of the society at large, a communications system interested in expressing and sustaining bigoted attitudes, a system of religion so other-worldly in its orientation as to be unrelated to the facts of existence, a system of law enforcement whose primary task is to protect existing institutions. Each of these works hand in glove with the others in sustaining the oppressiveness of the society. Wright, of course, intends for readers to see that oppressiveness in operation and therefore put forth effort to end it.

Just as we see Jake in *Lawd Today* functioning within a social framework inimical to his ends and aspirations, so we see Bigger Thomas in a similar situation. Neither fully understands his relation to his environment. The difference between them, aside from minor considerations such as age, economic class, and so on, is the difference in Wright's attitude toward them rather than in their essential characters. Whereas Wright's attitude toward Jake is fairly consistent in the novel from beginning to end, his attitude toward Bigger undergoes a change, and that change is a barometer indicating the extent and limitations of the sociopolitical aspect of the novel. The beginning of *Native Son* differs markedly from the end in relation to tone, the attitude that Wright expresses toward Bigger. In the first section of the novel, Wright deals with Bigger objectively in the sense that Wright expresses comparatively little sympathy for him personally. Through the second and third sections, Wright's perspective on Bigger becomes increasingly sympathetic, the distance between author and character diminishing all the while. To put this another way, when Wright deals with Bigger in the first section, he treats him as a sociological entity, describing through his case the "plight of the black man in America" and seeing him thereby as from a great distance. The more specifically human Bigger becomes, the closer Wright identifies with him and the less objective the tone. Eventually the prevailing tone of the first section is taken over in the third by Max, who continues the sociopolitical level of discourse, especially during the courtroom scenes, and the voice of the writer tells us in contrast about the most significant aspect of the novel: Bigger Thomas's increasing awareness of who and what he is and how he stands in relation to the forces operative around him.

The distinction I have made between Max and the author in the third section is not entirely satisfactory; for the tone underlying Max's voice is just as much the voice of the writer, inasmuch as it is controlled by the writer, as the voice underlying Bigger's exploration of his inner self. The significant point is this: Max expresses attitudes inseparable from the attitudes of the author. Indeed Max is Wright's spokesman, but Wright is a complex man. Max does not say all that Wright has to say. He says what Wright has to say on an ideological level, not what he articulates as an existential human entity, a distinction that Wright frequently maintained. This distinction is not apprehended by those critics who read *Native Son* as an intended but failed dramatization of Marxist values.[24] The novel is not finally Marxist in perspective, even if we grant the truth and significance of Max's various orations. Max is indeed a Marxist, but much of what he says might as well have been spoken by liberal-thinking people of a variety of persuasions. A liberal of any kind might have thought as Max thought, but this is not the most salient point. Even if we grant that Max's stance is Marxist in essence, the fact still remains that it is in competition and conflict with that of Bigger Thomas. Max sees things in large social perspective; Bigger sees things in personal, private perspective. During one of their conversations the following dialogue occurs:

> Max: "Well, this thing's bigger than you, son. In a certain sense, every Negro in America's on trial out there today."
> Bigger: "They going to kill me anyhow."[25]

Which view is Wright's?

Both are his truly, but given the two, Wright indicates in a number of ways that one is of greater ultimate significance than the other. The two are not mutually exclusive, although logically they may not be entirely compatible. Each represents a different perspective, but what is important is that Wright's greater weight of sympathy at the end of the novel is with one point of view rather than the other. Specifically, if we weigh the perspectives at the end of the novel, if we assess the tone during the last pages, we find that they are nearly balanced but not quite. Bigger's voice is the weightier one; his perspective is of greater truth and significance. In the last scene of the novel, Wright has the choice of indicating in the exchange between Bigger and Max the degree to which his sympathies lie with the perspectives represented by the two men. In his focus on Bigger and in the manner in which Bigger attempts to come to terms with his situation, Wright sympathizes most with the man who is in the more critical situation. Bigger faces impending doom, and the generalizations Max makes in an effort to comfort him, generalizations that clearly do not serve, indicate that Max, with his political philosophy, ultimately has nothing to offer Bigger. Wright does not reject Max, does not diminish the value of his social and political orientation; he simply indicates its limitations. The point of the last scene, a point that even Max recognizes and articulates, is that one dies alone and that one must come to terms with that fact. Max is so shaken because he is horrified by Bigger's imposition and acceptance of his own definition of self: "What I killed for, I *am*!" [Wright's emphasis]. It is this from which he recoils, not from Bigger per se. The simile, given the meaning that its referent has in the total context of the novel, contained in the line, "Max groped for his hat like a blind man," should not be lost. Again Wright does not thereby reject the socialist vision; rather he indicates what seems to him its natural limitation.

The character of Wright's fiction would suggest that his break with the Communist party, prefigured and reflected in his work, involved as much inner turmoil as is suggested in his recital of it in "I Tried to Be a Communist," and probably even more.[26] That is, I doubt that what might be apparent to a sensitive reader of his fiction, his resistance to social definition of individual character, was entirely understood or realized by the man himself. The third section of *Native Son* contains elements that are antithetical to Marxist ideology. I do not think that Wright was consciously or intentionally heretical, for in the book the Marxists are generally highly regarded, more highly, in fact, than most others in that world. But beyond that, it is of paramount significance that Wright was involved in writing "The Man Who Lived Underground" in 1941, the year preceding his break with the party.[27] In comparison with *Native Son* and the works preceding that, "The Man Who Lived Underground" is the least ideologically based, the most symbolic, the most subjectively conceived and oriented, and, up to the time of its writing, the least racially and socially focused work.

With "The Man Who Lived Underground" and in all his fiction thereafter, Wright was concerned with the interior state of being, with the quality of consciousness, of his central character. He was not disregardful of the facts of social environment, but by the time his thinking had led him to conclude that the state of consciousness of the individual may determine the nature and quality of his life and the meaning of his particular circumstances, his thinking had shifted from the Marxist idea that environment determines the character of consciousness to its opposite. That is, he did not simply reverse his belief but began to explore the implications of the opposite belief, an exploration that was to preoccupy his major fiction. He could not abide the notion that Bigger Thomas (himself and all black people insofar as Bigger represents these) was so entrapped by his environment as to be totally a victim. The way out for Bigger was through the exercise of consciousness beyond the boundaries sanctioned by the system of institutions, of ethics and morality, beyond, in short, good and evil. The ramifications of this conclusion in relation to a social context became almost obsessional with Wright. Time and time again he dealt with the possibility of the unfettered consciousness whose only antagonist is conscience. "The Man Who Lived Underground" shows the development of consciousness beyond ordinary limits and the fate of that consciousness in a social context.

Because of the nature of his experience once he goes underground, Fred Daniels, the protagonist, sees the functioning of society in a distant, uninvolved, and seemingly objective way. Had he not by circumstance become a fugitive, it is unlikely that this uneducated, not overly intelligent, but resourceful man would ever have had occasion to perceive the world as he does. As it is, however, he is forced to see without being seen (or without being recognized), to look at the operation of the world as one uninvolved. The result is a strange disengagement that allows him to see behind appearances. He comes to recognize the arbitrariness of certain social values and generalizes his particular experiences to include the whole range of institutions. He discovers, for example, that social identity does not reside in the quality of individual personality but in circumstance. By stepping into the sight of others, he becomes a projection of his observers' expectations, a moviegoer on one occasion, a clerk in a grocery on another. He observes circumstances, which he himself has created, turn an innocent watchman into a thief. In his isolated situation he comes to discover that money and gems have no inherent value despite the role they play in the functioning of the society. We may infer the conclusion on his part that social organization is arbitrary, itself the result of necessity and without reality beyond that attributed to it by people. For this reason he feels the nearly irresistible urge to laugh when he observes worship in a church; from underground it appears a formal exercise, empty, devoid of meaning. Fred Daniels wishes to deliver his message to the world above. He does not have the language to articulate his experience; so he wants to show it to others. Unfortunately he decides to reveal his new-found knowledge to the police, whose function, we may infer from the story, is to prevent such knowledge from spreading. "You've got to shoot his kind," says the policeman *Law*son, "they'd wreck things."

But how would "they wreck things"? What is the message that Fred Daniels wants to bring to the world, the message of such significance that he must be murdered to prevent its delivery? The message is that all people are free, that reality is a social construction having no essence in itself; that social constraint, morality, all social scales of value are arbitrary and have no authority, that the total social scheme exists only on the basis of faith and belief. The function of the police, then, is to protect and sustain the illusion of reality. Fred Daniels would not alter that illusion, as reformers might, but would subvert it altogether. His kind would "wreck things."

Black Boy may need justification for being included in a consideration of Wright's fiction. This is neither the time nor the place to present that justification, but ample reasons exist for treating it as fiction despite its being ostensibly autobiographical.[28] For example, its form, its symbolism, and its obvious manipulation of Wright's past for the sake of putting forth a clearly conceived theme suggest fictional means. More pertinent, however, is its thematic relation to Wright's fictional works, its insistence, as in "The Man Who Lived Underground," on the subjective experience of the individual as more real and significant ultimately than social schemes for organizing reality. This is the message of *Black Boy* as well, but not its only message.

Black Boy has a social purpose of a particular kind as well. Its readers are intended to come away from the book with a deep knowledge and understanding of the effects of racism on the personality, of the ways in which racism deeply affects personal and familial relations, of the pervasiveness of racism and of racism's total insidiousness. *Black Boy* lays bare the bones of racism, revealing the extent to which its influence pervades the home, the church, the school, business, law enforcement agencies—indeed all facets of life, institutionalized or not.

The title of the book seems intended to suggest that the experiences recounted represent experiences encountered by all "black boys," and by implication all black people. Hence we are led to believe that the central character is intended to be representative. In large measure that is true, but in some significant ways it is not true. The narrator makes it clear that he is exceptional in his environment, that his case is indeed unique. This element runs counter to the book's ostensible intention. The implication that Wright was the only person in his environment to resist the influence on him of oppression leads to some rather untrue, unpleasant, and ahistorical conclusions that Wright probably would not have intended to suggest. I am sure that *Black Boy* was not intended to be a primer explaining why "they" (black people) are as "they" are, although elements of the book imply this. The famous passage that Ellison quotes in his exchange with Irving Howe, for example, expresses the notion that black people have missed the essential spirit of Western civilization.[29] That passage stems from a mood and is contradicted by the narrator's description of the family who own the rooming house he lives in when he goes as a young man to Memphis. But it is also consistent with the facet of the book that sees black life as entirely warped and without redeeming virtues.[30]

The problem under consideration here makes clear a certain dichotomy in Wright's thinking, an ambiguity in the book's meaning. On the one hand he wishes to show the effects of racism in the South on the personalities of black individuals and to show it in such a way as to reveal its utterly damaging character. On the other hand he knew himself to be an exception to the generalization (a fact made manifest in his capacity to write the book), for his own experience told him that he had somehow escaped the most destructive intentions of the oppressors as described in the book. Wright might have accounted for his ability to resist the negative influences exerted on him by his environment in any number of ways. It might have been attributed to some individual, to his mother or someone else; it might have been attributed to the social class of his family. As it stands, however, Wright attributed his ability to resist to the conscious exertion of his own individual will. The autobiography is then, besides its being protest against Southern society, the history of the willful creation of Richard Wright by himself—hence the extreme emphasis in his work on choice and on the responsibility of the individual to and for himself; hence the sense conveyed by the book of the impingement upon a single consciousness of the events described (and its similarity to Joyce's *Portrait of the Artist*); hence the subjective element of the book; and hence, finally, the quality of the book quite aptly described as existential.

Black Boy reveals the roots of Wright's existentialism. If I read the earlier book *Native Son* correctly, and I think *Black Boy* makes that reading more credible, then the existential element of that book is as natural as air and right out of Wright's experience. The narrator learns to distrust "everything and everybody"; to rely upon his own sense of how things are, to believe only what is acceptable to his own sensibilities. (His attitude toward religion as expressed in the book is an example.) For him, existence, without doubt, precedes essence. This further implies that Wright's existentialism is not derived from his association with French intellectuals but was instead home-grown, right out of the American South.[31] Since Marxism and existentialism are incompatible in so many ways, it is no wonder that Wright was never a very good (convinced) Marxist, that so much of his work should have been considered suspect by the party, and that the personal, subjective, apolitical element I have been discussing should have been so frequent in his most political fiction.

The Outsider, the book generally recognized as being existential, is an exploration of some of the implications of the earlier fiction.[32] In a narrow sense of the word, the novel is not so much political as antipolitical, a repudiation of Marxism and fascism as well. Viewed from the perspective suggested in this context, however, *The Outsider* is anarchistic in its implications, although the anarchic perspective seems to be rejected at the end in favor of a kind of humanism.[33] The book has a number of racial implications, although it is less a book about race as such than any book preceding it. The novel relates to *Native Son*, "The Man Who Lived Underground," and *Black Boy* in its positing of a character, a black man, who rejects traditional systems of ethics and morality and who then explores (through thought and action) the implications of living beyond law and moral restraint. The impulse to reject preexistent systems of value is perennial in Wright's psychology, and if my line of argument is correct, that impulse has manifested itself as the expression of subjective and private realities in opposition to codes or systematized beliefs. *The Outsider* is no exception to this assertion. In this novel no such opposition exists except at the novel's conclusion. The extent to which Wright is at one with his subject can be seen by assessing his attitude toward his hero. He is at one with him throughout the novel. As a matter of fact, the prior element of contradiction—Wright's personalism and individualism as opposed to systems of belief—becomes part and parcel of the novel, the subject indeed, with which it deals. At the conclusion Wright implies that Cross's course was the wrong one, but at the same time he says (or, more precisely, the tone says) that he too was wrong, that the direction of his own thinking was erroneous.

Before he becomes "an outsider," Cross Damon is, of course, an insider; he follows generally the codes of conduct sanctioned by social institutions and is thereby trapped within the confines of a difficult, unbearable life. Imaginative and intelligent, he takes the opportunity to escape, to throw off the burdens of institutional life. He changes his identity, murders a man who could betray him, escapes to another city, and eventually becomes relatively free, an outsider. In bludgeoning to death two men, one a Fascist and the other a Communist, he expresses his freedom from political ideology and morality. He is also an outsider because of the nature of his vision. Being black and an intellectual, he has special insight into the society: He is at once a part of it and not a part of it and able, because he is an intellectual, to see the ramifications of his situation.

Although Wright ostensibly intended *The Outsider* to be non-political, the novel could not help but be political in that it is a restatement of an about-face from a previous political commitment, however tenuous and incomplete that commitment was.[34] The novel turns out to be very political in that it advocates (up to its final scene) a more thorough repudiation of social organization than ever before. It puts forth a visionary element in that it projects the rise in Nietzschean fashion of a group of superconscious men of such vision as to allow them to see things truly and straightforwardly. Theoretically this would be (again up to the final scene of the novel) good, for these men of vision could run affairs better than the myopic, currently existing rulers. But this perspective pushes Wright toward fascism, an untenable position for him, yet the direction he moves in in reacting against Marxism. The implications of his thesis are finally intolerable, and Cross Damon's world, as sympathetic as Wright has been to him, begins to crumble. Damon's anarchy becomes terrible and terrifying in its consequences. Wright himself discovers that he is not quite as free as he thought he might be. He kills off Cross Damon and has him repudiate his direction:

> "I wanted to be free . . . to feel what I was worth. . . . What living meant to me. . . . I loved life too . . . much. . . ."
>   "And what did you find?"
>   "Nothing. . . . The search can't be done alone. . . . Never alone. . . . Alone a man is nothing. . . . Man is a promise he must never break."[35]

Consider what this means. Early in life Wright had recognized that institutions are not by nature necessarily sustaining of the individual. By the time he was sixteen, he was fairly certain that the individual was likely not merely to be unsustained by institutions but that they might indeed be arrayed against him. When Wright goes to Chicago and discovers Marxism, he becomes aware of the possibility that institutions might be rearranged in such a way as not to be destructive of his particular life and personality. He also discovers, however, that the matter has essentially to do with rearranging institutions and not doing away with them, and his awareness of the racism of many American Marxists causes him to hold back from any kind of total commitment to another institutional scheme. His faith and belief in himself allow him to hold back—to believe that truth lies within his own awareness and sensibility—this, exclusive of institutional claims. *The Outsider* becomes then Wright's exploration of this basic assumption. His exploration in his fiction of the ramifications of that assumption led him not only to repudiate it but to fall back on humanism in response.

Perhaps the most interesting element of *The Outsider* is the depth and scope of its repudiations. As has been suggested, Wright was fascinated with the idea that social reality is an arbitrary construct and that identity, dependent as it is on social definition, is also arbitrary and if not utterly unreal, at least without a basis beyond that arbitrary social framework. If a person understands this, sees behind the scene, he or she is free to choose an identity through will. How free then may an individual be? Entirely free, subject only to biological and physiological limitations. This is the conclusion Wright's thinking led him to, and the question dealt with in *The Outsider* is whether this is indeed the case.

Wright ultimately answers the question through the outcome of the novel's plot. He has effectively repudiated the claims of communism and fascism to be adequate means of describing and dealing with reality by his obviously sympathetic attitude toward Cross Damon's conception of and actions against Communists and Fascists. Cross, the existential anarchist, sees through these ideologies and from, we are led to believe, a superior, more adequate vantage point. The final judgment, however, is against him, against anarchy, and against existentialism as he conceives it. Cross sees the flaw in his assumption to be in having attributed too great a capacity for will to exert itself independently of and in a manner antagonistic to other forces operative in the total psyche. His mother has bequeathed him, he tells us early in the novel, his sense of dread, a sense stemming from the conflict of desire and conscience, a heightened desire born of conscience's opposition to it, and a painful consciousness of the conflict. His ability to act consciously, apparently unconstrained by morality, is in response to an utterly rigid sense of morality. In the end, and this contributes to the resolution of the novel's plot, conscience emerges victorious, and he repudiates the conclusions about freedom arrived at through the functioning of consciousness alone. Whereas he had escaped the chastisement of his mother for his negative actions early in the book, he comes finally to judge himself, and in her terms. He thus undercuts the value system he has propounded throughout the novel, denying the worth and validity of the outsider's perspective. The significant determining factors come not to have their sources in the functioning of consciousness or the exercise of will. Rather values are not ultimately derived consciously but exist in some anterior chamber of the psyche and are incapable of being extinguished ultimately by will. Hence *The Outsider*, Wright's existential novel, comes to be his antiexistential novel, a clear denial of the viability of existentialism as a satisfactory basis for living. Through this novel Wright concludes that the nature of human character and of existence lies not in the functioning of consciousness and willfulness but in preconsciousness or unconsciousness. That Wright had such thoughts at hand is evidenced by the implication rendered early in the novel that Cross's motivations are more Oedipal than cerebral. The sexual component of the relation between Cross and his mother and her dominance over him lead to the possibility that his real problem is to free himself from her (perhaps by marrying someone as much unlike her as possible) and to achieve the right to authority and independence by asserting his will, by doing whatever he freely chooses to do. Here Wright turns away from politics and philosophy toward psychology as a means of defining the nature of character and existence. And it is significant to note his focus on the individual and not on groups, an interest the genesis of which can be traced to the ending of *Native Son*.

Savage Holiday, the novel following *The Outsider*, is not anomalous, a pot-boiler, simply written to make money.[36] It is admittedly not a very good novel, but it is a serious novel. It reveals the next step in Wright's thinking, the link to the earlier novel being the Freudian implications of the relation between Cross Damon and his mother. Wright asks in *Savage Holiday*, what if the nature of will and the character of consciousness—circumstance providing the context of their operation—are determined by early environment? What if Cross Damon's ostensible search for meaning is no more than an unconscious attempt to free himself from his mother? *Savage Holiday* pursues the question raised in the preceding novel and is thereby a continuation of Wright's interest in interior states of being and in the nature and quality of conciousness, though from a somewhat different perspective than before.

In *Native Son* Bigger Thomas fumbles his way half-consciously to the conclusion that individuals may choose to be as they exist at any given moment in time, a choice exclusive of institutional claims to define and judge the value and character of individual thought and conduct and, of course, individuals themselves. Fred Daniels exhibits the individual consciousness divesting the world of social, moral, religious, and legal values through the random experience of a disengaged observer. The central figure of *Black Boy* evades the constricting influence on him of institutional values through willfulness, simply refusing to heed environmental pressures. His response is defensive and his definition of self negative in that he knows more what he is not than what he is. Cross Damon of *The Outsider* sets about consciously to construct the character and circumstances of his life, his values, and his identity. The possibility and desirability of such an undertaking are, of course, negated finally in the novel. *Savage Holiday* is like the preceding major fiction from *Native Son* on in that it deals with the obsessive question in Wright's thinking: What are the dangers, limitations, and possibilities of consciousness functioning outside the confines of institutionally imposed limits? In *Savage Holiday* Wright indicates rather explicitly his concern with the relation of individuals to institutions:

> The majority of men, timid and unthinking, obey the laws and mandates of society because they yearn to merit the esteem and respect of their law-abiding neighbors. Still others, reflective and conscious, obey because they are intelligently afraid of the reprisals meted out by society upon the breakers of the law. There are still other men of a deeper and more sensitive nature who, in

their growing up, introject the laws and mandates of society into their hearts and come in time to feel and accept these acquired notions of right and wrong as native impulses springing out of the depths of their beings and, if they are ever tempted to violate these absorbed codes, act as though the sky itself were about to crash upon their heads, as though the very earth were about to swing catastrophically out of its orbit.[37]

Wright seems to have convinced himself that the actions of individuals do indeed require restraint. This is explicit in the conclusion of *The Outsider*. *Savage Holiday* suggests that even the individual who has most thoroughly internalized institutional values may not necessarily be constrained by them (the psychological state of the human organism is a prior consideration) and that the willful aspect of consciousness may be circumscribed by unconscious elements. Hence *Savage Holiday* is as *anti*existential as *The Outsider*; it vividly demonstrates the individual subjected to circumstances beyond his or her capacity to will. Erskine Fowler unwittingly is responsible for the death of Tony Blake; he kills Mable Blake; he surrenders to the police. The first of these acts is gratuitous; the second an act of compulsion; the third the result of prior conditioning. No one of them is the result of the free, or even partially free, exercise of willfulness. Governed as he is by guilt, pushed out of his job, which allowed him to keep his compulsions in check, Erskine Fowler stands at the opposite pole from Bigger Thomas, who is totally free psychically at the end of *Native Son*. The one book, then, is an ironic inversion of the other: Bigger Thomas is poor, black, without social status but free; Erskine Fowler is financially well off, white, successful but enslaved.

It is not surprising, therefore, that *Savage Holiday* should be essentially raceless, a novelistic construct dealing with considerations seen to be more basic than the social. Race, social class, economic status, and politics are peripheral considerations. The character and state of Erskine Fowler's psyche is the more salient matter. At this point the implications of *Native Son* and *Savage Holiday* coincide. The difference between them lies in Wright's interpretation of the meaning of the experiences of the two central characters. Bigger says in effect, "I am what I am and I accept that fully"; Fowler says, "What I am is evil and must be realigned with an external system of values." In the one case existence precedes essence; in the other the contrary prevails.

What then does *Savage Holiday* tell about Wright's politics? It is a confirmation of Wright's statement in the immediately preceding novel, *The Outsider:* The character of human nature is such that the individual cannot be trusted to formulate his or her own private system of values exclusive of traditional humanistic ones. The later novel goes one step further: Not only is human nature so limited as to require the restraint imposed by a general humanism, but it needs the specific direction, formulation, and control of currently existing institutions. This implies a different perspective from Wright's earlier analyses of the nature of institutions and the proper relation of individuals to them. Earlier works—*Uncle Tom's Children, Native Son,* and *Black Boy*—show the role of institutions in sustaining oppression. *Savage Holiday* sees currently existing institutions as a necessity for organizing and controlling human behavior. No irony or ambivalence is apparent in Wright's attitute. If liberalism is defined as being founded on the notion that individuals are constantly in a state of becoming and that human nature is unfixed, and conservatism as the notion that individuals, given a fixed nature, can be worthwhile only insofar as they act within the limits defined by institutions, then the political implications of *Savage Holiday* make it clear enough where Wright stands at this point in his career.

The Long Dream, the last of Wright's novels, is perhaps difficult to assess in its political dimension, for it may too easily be (and has most frequently been) read as a weak attempt on Wright's part to recapture the character and quality of his earlier fiction of social protest.[38] The novel, on the contrary, is not that at all and if read as such cannot but be judged as weak. Having retreated from the political stance outlined in his "Blueprint for Negro Writing," having lost his confidence that the ultimate quality of the individual human life is determined by forces outside the control of individuals, and having concluded that the experience of the discrete individual, qua individual, is finally more significant than group experience, economic class, or social status, Wright wrote a novel whose primary concern is with character and personality.

Seen from this perspective, *The Long Dream* makes far more sense than if seen in a social dimension alone. It clears up the question of the blurred distinction in the novel between oppressed and oppressor. Certainly if Tyree, Fishbelly's father, is a victim of oppression, he is no less an oppressor, for he is responsible for the slum tenements he owns; he is responsible for the prostitution among black people in the city. This perspective also clears up the otherwise obtrusive, unessential focus on Fishbelly's early life and character (for example, the source of his name and observing his father having intercourse). And, finally, it accounts for the sharp focus throughout the book on the one central character to the exclusion of the others except as they impinge directly on his life. If the book were more socially oriented, we might expect Fishbelly to be less unique, and we might expect a more developed emphasis on and broader analysis of the pervasive effects of racism on black people.

The point I wish to make is subtle. Whereas I do not wish to give the impression that *The Long Dream* is not literature intended to be critical of the society in which its events occur, I do suggest that its focus is upon the private experience of an individual who exists in that corrupt and oppressive society. The social setting is a given. There is no hope or possibility of its ever changing, and Wright establishes its reality only to explore the character of an individual who develops in it. Wright's focus on character is further evidenced by his conception of the project of which *The Long Dream* is only a part. It was intended to be the first part of a trilogy. The second volume (unpublished) depicts Fishbelly's experiences in Paris after his escape from the South.[39]

Perhaps the point is even clearer if we compare *The Long Dream* and *Native Son* in regard to their focus. Fishbelly is detailed in far more depth than Bigger Thomas. Whereas with the later novel a case could be made for the novel's describing the coming to maturity of its central character, the primary factor being his relation to his parents, especially his father, no similar theme could reasonably be argued for the earlier novel. There is a certain similarity between the two books if we consider Wright's shift in focus during the final section of *Native Son* to the character of Bigger's interior state. Even so, the fact of Bigger's existence as a representative figure, as a social being, runs parallel to that deeper current. The seed of *The Long Dream* exists within the earlier novel, yet the point remains that Bigger Thomas's life serves to depict the potentially utterly damaging character of racism; Fishbelly's life serves as no such exemplum. Bigger is trapped and finally killed by his environment; Fishbelly escapes.

Fishbelly's social and economic class likewise points to Wright's interest in his unique character. None of Wright's other major characters (with the exception of Erskine Fowler in *Savage Holiday*) is of relatively similar socioeconomic class, and since race and class were so inextricably intertwined in Wright's earlier work, we might assume that he is working from other premises here. The casual reader might well miss Wright's insistence on the role of class in the novel, but it is nevertheless there. Note, for example, Fish's shame in facing his friends after he has not passed his high school examination, the aspiration levels of his friends (Sam wants to study law; Zeke, business administration), Tyree's insistence that Fish be educated, Wright's description of the two areas in which the black citizens of Clintonville live (Fish's family lives in Addison Addition among other petit bourgeoisie; the unskilled, untrained, "illiterates and semi-literates" live in Ford's Ridge). Fish is taught to distinguish between himself and those of a lower social and economic level:

> Through a haze of heat loomed Mr. Jordan's store, whose front porch was crowded with loitering railroad workers. He readied himself to be laughed at, scorned. His parents had cautioned him against these roustabouts. "Son, they your *color*, but they ain't you *kind*," his mother had told him. "I touch 'em only when they *dead*, Fish, and I wouldn't do that 'less I was paid," his father had drawn the line.[40]

The class emphasis of the novel is intimately related to Fish's character, suggesting again that he is not representative of black people in general, that factors other than race have been responsible for creating him. Class puts him in the situation in which he finds himself at the end of the novel, and access to the resources available to him as a member of his class allows him finally to escape.

That Wright's focus is on individual character in *The Long Dream* is also apparent if we compare the nature of familial relations in the novel with those relations in *Black Boy*. In the autobiography it is made clear that the character of interrelationships within the family is determined by the social milieu in which the family lives. For example, when the young Richard is injured in a cinder fight with white boys, his mother beats him because she is fearful of the consequences of his fighting whites. Likewise she slaps him at another point when he questions her about his grandmother's racial identity. His mother's inability to feed and clothe him adequately and her eventually placing him in an orphanage are direct results of the influence on his family of the environment. Social factors do indeed influence Fishbelly's character (such as his early knowledge and resulting fear of lynching), but primarily his character is accounted for by reference to particular psychological factors having to do with private as opposed to social experience. His observation of his father's copulation with a woman in his funeral parlor is an example. No class or racial factor is present there. Fundamental aspects of his character stem from relations within the family unit alone, as when Fishbelly recovers from the serious burns he receives after falling on a hot stove.

> Fishbelly now felt justified in burrowing himself into his mother; and she, wallowing in guilt, let him. The comfort he drew from her was sensual in its intensity, and it formed the pattern of what he was to demand later in life from women. When he was a man and in distress, he would have to have them, but his need of them would be limited, localized, focused toward obtaining release, solace; and then he would be gone to seek his peculiar, singular destiny, lonely but affable, cold but smiling, and strongly insulated against abiding relationships. [P. 60]

Insofar as Wright's focus in *The Long Dream* is on character and on the unique quality of character, his novel's emphasis is not on class, race, or other matters of a social and political nature. It is no wonder that the protesting edge of Wright's fiction seemed blunted by the time he wrote his last novel. It is social protest by default only, not by design. *The Long Dream* follows logically Wright's line of development as a novelist as he moved away from his earlier conception of literature as a weapon with which one could fight oppression. (Compare, for example, the above quotation from the novel with Wright's Freudian analysis of Erskine Fowler's character in *Savage Holiday*.) As Wright's politics changed, so did his fiction. Or to put the matter in another way, the less committed he was to a political ideology, the less politically ideological was his fiction.

Although Wright's fiction moved during his career from a greater to a lesser emphasis on external reality, from a primary concern with the nature and quality of environment to a focus on the psyche of the individual in a social environment, Wright never became so subjective as to lose sight of the relation between character and environment. In the same way he never ceased to be a political man, despite his inability to commit himself to any existing ideology or party. His reliance on personal impression, on the barometer of his own psyche, probably is the result of that quality of personality which from the very beginning caused him to be suspicious of "objective" frames of reference. His social and political analyses could only be highly personal since he had no "objective" ideological frame of reference. He knew this and felt some melancholy because of it. Nonetheless he saw no alternative. He was leftist in his thinking always, but the bent of his politics (implicitly expressed in his objective emphasis even at his most subjective) found more explicit expression in his nonfiction than in his fiction. *The Color Curtain; White Man, Listen; Black Power;* and *Pagan Spain* are apt testimony to his leftist thinking, his hatred of fascism and colonialism, his sympathy for economic arrangements of a socialist character, his awareness of the limitations of Western institutions— leftist but by no means doctrinaire Marxist.

Hence if we were to think of the body of Wright's fiction in terms of its political orientation, a pattern is discernable, but the nature of the change in his fiction is not so easily described. We could say, for example, that his fiction becomes more conservative and even in a sense rightist. To some extent that is indeed the case. It is important, however, to remember that such an evaluation operates within the confines of the system of his own fiction and consequently does not mean anything absolutely. Wright's most "conservative" novel may well stand in relation to any given novel by another author as Karl Marx to George III. Wright was not a Dreiser or a Steinbeck, men who in their youths protested against the lot of the dispossessed but who in later years recanted and joined the forces of the oppressor. His integrity was greater. The strength of his social vision, the "length" of his "dream," is attested to in his last novel, *The Long Dream,* where it is apparent that no personal and private concern of his own could overshadow the social fact of a system of institutions inimical to the fulfillment of the legitimate desires of the individual, especially, as in the novel, a black individual. His was the uniquely rebel spirit, alone, driven finally into himself, and unable constitutionally to assent to anything that he did not understand and believe. Yet this isolated man was social enough in his commitment and orientation to realize that the interrelation between society and the individual is such that no "separate peace" is ever wholly possible.

NOTES

1. Wright, "Blueprint for Negro Writing," *New Challenge* 2 (Fall 1937): 53-65. Reprinted in *Richard Wright Reader*, ed. Ellen Wright and Michel Fabre (New York: Harper & Row, 1978), pp. 37-49. An expanded version of the essay was printed for the first time in John A. Williams and Charles F. Harris, eds., *Amistad 2* (New York: Random House, Vintage, 1971), pp. 3-20.

2. Williams and Harris, *Amistad 2*, p. 10.

3. Ibid., p. 19.

4. See *Richard Wright Reader*, pp. 45, 48.

5. See my Introduction, p. 9.

6. *Richard Wright Reader*, p. 42.

7. Ibid., p. 44.

8. Richard Kostelanetz deals quite specifically but in significantly different ways with some of the issues I raise here. In any case, anyone interested in the politics of Richard Wright's fiction should see his essay, "The Politics of Unresolved Quests in the Novels of Richard Wright," *Xavier University Studies* 8 (1969): 31-64.

9. See Richard Wright, "I Tried to Be a Communist," *Atlantic Monthly* 159 (August 1944): 61-70. Michel Fabre, *The Unfinished Quest of Richard Wright* (New York: William Morrow, 1973), pp. 228-31, further discusses Wright's conflict with the Communist party and corrects some of the "facts" reported in Wright's account of his relations with the party. See also Constance Webb, *Richard Wright: A Biography* (New York: G. P. Putnam's Sons, 1968), pp. 139-57.

10. Two salient questions arise here: Wright's existentialism (see p. 42 below) and the meaning and motivation of his involvement with the Communist party. Both are closely related to what Fabre, *Unfinished Quest*, refers to as Wright's "individualism" (p. 137) and his "spirit of rebellion" (p. 5). Robert Bone, *The Negro Novel in America* (New Haven: Yale University Press, 1958), p. 143, refers to the "stubborn and uncorruptible individualism [which] kept him [Wright] in constant conflict with the party bureaucracy."

11. See George E. Kent, "Richard Wright: Blackness and the Adventure of Western Culture," *CLA Journal* 12 (June 1969): 335-39 for a more extended analysis of *Lawd Today*.

12. In its original 1938 version, *Uncle Tom's Children* contained only four stories. The fifth, "Bright and Morning Star," was added (along with "The Ethics of Living Jim Crow") to the 1940 edition and has appeared subsequently.

13. Keneth Kinnamon, *The Emergence of Richard Wright* (Urbana: University of Illinois Press, 1972), pp. 85-86. Kinnamon's study is by no means limited to symbolic analysis.

14. Clifford Hand, "The Struggle to Create Life in the Fiction of Richard Wright," in *The Thirties: Fiction, Poetry, Drama*, ed. Warren French (Deland, Fla.: Everett/Edwards, 1967), pp. 83-84, sees the spiritual as "at best irrelevant and possibly incapacitating in Mann's struggle to live."

15. Compare Kinnamon, *Emergence*, p. 93.

16. Compare Kent, "Richard Wright," p. 332.

17. Readers have sometimes mistakenly seen Sarah's seduction as a rape. See, for example, Kostelanetz, "Unresolved Quests," p. 34. Hugh Gloster, *Negro Voices in American Fiction* (Chapel Hill: University of North

Carolina Press, 1948), p. 225, interprets the relation between Sarah and the salesman as mirroring exploitation of black females by white males.

18. Richard Wright, "Long Black Song," in *Uncle Tom's Children* (New York: Harper & Row, Perennial Library, 1965), p. 106. Subsequent quotations are from this edition.

19. Kinnamon, *Emergence*, pp. 96-97.

20. Alternative interpretations appear in Fabre, *Unfinished Quest*, p. 164, and Webb, *Richard Wright*, p. 166. My particular reading is based on Wright's discussion of black institutions in, for example, "Blueprint," Williams and Harris, *Amistad* 2, pp. 8-9: "And any move, whether from progress or reaction, must come through [black institutions] and them alone for the simple reason that all other channels are closed. Negro writers who seek to mold or influence the consciousness of the Negro people must address their messages to them through the ideologies and ideals fostered in such a cramping and warping way of life."

21. Edward Margolies, *The Art of Richard Wright* (Carbondale: Southern Illinois University Press, 1969), pp. 68-69.

22. Kent, "Richard Wright," pp. 322-43, esp. p. 334, arrives at a similar conclusion in his discussion of what he identifies as "the nationalistic impulse" in *Uncle Tom's Children*.

23. See Donald B. Gibson, "Wright's Invisible Native Son," *American Quarterly* 21 (Winter 1969): 736-38. The following discussion of *Native Son* is based in large part on this essay.

24. Bone, *Negro Novel*, pp. 150-51, and John Reilly, afterword to *Native Son* (New York: Harper & Row, Perennial Classics, 1966), pp. 394-95, 396.

25. Fabre, *Unfinished Quest*, p. 239.

26. See n. 10.

27. Fabre, *Unfinished Quest*, p. 239.

28. In its opening chapters, ibid., points out some of the discrepancies between *Black Boy* and Wright's actual life.

29. Ralph Ellison, *Shadow and Act* (New York: Random House, 1964), pp. 118-19. The passage occurs in *Black Boy* (New York: Harpers, 1945), p. 33.

30. In a seminar on Richard Wright that I conducted at Harvard University in the spring of 1975, a student, Celia Colbert, suggested that Wright's enigmatic criticism of black people makes sense if one substitutes the first person singular pronoun for "Negroes," especially given the preceding episode during which Wright has been humiliated by his estranged father. See also Ellison's analysis of this passage in his review of

Black Boy, "Richard Wright's Blues," *Antioch Review* 5 (Summer 1945): 323-24.

31. See Gibson, "Invisible Native Son."

32. Although our conceptions of the relation between *The Outsider* and Wright's earlier work differ markedly, Darwin Turner feels that the later novel relates to earlier fiction, especially to *Native Son*. Turner, *"The Outsider*: Revision of an Idea," *CLA Journal* 12 (June 1969): 310-21. Hand, "Struggle to Create Life," articulates a more specific relationship: *"The Outsider* explores the meaning of the freedom Bigger achieves just before his death" (p. 86).

33. See Fabre, *Unfinished Quest*, pp. 322, 374. Nick Aaron Ford, "The Ordeal of Richard Wright," *College English* 15 (October 1953): 90, treats Cross Damon's repudiation of his direction as a philosophical inconsistency standing at odds with the novel's existential assumptions.

34. Webb, *Richard Wright*, p. 307.

35. Richard Wright, *The Outsider* (New York: Harper & Brothers, 1953), p. 404.

36. Nathan A. Scott, "Search for Beliefs: Richard Wright," *University of Kansas City Review* 23 (Winter 1956): 135n, thinks the novel unworthy of serious consideration: "In 1954 Avon Publications brought out, between its typically lurid covers, a curiously incoherent little potboiler, *Savage Holiday*, which is available only in this paperback edition and about which the less said the better."

37. Richard Wright, *Savage Holiday* (New York: Award Books, 1965), p. 33.

38. Fabre, *Unfinished Quest*, p. 466. See Saunders Redding's assessment of the novel, "The Alien Land of Richard Wright," in *Soon One Morning: New Writing by American Negroes*, ed. Herbert Hill (New York: Alfred A. Knopf, 1963), pp. 50-59.

39. Fabre, *Unfinished Quest*, pp. 475-82.

40. Richard Wright, *The Long Dream* (Garden City, N.Y.: Doubleday, 1958), p. 20.

2

Ralph Ellison's
Invisible Man:
The Politics
of Retreat

"I wasn't, and am not, primarily concerned
with injustice, but with art."
—Ralph Ellison[1]

"Who knows but that, on the lower
frequencies, I speak for you?"
—Ralph Ellison[2]

THE FAMOUS EXCHANGE several years ago between Irving Howe
and Ralph Ellison is of abiding interest because of the values,
attitudes, and ideas that lay beneath the surface of their commentary.[3] Although ostensibly talking about literature—specifically
about Ellison's and James Baldwin's relation to Richard Wright—
they were essentially arguing over the nature of reality. They were
arguing a question whose resolution forms the basis of the political
orientation of individuals and, more complexly, of groups. Underlying Howe's analysis of and evaluation of the work of the three
writers is the assumption that human beings are essentially the
result of the influence on them of heredity and environment, that

men and women are social creatures whose nature and character are molded by societal experience, and that the writer's duty is to seek to influence the society so as to improve it and thus improve the lot of people. Ellison, on the other hand, argues the individualist's position—that human beings are creatures of will and their lives are what they make of them, that individuals determine the nature of reality exclusive of social considerations, and that the writer's responsibility is to self and only to society insofar as art is broadly humanistic in function.[4] Writers, from Ellison's perspective, are above social science, politics, and economics, their domain being the inner landscape, the private, psychic experience of the discrete individual. Their concern with the social is important only as it bears on that experience. To put their difference in another way, it may be said that Howe locates reality in the external, material world; Ellison, in consciousness, in mind. On the one hand, reality is what it makes you; on the other, what you make it. This divergence of values lies at the heart of the disagreement between Ellison and Howe.[5] Ellison's *Invisible Man* is the fictional presentation of his perspective on reality, its ramifications fictionally articulated, its burden repeated and developed again and again in essays and interviews subsequent to the novel.

It is quite fitting, therefore, that the narrative method Ellison chooses is as it is, for the method is in consonance with the argument of the novel. The prologue takes us, as it progresses, deep within the psyche of the narrator, so deeply that logical relationship is ultimately no longer maintained, and we are given the impression that we are participating entirely in dream or fantasy. The mind revealed is disturbed and agitated. The impression rendered is not of total incoherence, but of thoughts that, although not logically related, center around some as yet unspoken, perhaps unconsciously realized, core. A relation exists between the character of the monologue, its dissonance and subjectivity, and the fact of the character's being underground. Without recourse to forced symbolic analysis on the reader's part, it is apparent that the narrator's physical retreat from the world is analogous to his retreat into himself, into his psyche. It is in this context, in the dim, half-lit regions of dream and fantasy, that the most objective and realistic episodes and events of the novel must be seen, for the whole narrative takes place in the disturbed mind of the narrator. The events are remembered and hence at one remove from their actual chronology. This is consistent with the value scheme underlying the novel: Everything that we see takes place not in the world, as is apparently the case, but in the memory of the participant observer. The epilogue, also an expression of the narrator's most private, subjective thoughts and feelings, differs from the prologue in that the consciousness revealed there is in a healthier state. Apparently the review of the past has created order in the narrator's mind, his discourse being more rational, more orderly, and less indirect and metaphoric. Although he seems more in control of his thought processes, at the end there is yet some question about the stability of his psyche. This focus on the psychic state of the central character is relevant to the novel's meaning and consistent with its underlying value scheme. Just as the narrative method points to the conception that reality is essentially subjective, the changed state of the narrator's psyche indicates the effect on it of all that has gone before. The whole point of the narrative has been to serve a therapeutic end. Hence the implication arises that the novel's interest is not in the social group but in the individual; not in the coming to terms with a social situation by any group of people, but in the psychological response of the specific individual to a societal situation. The interest has been as the narrator's former professor of literature has said of *Portrait of the Artist*: "Stephen's problem, like ours, was not actually one of creating the uncreated conscience of his race, but of creating the *uncreated features of his face*. Our task is that of making ourselves individuals."

The narrative method also tends to support Ellison's assumptions about the primacy of the inner experience of the discrete individual through the tone of the narration, which has the effect of further distancing the actual events of the narrative from reality. That is, the narrative could have been delivered straightforwardly. As it is, however, the events of the narrative are presented through the retrospective consciousness of the narrator and at the same time through his earlier, naive perspective. The narrator understands certain things that the central character in the time present of the narration does not understand. For example, at the beginning of the second chapter, where the narrator evokes a somewhat romantic vision of the college, he apparently did not at the time understand the significance of the fact that a road from the campus leads to the insane asylum. He only understands in retrospect. Another example of the dual consciousness through which the narration is delivered is the narrator's observation on the campus of the statue of the Founder, "his hands outstretched in the breathtaking gesture of lifting a veil that flutters in hard, metallic folds above the face of a kneeling slave; [he stands] puzzled, unable to decide whether the veil is really being lifted, or lowered more firmly into place; whether [he is] witnessing a revelation or a more efficient binding" (p. 28). The central character could not possibly have raised this question at the time he resided at the campus; but in retrospect, having a different perspective on the meaning of his campus experience, he sees it in another light. Likewise, when a coed tells him to deliver a message to her boyfriend, "The grass is green," he understands what it means later (his understanding being evinced by his having chosen to relate it) but not earlier at the time he actually hears it. In the tone throughout are evidences that the consciousness of the narrator of the tale is at once naive about and knowing of the past and the future. The effect is distorting, and the implication is that the meaning of the experience of the central character is primarily centered on its effect on him and him alone and not on its social dimension. I say "primarily" because some qualification need be made, a matter for later consideration.

The conception of invisibility is integral to the meaning of the prologue and of course to the whole novel because it too stems from Ellison's basic orientation. Since the novel's publication, the term *invisible* has taken on a meaning of its own and may therefore be confusing in relation to the special meaning that it comes to have in the novel. It has been not uncommon to describe black people as invisible, meaning that we are ignored or neglected in various ways, but this is not what Ellison means. Rather, as the example he gives at the beginning of the prologue of the response of the man whom he accidentally bumps indicates, invisibility occurs as the result of the definition of individuals solely in terms of what they appear to be (belonging to a specific race or class, for example). The final line of the novel, "perhaps, on the lower frequencies, I speak for you," generalizes the conception to mean definition based on any social criteria—one's dress or occupation, or for that matter any other objective basis which does not recognize uniqueness or individuality. The novel posits something ostensibly more real than social definition. We are told this in the first paragraph of the novel proper:

> I was looking for myself and asking everyone except myself questions which I, and only I, could answer. It took me a long time and much painful boomeranging of my expectations to achieve a realization everyone else appears to have been born with: That I am nobody but myself. [P. 13]

This opening statement and subsequent events direct us to read the novel as an account of a person whose progression through it causes him to divest himself of social roles entirely, the implication being that his essential self is other than social. This stands in contrast to what most people have meant when black people have been said to be invisible. At the same time, Ellison apparently does not intend what is usually meant when people have ascribed some level of being beyond the social; he does not ascribe a soul or any metaphysical mode of individual being. His ascription is, rather, psychological. The essential core of a person is a discrete self, a psyche, an entity that has the potential of distinguishing itself from its surroundings. Once achieved, once so separated, the world may, as the central character observes in the epilogue, "become one of infinite possibility" since all social values and social authority have been discarded or subverted. No wonder he says, "No, but the next step I couldn't make, so I've remained in the hole," for the next step means creating his own reality independent of others'. Toward that way lies madness. The important element here (despite the qualification that this aspect of the analysis deserves here and will later receive) is the tendency toward Platonism. It is not by any means a specifically Platonic perspective that the central character discovers and values, yet the same relation is implied of self to social reality as Platonism describes of the Real to material reality. Hence, in relation to the degree to which it is believed, Ellison's conception of the truth of invisibility diminishes the significance of social reality and assigns to the individual human psyche a greater burden than it can perhaps bear.

The implications of the conception of invisibility generated in the context of the novel are of political consequence, for they raise questions and indeed supply certain answers about individuals and their relation to society. The presentation of the conflict between the central character and his society, of the distance between him and every other individual in the world, is an expression of value, not in that in Ellison's opinion such a relationship is desirable, but in that he insists that the central character comes to understand his real relation to everyone around him. The description assigns value to the perception. The perception that reality is a function of individual consciousness suggests in the context a total relativity of value. Recognizing this as problematical, and somewhat dissatisfied with it as the logical conclusion of his thought and experience, the central character begins to posit value when he says certain things in the epilogue: when he states that "in spite of all I find that I love"; and when he implies, attributing the thought to what his grandfather might have meant by his deathbed advice, that American democracy as defined by its basic doctrines is worthy of affirmation. These are indeed simply posited and not in any but the most tentative and indirect manner. Because they stand in diametrical opposition to the individualistic implications of the whole novel, they are given no support beyond their statement. Those individualistic implications, part and parcel corollary to the conception of invisibility and so strongly stated as to negate the value of love and democracy, mean that race is an individual and not a group problem and that in order to deal with racial oppression, oppressed individuals need to alter their own particular consciousness, need to discover, as the central character does, that they are nobody but themselves. If one denies the true and real existence of racial and class distinction, then one may say that such categories are inoperative and consequently irrelevant. Practically speaking, such

an attitude reflected in social policy would call for the entire disregard of individuals as members of groups or classes.[6] Denial of
race and class distinctions also points to the entire meaninglessness
of group identification and suggests instead the desirability of
individual definition. These implications are all borne out in the
novel's plot, scene, and character.

The action of the novel occurs in three distinct geographical
locations: the small Southern town of the hero's early life; the
college, a community in and of itself and somewhere in the South
other than his hometown; and New York City.[7] Such a structure
does not in itself contribute to the author's expression of values
except in the way in which it is used, in the way that plot and
character are developed within the structure. The first section
comprises the first chapter alone; the second, chapters 2 to 7; and
the third, chapters 7 to 25, the second and third sections overlapping in chapter 7.

The first chapter reports the dying words of the grandfather,
significant because they express a theme whose importance is such
that the enigma of the central character's life cannot be unlocked
without his first untying that Gordian knot. The grandfather's
statement is first of all a paradox akin to the riddle of the Sphinx
put to Oedipus; akin in the sense that the central character's resolution of his situation depends upon his capacity, individually, to
assert a certain intellectual prowess:

> "Son, after I'm gone I want you to keep up the good
> fight. I never told you, but our life is a war and I have
> been a traitor all my born days, a spy in the enemy's
> country ever since I give up my gun back in the Recon
> struction. Live with your head in the lion's mouth. I
> want you to overcome 'em with yesses, undermine 'em
> with grins, agree 'em to death and destruction, let 'em
> swoller you till they vomit or bust wide open." [Pp. 13-14]

But more to the point is the absurdity of the statement, its pitiful
expression of utter impotence, its underlying acknowledgment of

the necessity of resistance to an intolerable situation and, at the same time, the futility of any resistance beyond an attitude so deeply concealed and suppressed as never to find expression outside the consciousness of the speaker. Reminiscent of Claude McKay's poem, "If We Must Die," in the sense that it suggests that resistance can only be at the expense of the life of the resister, it differs from McKay's poem in that its advocacy of resistance is attitudinal alone and not even imaginatively actual, physical, but wholly metaphorical.[8] The grandfather advocates a private and subjective war, so private and so subjective that the enemy does not even recognize that he is at war. He is a spy with no country, with no superior or even side to which to report. When the central character believes late in the novel that he puts his grandfather's advice to the test in his dealing with the Brotherhood, he discovers that it does not work. But what he does then is not what the grandfather has said, for the grandfather's strategy works only within himself, having no practical consequences outside the perimeter of his own consciousness. It does allow him to maintain a certain integrity, although a wholly personal and private sense of wholeness and strength of character. The grandfather says in his deathbed advice that objective political, sociological relation between black and white is not nearly so real as his imagined re-creation of that relation. It is all in the mind, and if he feels he is at war, he is indeed at war though he fires no bullet, files no report, and engages in no acts of espionage. The grandfather has retreated from the world and posits his fantasy as reality, displacing commonly conceived reality. The shades must be drawn because the grandfather is a heretic who firmly believes that his freedom lies in his capacity to imagine, to transmute external reality by an act of imagination. Theoretically he is right in that social reality depends upon faith and belief of individuals in a society that things are such and such, but practically he is wrong in that his imaginative definition has no significance whatsoever beyond himself in the world. The central character, though apparently he does not consciously know it, becomes his grandfather in his rejection of and retreat from the world. He does in fact, as he says he has been told, "take after" his relative.

The chief episode of the first chapter, the battle royal, is revealing in its expression of the value structure of the novel, its major import being that it is a statement of the central character's sense of self, of the public definition of him by the society, and of the interrelation between the two as delineated in the action. The central character sees himself as an individual, distinguished from other participants in the battle by his particular purpose in being there. He is there to deliver an oration; they to entertain the "town's leading white citizens." It turns out, however, that the distinction is meaningful only to him:

> "I didn't care too much for the other fellows who were to take part. They were tough guys who seemed to have no grandfather's curse worrying their minds. No one could mistake their toughness. And besides, I suspected that fighting a battle royal might detract from the dignity of my speech. In those pre-invisible days I visualized myself as a potential Booker T. Washington. But the other fellows didn't care too much for me either and there were nine of them. I felt superior to them in my way, and I didn't like the manner in which we were all crowded together into the servants' elevator." [P. 15]

The attitude of the white citizens toward him does not differ significantly from their attitude toward the other combatants; he, despite the ostensible purpose of his being there, is treated no less inhumanly than they. Interestingly enough, he does not seem to understand what is happening to him, accepting the situation uncritically and as not entirely abnormal. He tries as hard as the others to collect the artificial money from the electrified rug:

> "And we snatched and grabbed, snatched and grabbed. I was careful not to come too close to the rug now, and when I felt the hot whiskey breath descend upon me like a cloud of foul air I reached out and grabbed the leg of a chair." [P. 22]

After all the humiliation of the battle royal, he still desires to deliver his speech, to impress these barbarians with his intellectual abilities. His response at the point where he feels he will not be allowed to speak is despair. From this point on, the irony occasioned by the disparity between his sense of self and their sense of him is intense. His mouth fills with blood, almost strangling him; yet he continues, though nauseated, because of his overwhelming "belief in the rightness of things." When finally he is given the gift of the briefcase, "in the name of the Board of Education," he tells us his reaction:

> "I was so moved that I could hardly express my thanks. A rope of bloody saliva forming a shape like an undiscovered continent drooled upon the leather and I wiped it quickly away. I felt an importance that I had never dreamed.
>   'Open it and see what's inside,' I was told.
>   My fingers atremble, I complied, smelling the fresh leather and finding an official-looking document inside. It was a scholarship to the state college for Negroes. My eyes filled with tears and I ran awkwardly off the floor." [P. 26]

This particular moment forms the climax of the first chapter and along with the denouement that follows—the central character's dream about his grandfather and him—establishes the pattern of action of the entire novel. The episodes following are not simply repetitive of the movement of the first chapter, differing as they do in their range, subtlety, and complexity. Just as the movement here is from the grossest external, physical manipulation—subtle in that his drive to fulfill his own desires causes him to be motivated toward doing the will of others—so the movement of the subsequent chapters is from external manipulation of him to internal self-manipulation as his own desires seem potentially capable of fulfillment through involvement with certain social structures. Each climax of the major episodes has the effect of pushing him off in a different direction until the final climax, the riot—the broadest,

most complex, most socially relevant climactic moment—thrusts
him back upon himself, into himself, and away from dependence
upon external criteria of truth, rationality, and reality.

The differences among the major episodes of the novel can be
measured by assessing the differences between the first and last
episodes. The exposure of the central character to the nude dancer
at the beginning is analogous to the experience with Sybil near the
end; the battle royal is analogous to the riot; his falling into the
open manhole and his decision to remain there analogous to the
dream concluding chapter 1. The intervening chapters expand upon
the central idea articulated in the first chapter until at the end a
reversal has occurred and the central character's private sense of
self assumes ascendancy over his social or public sense of self when
he discovers, in his words, that "I am nobody but myself."

The center of the second section, whose action leads up to and
away from that center, is the Golden Day episode. The central
character's various encounters during the section with Norton,
Trueblood, the vet (at the Golden Day), and finally Bledsoe reflect
on his situation and character, revealing his respect for and awe
of the forces responsible for suppressing his individuality and at the
same time his incomprehension of the intentions toward and relation to him of others. A good deal is indicated about the point of
this section and about the novel in general in a review of Gunnar
Myrdal's *An American Dilemma* (written by Ellison in 1944 though
unpublished until years later) in which Ellison says that after the
Civil War:

> The conditions for the growth of industrial capitalism
> had been won and the Negro "stood in the way of a
> return to national solidarity and a development of trade
> relations" between the North and the South. This
> problem was not easy to solve. . . . In order to deal with
> [it] the North did four things: it promoted Negro educa-
> tion in the South; it controlled his [*sic*] economic and
> political destiny, or allowed the South to do so; it built
> Booker T. Washington into a national spokesman of
> Negroes with Tuskegee Institute as his seat of power;

and it organized social science as an instrumentality to
sanction its methods.[9]

The importance of this analysis to the meaning of the novel cannot
be overstated. It forms the conceptual framework out of which the
novel arises, the novel being an expansion of the idea and the
application of its implications to the life of a specific black individual. Clearly, for example, the characters of Norton and others
have their inception in Ellison's analysis of the relation between
industrial capitalism and black people. Norton is the idea articulated
above, and although he possesses particularizing characteristics, his
motives, actions, and attitudes stem more from the idea governing
his conception than from his particular character. Norton is a
force, and since forces are impersonal, it is no wonder that in the
dynamism of his relation to black people they should be hardly
people at all but ciphers, mere entities to be manipulated in the
interest of achieving certain economic goals. When he says to the
central character, "You are my fate," he means that the successful
expansion of industry and his continued success as an industrialist
are dependent on whether the central character is molded in such a
way as to serve the ends of Northern industry. Norton's concern
with whether the hero has read Ralph Waldo Emerson reflects the
interpretation of Emerson as the apostle of American nationalism
and capitalism, his doctrine of self-reliance ("Self-reliance is a
most worthy virtue," Norton says), a justification for laissez-faire
capitalism.

When the narrator first describes Norton, he describes him, not
as he is understood at the time of his appearance to him at the
college, but as he understands him retrospectively: "A Bostonian,
smoker of cigars, teller of polite Negro stories, shrewd banker,
skilled scientist, director, philanthropist, forty years a bearer of the
white man's burden, and for sixty a symbol of the Great Traditions" (p. 29). At the time the central character first encounters
him, however, Norton is seen as so awesome, so powerful, rich,
and so knowledgeable, so far above him in all ways that he could
not begin to be able in the least way to understand his relation to
Norton beyond the relation assumed by him and the college to be

the proper one. The vet accurately assesses the central character's vision in saying that Norton is "not a man to him but a God, a force."

This view is corrected in the epilogue when the narrator again encounters Norton years later in the subway. The awe returns for a moment, but then he sees Norton not as the powerful philanthropist but as "an old gentleman . . . thinner and wrinkled" and lost. He accuses Norton of being ashamed because he is lost. "If you don't know *where* you are, you probably don't know *who* you are," he says irreverently. He mocks Norton's earlier words: "But I'm your destiny, I made you. Why shouldn't I know you?" (p. 91). The assumptions he initially made about Norton and the assumptions Norton made about him no longer prevail. For the central character, reality lies not in what Norton is but in how he is perceived. The Norton perceived at the end is the same person perceived at the beginning. The difference is in the changed perspective of the observer.

The same point about the relativity of perspective and its bearing on the character of truth or actuality is vividly made by the Trueblood episode. Trueblood's narrative recounts his violation of one of the most basic rules of conduct of the general society: the prohibition against incest. Moreover, issue results, a horrendous fact because the act is continually reflected in its issue. In the dream he has during the incestuous act, he violated the Southern and American proscription against sexual contact between black males and white women. As the narrative is related, the two acts, sexual intercourse with the white woman in the dream and, simultaneously, with his daughter in actuality, are inseparable—the one being coterminous with the other, the dream inseparable at each moment from the act; the act inseparable at each moment from the dream. Ironically Trueblood's white Southern neighbors and Mr. Norton as well are not outraged and indignant on hearing the tale; instead they reward him because his narration of the dream has determined their perspective on it. The narration is such that the whites hearing the story cannot judge Trueblood negatively any more than if he were narrating dream alone. At the same time, the narration confirms the conception of the white audience of the black as being incapable of moral restraint, and it in part fulfills the desire of fathers in general to possess their daughters sexually. In hearing the story, its audience hears what it wants to hear, what it needs to hear. The point is made in the contrast between the central character's response to the narration and Norton's. The central character is not captured by the tale, for he sees its meaning as detrimental to his own best interests: "How can he tell this to white men, I thought, when he knows they'll say that all Negroes do such things? I looked at the floor, a red mist of anguish before my eyes" (p. 45). But even so, he judges Trueblood practically, but not morally. Practically no one, not even the people at the college who feel so threatened by Trueblood, judges the violations of law and morality as such. What incest is, apparently, depends on how it is viewed. Ellison proves this point in the telling of the tale: even the reader, like most of the characters in the tale, does not, no matter what his moral views, judge the act itself. The responses of Kate, Mrs. Trueblood, her female neighbors who succor her after the event, and the black minister whom Trueblood later consults are different from those of all the others around. They judge the morality of the act of incest, and they judge the perpetrator and find him wanting:

> "And I'm still settin' there when she comes back with some women to see 'bout Matty Lou. Won't nobody speak to me, though they looks at me like I'm some new kinda cotton-pickin' machine. I feels bad. I tells them how it happened in a dream, but they scorns me. I gits plum out of the house then. I goes to see the preacher and he don't believe me. He tells me to git out of his house, that I'm the most wicked man he's ever seen and that I better go confess my sin and make my peace with God. I leaves tryin' to pray, but I caint. [P. 51]

Trueblood himself, after thinking for days "'bout how I'm guilty and how I ain't guilty," concludes finally "that I ain't nobody but myself and ain't nuthin' I can do but let whatever is gonna happen happen" (p. 94). His is among four distinct interpretations of the incestuous act and, finally, in the novel's context, the most significant one. If we see the act in relation to the central character's statement at the beginning of the first chapter that he had to discover that he is nobody but himself, and his insight while eating a yam on the street in Harlem, "I yam what I yam," then the episode demonstrates the author's initial assumption: The nature of reality is dependent on the perception of the discrete individual. Trueblood's "I ain't nobody but myself" is what it takes the central character many years and much pain to learn.

Norton is so shaken by the narrative not only, as so many critics have said, because he too has had sexual inclinations toward his daughter but because his whole conception of the world as reflecting an orderly arrangement of things and himself as one who assists in the sustaining of that arrangement is called into question. His exclamation, "You have looked upon chaos and are not destroyed!" (p. 40) indicates astonishment that Trueblood's infringement should not have been punished by some controlling agency beyond. By the time he has heard the completed tale, he is in a faint and weakened condition because Trueblood's power of narration has drawn him into complicity. Norton tells us that his "real" work has been not his banking and research but his "first-hand organizing of human life," and this is dedicated to the highly idealized memory of his daughter, "rare, a perfect creation, a work of the purest art. A delicate flower that bloomed in the liquid light of the moon. A nature not of this world, a personality like that of some biblical maiden" (p. 33). The effect of Trueblood's narrative is to raise doubts in Norton's mind about the character of his emotional relation to his daughter and his conception of himself, for through empathy with Trueblood, the sexuality inherent in his relation with his daughter is dredged up from the deeper recesses of his mind. He is shaken to the core of his being, not only because he sees that Trueblood is not struck down for his "monstrous" act, but more so because he is unable finally to distinguish between Trueblood and himself. Trueblood has been "true to the claims of the blood." Norton, whose life has been centered around the ideal, is, through the influence of the narrative, reclaimed by the blood. The Golden Day episode continues Norton's descent into the world's sexuality, physicality, and violence from which his ideals, his money, and his social position have heretofore shielded him. Interestingly enough the obverse of Norton's idealism (as critical as the author is of that) is unsatisfactory, false, mad, chaotic, and unbearable.[10]

Norton's experience at the Golden Day during the third chapter of the novel is a rendering of the obverse of the sense of order deriving from his idealism, a dialectically opposite alternative called forth by the challenge to order and idealism occasioned by Trueblood's narrative. The veterans, black veterans of the battle of life, are leaderless and lacking the restraints ordinarily imposed by internal or external authority. Norton therefore is divested of the respect accorded to him (but not per se belonging to him) by those who know and value his social identity. The veterans and the prostitutes, outcasts both, have no stake in recognizing or sustaining Norton's power, a power whose only source lies in the recognition and acceptance of his social identity, a power whose manifestation consists in its capacity to elicit respect.

The prostitutes and the character referred to as the vet make clear the implications of the episode by means of their articulation of the central character's perspective through contrast with their own. Both he and they observe and interpret Norton's identity; both see a totally different reality. "He's only a man," the vet says, "Remember that. He's only a man."

> I wanted to tell him that Mr. Norton was much more than that, that he was a rich white man and in my charge; but the very idea that I was responsible for him was too much for me to put into words. [P. 66]

The women too see him as a "rich white man," but in contrast to the attitude conveyed by the central character in making the same observation they see him irreverently as a "rich ole white man" with "monkey glands and billy goat balls." The vet speaks of him as a "trustee of consciousness," a description having no meaning to the central character. Hester, one of the women, pats Norton on the cheek, expressing far more familiarity and lack of respect than he has known or desires. The vet, perceiving Norton as a man and an equal, acts toward him in a way contrary to the rules governing interaction in this environment between a black man and a white man, especially a white man of Norton's "stature":

> The one thing which I did know was that the vet was acting toward the white man with a freedom which could only bring on trouble. I wanted to tell Mr. Norton that the man was crazy and yet I received a fearful satisfaction from hearing him talk as he had to a white man.[11] [P. 71]

The character of the vet's words, the tone and diction of his speech, makes it clear that his attitudes, his evaluation of the central character and Mr. Norton, are reflective of the author's own system of values within the context of the novel.

> "But seriously, because you both fail to understand what is happening to you. You cannot see or hear or smell the truth of what you see—and you, looking for destiny! It's classic! And the boy, this automaton, he was made of the very mud of the region and he sees far less than you. Poor stumblers, neither of you can see the other. To you he is a mark on the score-card of your achievement, a thing and not a man; a child, or even less—a black amorphous thing. And you, for all your power, are not a man to him, but a God, a force. . . . He believes in you as he believes in the beat of his heart. He believes in that great false wisdom taught slaves and pragmatists alike, that white is right. I can tell you *his* destiny. He'll do your bidding, and for that his blindness is his chief asset. He's your man, friend. Your man and your destiny. Now the two of you descend the stairs into chaos and get the hell out of here." [P. 73]

The vet is not precisely the person who the central character finally becomes in the epilogue, yet certainly he is undifferentiated from

the central character of the prologue whose psyche is apparently
healed, finally, through the therapy of the objectification and
ordering of tangled, partially understood thoughts and feelings.
There is indeed some question about the psychic wholeness of the
central character as he appears in the epilogue. He is, in any case,
"better," if not well. His view of Norton at the end is not unlike
the vet's earlier view. The implication of the vet's perceptiveness,
that "in madness is divinest sense," raises the question whether the
awareness and understanding evinced by the central character
finally can issue only out of madness. Such extreme individualism
is a manifestation of pathology. The apparently settled state of his
mind is true and of value within the context established by the
writer; yet clearly he can see and interpret the world as he does only
by rejection of social reality, a state thoroughly enough described
in psychiatric literature on psychosis.

The time in the second section from the central character's
departure from the Golden Day to his arrival in Harlem constitutes
a falling away of the action from the climax of the section, which
occurs specifically when the vet says, "I'm sick of both of you
pitiful obscenities! Get out before I do you both the favor of
bashing in your heads!" (p. 73).

The depiction of the character of the college, of Bledsoe, and of
the dismissal are background describing who the central character
thinks he is, why he conceives of himself as he does, and how,
given these factors, he progresses. The section describing the college reveals the depth of the central character's involvement in that
institution, an involvement so intense that when he compares his
leaving to "the parting of the flesh," the comparison is not quite
so hyperbolic as it might appear. Of course all groups and institutions have their ritual means of ensuring the identification of the
meaning and goals of the institution with the individual's own sense
of his meaning and goals. The college represents a rather special
situation in this regard, given its particular history and character.
It is significant that the college is for blacks, located in the rural
South, and founded after the Civil War. For thousands of black
people, such colleges historically represented the only way out of
extreme rural poverty. The central character's early sense of him-

self as "a potential Booker T. Washington" should not be taken lightly in view of the fact that Washington's rise from slavery to a position of influence and power was a phenomenon generally well known among black people in the earlier twentieth century and ostensibly indicative of the greatest of possibilities that lay ahead for intelligent, aspiring black youth. The way lay through the college, the type of college founded by Washington, prototype of the college of the novel, being living proof of the potential to realize the idea.

The central character has been so thoroughly imbued with the dream articulated by Homer A. Barbee (Homer, the historian, the transmitter of the true past), he believes it so intensely and entirely, that he is incapable of seeing it as other than his own knowledge and point of view, for in the myth of the past of the college is the enunciation of his own future possibility. He has no hopes or dreams whatsoever beyond those potentially possible through his association with the college, hopes and dreams sustained and renewed through the semireligiosity transmitted during the chapel scene, where we see the enactment of the annual Founder's Day, a day in fact celebrated at most such colleges as that of the novel to honor the founder of the particular college.

Central to the celebration of these Founder's Days is the annual oratorical tribute, delivered in *Invisible Man* by Barbee. Ellison's rendering of the oration may be imaginary, but the style and the language are such that it is by no means distant from actual Founder's Day orations. Following is a transcription of a Founder's Day oration delivered on the occasion at Hampton Institute in 1898. Booker T. Washington attended that school, and although the founder here referred to is General Samuel Chapman Armstrong, the similarity between it and Barbee's tribute bespeaks a common tradition:

> This day is reverently set apart by us to recall the life of our Founder and to repeat to ourselves the lessons of his teaching. It is a familiar story which we love to tell to each other from year to year; but it is a story very difficult to tell with the moderation of statement of which

our Founder would approve. . . . It is not my purpose
here today to review in detail the movement of General
Armstrong's life. Yet no one can recall his personal
history without a new impression of the mysterious way
in which a living God sometimes unfolds before a man
by slow degrees the special work which is to be given to
that man to do. Looking back on General Armstrong's
career we see him prepared by each step from its beginning for the destiny that was before him, . . . By
degrees his mission began to call to him. "A day
dream," he once wrote, "of the Hampton School nearly
as it is, had come to me during the war a few times. . . .
The thing to be done," he goes on "was clear: to train
selected Negro youths who should go out and teach and
lead their people; to teach respect for labor, to replace
stupid drudgery with skilled hands, and to those ends to
build an industrial system." Such a day dream, so
described, calls back to one's mind a scene which many
travellers remember with special emotion among the
sacred places of Palestine.[12]

It was this thinking and sentiment with which students at the college were imbued, students who were extraordinarily receptive
because they came to the college with nothing, wanting a great
deal, and hence were psychologically ready to adapt to a scheme of
values that gave them a hitherto unknown place in and relation to
the larger society. Reverend Barbee's oration reflects the mythological basis on which belief in the college and its ostensible ends is
founded.

Dr. Bledsoe, however, in his conversations with the central
character following the chapel scene, expresses opinions, ideas, and
values standing in contrapuntal relation to those expressed by
Barbee. Bledsoe's attitudes and orientation represent the truth
beneath the appearance, the structure behind the facade, the bone
beneath the flesh. The oration is the public face of the institution;
Bledsoe's revelation, the mechanism behind. The terrible truth in
the relationship between appearance and reality (and yet another

way of describing the central problem of the novel) is that from Ellison's perspective the one is dependent upon the other; neither the face nor the mechanism is or can be pure, and therefore both are corrupt. The road leading off the campus to the insane asylum undercuts and corrupts the beauty of the campus. The statue of the Founder reflects impurity because it is "bird-soiled," its soiled state inseparable in the central character's mind from the statue's representational meaning. In the same manner the dying words of the grandfather in the first section ("Live with your head in the lion's mouth," and so on) represent courage and cowardice; daring and defeat; impotence and strength; vulnerability and impregnability. The problem that the central character sets for himself is to distinguish what by definition is incapable of distinction. He defines at the beginning of the novel the problem of separating the terms of the grandfather's statement, as analysis requires. No clear distinctions, however, are to be made. There are no interstices between the terms, no seams in the garment. The grandfather was "the meekest of men"; yet he says, "Live with your head in the lion's mouth." Between the act—the fact of the character of the grandfather's life—and the idea—danger of annihilation—is no distinction: the shadow and the act are one as the dancer and dance are one. The Founder's Day oration is shadow; Bledsoe, act. At one and the same time Bledsoe is shadow, the Founder's Day oration representative of act. Neither is real, yet both are real. Each has its mutually dependent effect upon the world.

It is from this perspective that the characters of the president of the college and the Founder are conceived. They are inseparable personages, each in varying degrees representing pure pragmatism and pure idealism, yet each partaking of the virtue (or limitation) of the other. This deduction is based on Ellison's purposely extracting biographical details from the life of Booker T. Washington and intertwining them with the characters of Bledsoe and the Founder. This begins early in the novel, in the second paragraph of the first chapter, where the narrator quotes directly from Washington's so-called Atlanta Compromise address of 1895: "free, united with others of our country in everything pertaining to the common good, and, in everything social separate like the fingers of the hand.''[13] Washington is mentioned by name in the fifth paragraph of the first chapter, and later, when the central character delivers his speech at the smoker, the only significant part of it rendered is also directly quoted from Washington's Atlanta address.

That the life of the historical figure is combined with the life of the fictional character Bledsoe is apparent in the parody of Booker T. Washington's arrival and acceptance into Hampton Institute as related in his autobiography, *Up from Slavery*. Washington indeed arrived at the college after trudging over two states and was instructed to clean a room. He cleaned the room very well and on that basis was accepted into the college. Ellison changes the facts somewhat in describing Bledsoe's initial arrival at the college as a young boy:

> I remembered the legend of how he had come to the college, a barefoot boy who in his fervor for education had trudged with his bundle of ragged clothing across two states. And how he was given a job feeding slop to the hogs but had made himself the best slop dispenser in the history of the school; and how the founder had been impressed and made him his office boy. [P. 90]

The central character's further impressions of Dr. Bledsoe clearly establish his relation to Booker T. Washington.

> I remembered the admiration and fear he inspired in everyone on the campus; the pictures in the Negro press captioned "EDUCATOR," in type that exploded like a rifle shot, his face looking out at you with utmost confidence. To us he was more than just president of a college. He was a leader, a "statesman" who carried our problems to those above us, even unto the White House; and in days past he had conducted the President himself about the campus. [P. 90]

Although couched in terms of personal impressions, these reminiscences are historically based.

But as the character of the opportunistic Bledsoe is based on the historical person Washington, so is the character of the idealized Founder. The statue described in the third paragraph of the second chapter is said to be of the Founder. It is, in the details of its description and in fact, a statue of Booker T. Washington on the campus of Tuskegee Institute. Later in the novel, however, the Founder and Booker T. Washington appear to be entirely separate people. "How would you like to be the new Booker T. Washington?" Brother Jack inquires of the central character. "Well, I guess I don't think he was as great as the Founder," he responds. "Why not?" Brother Jack asks.

> "Well, in the first place, the Founder came before him and did practically everything Booker T. Washington did and a lot more. And more people believed in him. You hear a lot of arguments about Booker T. Washington, but few would argue about the Founder." [P. 232]

Their distinction, however, is only apparent. If we recall the passage quoted earlier about the relation of Northern industry to the South and Ellison's comment there about Booker T. Washington, the relation between him and the fictional Bledsoe becomes clear.[14] The North, Ellison says, "built Booker T. Washington into a national spokesman of Negroes with Tuskegee Institute as his seat of power." The dual aspect, then, of the characters of the Founder, Bledsoe, and Booker T. Washington becomes clear. ("For has not," Barbee says, "your present leader become his [the Founder's] living agent, his physical presence?") Booker T. Washington was in fact the Founder of Tuskegee Institute; yet it has never been in his role as Founder that controversy (contemporary and later) has surrounded him. The argument was never whether Tuskegee should have been founded but rather what its particular educational policy should have been and what by implication should be national educational policy in relation to black people. Insofar as Washington had in mind to serve what he considered the national interest at the expense of black people, his role and character have a sinister, pragmatic, opportunistic side. Insofar as he founded and maintained one of the earliest and most significant educational institutions for black people in history, his role and character are entirely commendable. These roles are separated in the novel in the characters of the Founder and Bledsoe. They are combined ambiguously and ambivalently in the character of Booker T. Washington. The central figurative projection of the complex relation among the roles is rendered in the statue of the Founder on the campus, which is either (or both) freeing or enslaving (or both or neither) the person kneeling before it:

> Then in my mind's eye I see the bronze statue of the college Founder, the cold Father symbol, his hands outstretched in the breathtaking gesture of lifting a veil that flutters in hard metallic folds above the face of a kneeling slave; and I am standing puzzled, unable to decide whether the veil is really being lifted, or lowered more firmly into place; whether I am witnessing a revelation or a more efficient blinding. And as I gaze, there is a rustle of wings and I see a flock of starlings flighting before me, and when I look again, the bronze face, whose empty eyes look upon a world I have never seen, runs with liquid chalk—creating another ambiguity to puzzle my groping mind: Why is a birdsoiled statue more commanding than one that is clean? [P. 28]

Central to the meaning of the novel is whether the central character is ever able to untangle the strands of the ambiguities and ambivalences that constantly thrust themselves before him during the course of his experiences throughout the novel. Surely the vet has the capacity to understand, holding as he does a position that allows him to see through the external trappings (his social position and race) to the dynamics of the relation of the central character to Norton and the relation of both to the college. May we see the vet, then, as spokesman for the author? Ellison uses the vet as a means of commenting on Norton (as well as an index of the state of the main character's psyche). The vet's severe criticism of Norton for his application of an idealistic system of values to the world, a system that does not take into account the humanity of those subjected to it, is delivered in such a manner as to make it clear that his analysis reflects the values of the author. That is, the vet is presented so as to invite credibility, speaking as he does with authority, logic, and sanity. The vet, however, despite the fact that there is nothing during the scenes in which he appears to contradict or undercut the logic of his utterance (except his being insane— *argumentum ad hominem* on the one hand; sense in insanity on the other) is yet representative of a position distinguishable from the author's in the total context of the novel. The vet differs from the central character of the epilogue in that the vet has only the capacity to be critical and no positive understanding, feelings, or assumptions sufficient to allow him to function in the world. The vet has defined himself in a totally negative way; he knows who he is not although not who he is. The central character, however, in the only statements in the epilogue that would suggest that he is not totally insane, feels tentatively toward positive identity through social relationship.

> Could he have meant . . . that we [black people] were to affirm the principle on which the country was built and not the men, or at least not the men who did the violence. . . . Or did he mean that we had to take the responsibility for it, all of it, for the men as well as the principle, because we were the heirs who must use the principle, because no other fitted our needs? . . . Or was it, did he mean that we should affirm the principle because we, through no fault of our own, were linked to all the others in the loud, clamoring semivisible world, that world seen only as a fertile field for exploitation by Jack and his kind, and with condescension by Norton and his, who were tired of being the mere pawns in the futile game of "making history?" [Pp. 433-34]

> Our fate is to become one, and yet many. . . . [P. 435]

> And I defend because in spite of all I find that I love. [P. 437]

> Perhaps that's my greatest social crime, I've overstayed
> my hibernation, since there's a possibility that even an
> invisible man has a socially responsible role to play.
> [P. 439]

In the context in which they occur, however, these statements are indeed tentative reflections at best.[15] The long statement that appears as a kind of paean to the democratic ideal is put in such a way that it cannot be directly attributable to the central character (and finally to the author), for the apparent statement turns out finally to be an extended question and not an answer. Hence, faced with the question whether the central character ever untangles the ambiguities that confront him, we need only quote his words regarding his grandfather's deathbed advice:

> "And my mind revolved again and again back to my
> grandfather. And, despite the farce that ended my
> attempt to say 'yes' to the Brotherhood, I'm still plagued
> by his deathbed advice. . . . Perhaps he hid his meaning
> deeper than I thought, perhaps his anger threw me off—
> I can't decide." [P. 433]

He finally understands Norton and Jack, and since the scene during which he experiences partial insight when he looks at the statue of the Founder is rendered retrospectively, we may even assume that he comes to understand that. But the resolution of ambiguities seems to lead finally only to deeper ambiguities. We may say, then, that the central character comes to see his experience as ultimately ambiguous (and in this too he differs from the vet), and if his identity consists in his discovering he is nobody but himself, the emphasis should be placed on "nobody."

By the time the second section ends and the third begins (the central character's leaving the college and arriving in New York), the major problems of the novel have been articulated. We have only to see their specific working out in the central character's reactions to his experience. Within the third section, the lines of action lead to two high points in the plot: the explosion at the paint factory and the Harlem riot. After the paint factory episode and the central character's release from the hospital, the line of action depicting his intertwined relation to Ras and the Brotherhood develops toward his plunge into the underground. The final denouement, including the epilogue, follows.

In the paint factory episode, the central character attempts to function in the world in a relatively uncomplicated way. The result of the experience, however, is to force him away from the world, away from social relationship, and into himself. He cannot simply live from day to day in the world because some aspect of his personality surfaces from time to time in the novel causing him unconsciously to resist definitions imposed on him by his social environment. Its form is of an uncontrollable impulse to resist what is required of him by defining forces.[16] Its first appearance is after the battle royal; in delivering his oration he shouts out "social equality!" when he consciously meant to say "social responsibility." It emerges during the hospital scene when, faced with the possibility of the annihilation of his biographical past, he thwarts the lobotomizing device and the doctors who would depersonalize him. It emerges again when he unintentionally breaks the metal bank at Mary's house (a caricature of himself in relation to the Brotherhood) and again when he unwittingly drops into the manhole. In this particular section of the novel, it shows itself when he unconsciously puts the wrong chemical into the paint cans, thus sabotaging the national whitewash of the nation's monuments and, by implication, its social and political ideals. And it again comes to the fore when he turns the wrong valve, blowing up the factory's works. From the author's perspective it seems to be his humanity, his "self," which at these times bursts forth, however momentarily, thus saving the central character from becoming the "cog," the "mechanical man," the "walking zombie" (all terms used by the vet), the bank at Mary's that functions at the flip of a lever, the dancing black doll that Tod Clifton sells, the creature of Norton and the college, the lackey of management or labor at the paint factory, the tool of the Brotherhood, the appendage of Ras. This assumption on Ellison's part of some core of identity underlying social identity is the basis of the central character's insistence that he will emerge from the underground, for having peeled away false (social) identities, a self, a decision-making, judging, intelligent self, assumedly remains. The paint factory episode is, then, the peeling away of yet another level of social identity, a process begun in the battle royal scene and reminiscent of it in the fight between the central character and Lucius Brockway, reminiscent because it is motivated by forces exterior to the characters' wills.

The machine in which the central character is placed during the hospital scene is intended to have the effect not simply of lobotomy but also of destroying his capacity to resist social demand, acquiescence to social requirements. For this reason the test of the machine's effectiveness consists of asking the central character questions whose answers reflect his most nearly basic sense of self. If the machine works, he is not supposed to remember the answers to the questions posed: "What is your name?" "Who are you?" "What is your mother's name?" He does remember, however, and, unknown to his interlocutor, thinks insulting responses.[17] Because his basic sense of self is undestroyed by the machine, he is prepared to deal with more highly complex social phenomena as shown by his involvement in the eviction and his consequent recruitment into the Brotherhood.

The central character's sense of the potential meaning for his life of his introduction to the Brotherhood must be measured against the outcome of the plot, against the moment at the end when, chased and threatened by black and white, he drops into the open manhole. His high hopes for achievement in the Brotherhood are expressed at the end of chapter 16:

> I thought of Bledsoe and Norton and what they had done. By kicking me into the dark they'd made me see the possibility of achieving something greater and more important than I'd ever dreamed. Here was a way that didn't lead through the back door, a way not limited by black and white, but a way which, if one lived long enough and worked hard enough, could lead to the highest possible rewards. Here was a way to have a part

in making the big decisions, of seeing through the
mystery of how the country, the world, really operated.
For the first time, lying there in the dark, I could glimpse
the possibility of being more than a member of a race. It
was no dream, the possibility existed. I had only to work
and learn and survive in order to go to the top. [P. 268]

The enormous psychological distance between this point and the
point at which the central character finds himself at the end of the
novel is a measure of the extent to which social involvement is
interpreted as destructive and threatening even (as in the case of
Tod Clifton) unto death.

The central character's relation to the Brotherhood is essentially
the same as to the college, both being analogous to his relation to
the society at large.[18] As does the college, the Brotherhood has its
facade masking an utterly divergent interior. The central character's
movement from the time of his involvement traces his eventual
understanding of the relation between the outer and inner aspects
of the organization and his response to that knowledge. The
problem of the disparity between the Brotherhood as it appears on
the surface and as it is underneath is more emotional than intellectual, for his faith has been so great, and he has to such a
degree internalized what he believed to be the values of the organization, that his psychic balance is threatened and his mind nearly
destroyed. He undergoes trauma (to put it in another way) because his sense of personal identity has been entirely enmeshed
with the ostensible aims and intentions of the Brotherhood. When
the organization betrays him, it has the effect of creating personal
and social disorientation, disequilibrium.

The depth of his commitment to the Brotherhood, stemming
from his recognition of it as the source of his identity and its
confirmation of his identity through its support and recognition,
allows the central character to resist the compelling exhortations of
Ras.[19] As his association with the college ostensibly would have
broadened his previously parochial life, so his involvement with the
Brotherhood will broaden his horizons even more. Ras offers what
appears to be a definition of self, narrowed and circumscribed by

its racial nature. Since there is no correspondence between what
Ras represents and wants and the central character's needs and
wants, there is relatively little ambivalence in his rejection of Ras.
Some degree of ambivalence is, however, reflected in his narration
of his experience with Ras in that Ras is presented in a not wholly
negative manner. His arguments for black nationalism are presented in a straightforward, convincing manner. They are the best
arguments for nationalism, and they capture for a moment the
imagination of the central character, who thinks, "He was an
exhorter, all right, and I was caught in the crude, insane eloquence
of his plea" (p. 282). Tod Clifton, though, is not so immune to the
argument. It is he who spins and strikes Ras when the Exhortor
says, "I am no black traitor to the black people for the white
people" (p. 284). Afterward, with tears in his eyes, Clifton tells the
central character, "It'll run you crazy if you let it" (p. 284). Ras's
implied accusation is finally seen by Clifton to be fitting when
Clifton discovers the treachery of the Brotherhood and indeed
becomes insane and is killed. Ras was in some sense right, and his
having been right is reflective in part of the narrator's attitude
toward him. This implied judgment, however, is modified by the
presentation of Ras "become the Destroyer":

> A new Ras of a haughty, vulgar dignity, dressed in the
> costume of an Abyssinian chieftain; a fur cap upon his
> head, his arm bearing a shield, a cape made of the skin
> of some wild animal around his shoulders. A figure
> more out of a dream than out of Harlem, than out of
> this Harlem night, yet real, alive, alarming. [Pp. 419-20]

The central character's spearing of Ras through his jaws in itself
constitutes a judgment—a negation and a denial. Again the negative definition, the assertion of what he is not, the final negation
and denial.

Rinehart is the diametrical opposite of Ras, his identity as fluid
as Ras's is fixed. The central character toys with the notion of
assuming the identity (nonidentity) of Rinehart but finally denies
that temptation because such a course could only intensify his

problem. Rinehart is anything to everybody and hence is nothing to anybody. His identity at any given moment rests entirely on the perceptions of those within his immediate presence. He is as he is seen to be at any particular time, his identity completely contextual. Since the central character's main problem has involved the imposition on him of others' senses of his identity, the manner of Rinehart can be no solution for him. Rinehart's identity is all surface, all social—"rind" and "heart"—but both outward; neither is underneath, behind, or within the other; both are continuous surface. Rinehart is invisible in the same sense that the central character has been invisible throughout the narrative. The difference is that as Rinehart he is consciously aware of the illusion he creates by virtue of the consciously assumed identity and mode of action. There is a paradox here. He may choose to be Rinehart, but, as his experiences as Rinehart reveal, he has no control over the particular response he engenders in those who observe him. That is, in choosing to be Rinehart he may choose nonidentity, and as "nobody" he is free of moral and social restraint and reality. Thus arises his sense of infinite possibility, which he experiences as Rinehart. Being nobody, he stands "outside the narrow borders of what men call reality" and in the realm of, as he says, "chaos" on the one hand or "imagination" on the other. Once he has had this insight, no participation in society is possible without its involving his "playing a role." Among the infinite roles possible for him, one is "a socially responsible role," as he says, but even playing such a role is unreal in some measure. His awareness of the meaning of Rinehartism allows him neither to embrace it nor to reject it. He says, therefore, at the end of the novel, that

> in going underground, I whipped it all except the mind,
> the *mind*. And the mind that has conceived a plan of
> living must never lose sight of the chaos against which
> that pattern was conceived. That goes for societies as
> well as for individuals. [P. 438]

He has thought himself into a corner, and no logic will allow him to stay or go, to remain underground or to emerge.

This, however, is not the whole story. The grandfather's death-bed advice has about it the character of Rinehartism in that it directs deception, the conscious assumption of whatever appearance is called for in any situation. Between the grandfather and Rine-hart, however, is an essential difference. Whereas Rinehart has no core, no center of self, no limits, no positive definition, the grand-father acts on principle, preserving a distinct coherence and integrity of self. The grandfather's expression of principle in his advice does not place him in the limitless realm of imagination or in the anarchic realm of chaos. Rather it places him in relation to higher principles, the principles articulated by the central character in the epilogue (quoted in part above), where it is speculated that the grandfather's words refer to the basic principles and ideals of American democ-racy. But again the central character cannot rest here, unable as he is either to embrace the grandfather's advice or to let it go. His perception of Rinehartism does not allow him to adopt the prin-ciples of his grandfather (assuming the advice to refer to democracy) and then simply live in the world because such a response can also result in his playing a role. Also, as has been pointed out above, the grandfather's private sense of self, or anybody else's private sense of self, has no necessary practical relation to a world in which the individual is powerless, at the mercy of the dynamics of a relentless social system.

The result is that the central character, with his insight into the meaning of the lives of his grandfather and Rinehart, is not simply impaled on the horns of a dilemma; he is torn between two equally paradoxical alternatives, equally committed at once to both and neither, each at once supporting and canceling out the other. He has indeed "whipped it all except the mind."

The problem we are left with, then, is that the central character has not discovered his identity but has rather discovered that he has no identity. He is nobody. His "perhaps on the lower levels I speak for you" completes the analogy to Emily Dickinson's

> I'm Nobody! Who are you?
> Are you – Nobody – Too?

Unless one wishes to pursue the argument that negation is one means of definition—an untenable argument here because negative definition rests on the assumption of a final positive, that what is being defined is something—then the meaning of the novel is finally that identity is a function of social circumstance and hence unreal, invalid, inauthentic. The argument, especially as articulated in such brilliant fictional terms, is compelling. It is no more compelling, however, than the paradoxes of Zeno, who quite logically proves that motion is impossible. That is, in that we do not in fact remain immobile despite Zeno's logic, we may not indulge the luxury of acting from the assumption that social reality, and the resultant terms of definition thrust upon us by society, is unreal. We must, in fact, and we do, act in the world, accommodating ourselves, however uncomfortably or inconsistently, to the disparity between self-identity and social identity, between who and what we think we are and who and what the world thinks we are.

Invisible Man, however, leaves us with the firmly established proposition that the only dependable source of truth, reasonableness, judgment, and reliability is the independent psyche of the discrete individual. Any reasonable person must admit that such a perception is true in some sense, but to take it to such a solopsistic extreme as the novel does leads to distortion and to the support of conservative, status-quo political and social values. The novel, in its insistence that the problem faced by the central character is private and personal, expresses values of a social character, for by implication each oppressed person in society must bear the burden of responsibility for his situation. Again, there may be an argument for such a proposition, but it is hardly a position favorable to the health of the dispossessed.

Concomitant with the expression of individualism as a value is the implication that group action is meaningless because group involvement diminishes individuality. Through the course of the novel, the central character has cut himself off from the possibility of group participation on any level. This suggests that racial and class solidarity are by definition meaningless and even detrimental to the well-being of individuals. Again this is true to an extent, but in its extreme it is not true. If it is true to the extent described in Ellison's novel, then the black power movement of the 1960s should have been repudiated as should any other move in the direction of racial group solidarity. Just as *Invisible Man* repudiates black nationalism through its interpretation of the character Ras, so Ellison has repudiated it subsequently.[20] I do not intend to suggest that Ellison should be a black nationalist but rather to say that his strong opposition to it has been in its form supportive of systems of belief and values inimical to black progress.

The novel also tells us that the victim can do nothing to alleviate social oppression. If the victim joins with others, he or she is likely to be manipulated in such a manner as to undercut personal aims, or he or she will define the self in such a narrow and provincial way as to distort or destroy individuality. He or she cannot discover identity because underneath it all there is not one anyway. One can only retreat into the cavern of the mind, for only there in the grotto of isolation exists unlimited freedom.

Ellison's rejection of the idea of the primacy of social experience is not unrelated to his insistence that he is an artist and not a politician or sociologist. The evolution of this attitude can be traced from his early days as a writer for *New Masses*. In 1940 when he held the opposite view, he could write in a review of Langston Hughes's *The Big Sea*, "In the style of *The Big Sea* too much attention is apt to be given to the aesthetic aspects of experience at the expense of its deeper meanings."[21] Less than a year later he said in a general critical statement about black writers, "The solution to the problem of publication [for black writers] seems to lie through the mastery of the intense ways of thinking and feeling that are artistic techniques."[22] I believe that Ellison was beginning to work out here a system of values antithetical to those he held at the time. This is attested to by comparison of his *New Masses* articles and reviews and later writings up to about 1946 with *Invisible Man* and subsequent essays, interviews, and speeches. *Invisible Man* marks the turning point, the point after which he begins to insist on the Americanness of black experience, on the importance of formal considerations in art, on himself as artist and not polemicist in his novel, on the relation between American art and American nationalism, and on the autonomy of art. It was only after *Invisible Man* that he could say with such aplomb in a comment about Malraux (1955), "Most of the social realists of the period were concerned less with tragedy than with injustice. I wasn't and I am not primarily concerned with injustice, but with art."[23] The social and political positions Ellison articulates in public forums almost all find their fictional representation in *Invisible Man*.

Despite Ellison's good intentions, as reflected, for example, in his appreciation of and sympathy for the black American past, the public policy implications of *Invisible Man* are murderous. The fact that he was called upon to testify before the Senate Subcommittee on Executive Reorganization should say something quite direct about the disparity between what he has thought his novel to be and what others conceive it to be.[24] Aside from whatever else it might be, *Invisible Man* is a social document that supports certain values and disparages or discourages others, and as such it must take its place among other forces that seek to determine the character of social reality. This is essentially the point Irving Howe wanted to make in his attack on Ellison. Unfortunately Howe's argument is tainted with racism (as when he refers to Ellison and Baldwin as "black *boys*"), and when Ellison joins the argument, he detects this and responds in kind. Hence the real issues are intertwined with extraneous, seemingly personal reaction and response. Ellison marshals the better argument; finally he devastates Howe by pointing out that some parts of Howe's response had been lifted from previously published work. Ellison won the argument; Howe, if we discount the racism of his position, was right. Ellison was wrong in that his novel indicates that victims apparently must start out by discovering what is wrong with them that they are victimized. If one starts out with the assumption that the poor, the dispossessed, the have-nots, the invisible are as they are because of some limitation they possess, then one will arrive at quite different conclusions, quite different social legislation, than if one begins by asking what is wrong with the society that there should be such victims. The question is one of emphasis, and Ellison has chosen to emphasize the responsibility of the victim for his victimization.[25] The novel makes myriad qualifications; hence the appearance of ambiguity. But the ambiguity is not true ambiguity, for the case is weighted on one side more than on the other. The novel says finally that the weight of social involvement is so destructive, so potentially devastating, that individual survival against it without loss of integrity is impossible. Therefore one cannot do otherwise than withdraw, retreat. On the one hand, retreat constitutes no politics at all; on the other, its effect cannot be but to sanction oppression by default, by refusal to oppose it. The feeling of powerlessness that leads to retreat is such a danger because its alternatives allow such narrow response: one may remain the powerless, underground victim; one may cast his lot with the oppressor. That is "the next step," which the central character of the novel cannot make. Making that step or not making it is secondary. More basic is the convincing case made in the novel for the necessity and desirability of withdrawal. This constitutes Ellison's politics of retreat.

NOTES

1. Ralph Ellison, "The Art of Fiction: An Interview," *Shadow and Act* (New York: Random House, 1964), p. 67. This chapter is based on an earlier exploration of Ellison's politics undertaken in *The Politics of Twentieth-Century Writers*, ed. George Panichas (New York: Hawthorne, 1971), pp. 307-20.

2. Ralph Ellison, *Invisible Man* (New York: Random House, 1952), p. 439. Subsequent quotations are from this edition.

3. Both arguments are reprinted in their entirety in Donald B. Gibson, ed., *Five Black Writers: Essays on Wright, Ellison, Baldwin, Hughes, and LeRoi Jones* (New York: New York University Press, 1970), pp. 254-95. Interpretations of the exchange contrary to mine are those of Robert Penn Warren, "The Unity of Experience," *Commentary* 29, no. 5: 91-96; and Robert Bone, "Ralph Ellison and the Uses of the Imagination," in *Ralph Ellison: A Collection of Critical Essays*, ed. John Hersey (Englewood Cliffs, N.J.: Prentice-Hall, 1974), pp. 108-11.

4. Let me note a qualification here. There is a curious inconsistency, worthy of exploration, in Ellison's conception of the function of literature. Although he has frequently argued over the years for the autonomy of art, he has developed the conception that American art is inseparable

from American culture and politics and is indeed "a function of American Democracy." This position is so curious because the arguments against black nationalism implied throughout Ellison's essays are the same ones that might be leveled against his American nationalistic stance. What remains unexplained is the denial of the one nationalism and the embracing of the other. See Ellison, "The Novel as a Function of American Democracy," *Wilson Library Bulletin* 41: 1022-27. The argument in the text follows the position implied in *Invisible Man* and in such essays in *Shadow and Act* as "The World and the Jug," pp. 107-43, "Hidden Name and Complex Fate," pp. 144-66, and "The Art of Fiction: An Interview," pp. 167-83.

5. To some extent the rancor of the exchange can be traced to the fact that it is indeed about such basic philosophical, moral, and political values.

6. One might feel that novels generally do not affect social policy. Without arguing that point here, let me report that Ellison testified before the U.S. Senate Subcommittee on Executive Reorganization in 1966. Senator Abraham Ribicoff of Connecticut concluded the session by reading the final paragraphs of *Invisible Man*, after which he made the following observation (revealing how good a reader he is): "What we are trying to do here is get rid of the stereotypes and cliches that you talk about. Again, as I said yesterday, we have to stop treating Negroes as a lump, and treat every Negro as an individual with his own personality, with his own standards, his own ideals and his own hopes and aspirations." If I ever meet the senator, I certainly hope he will treat me as an individual; I will certainly treat him as one. But insofar as he functions as a lawmaker I hope he will treat me as a "lump" and not attempt to formulate legislation that makes no distinctions among groups as the novel and, apparently, Ellison's testimony encouraged him to do. I withhold comment on the implications of Ellison's being called before the committee, given his insistence that he is an artist and not a politician. See "Harlem's America," *New Leader* 49 (September 1966): 22-35, for a transcription of Ellison's testimony.

7. Ellison's description of the novel's structure is different. He conceived of the form of the novel in terms of the development of the central character's consciousness "from purpose to passion to perception." Ellison, *Shadow and Act*, pp. 176-77.

8. The distinction here must be a matter of degree. McKay's poem is metaphorical in that its reference is broader than its literal meaning. Its literal meaning lies within the realm of possibility, whereas there is no possible literal level of meaning of the grandfather's words.

9. Ellison, *Shadow and Act*, p. 306.

10. This suggests one way of seeing the major conflict of the central character of the novel. Torn between an idea of the world and things as they are, between idealism and an actuality that does not conform but in fact contradicts it, he retreats into himself, into his mind, and believes he has therefore discovered his identity. He cannot emerge into the world at the end of the novel because he has rejected the world of material reality in favor of mind, of idea. The sense of irresolution that so many feel at the end of the novel comes about because the novel has amply and convincingly demonstrated that resolution is impossible within the novel's terms. "Resolution" would mean reconciling in some way the disparity between idea and actuality. At the very least this might involve a recognition of the existence of the problem itself. The novel ends, however, indicating that what it has gone to such lengths to describe as a problem may simply be dismissed by the central character's assertion that the problem is resolved.

11. The ambivalence of feeling expressed by his "fearful satisfaction" represents a trait of personality that is found throughout the novel, a kind of resistance to the forces, internal and external, that would have him be as others would have him.

12. Francis Greenwood Peabody, *Founder's Day at Hampton* (Boston and New York: Houghton, Mifflin & Co.; Cambridge, Mass.: Riverside Press, 1898), p. 3.

13. Booker T. Washington, *Up from Slavery* (New York: Bantam Books, 1963), p. 156. The exact quotation is as follows: "In all things that are purely social we can be as separate as the fingers, yet one as the hand in all things essential to mutual progress."

14. See n. 9.

15. "One asks this hero how he is to come out and be socially responsible? Upon what ground in reality can he affirm *any* positive principle? Just what is he going to do? Everything in the novel has clarified this point: that the bizarre accident that has led him to take up residence in an abandoned coal cellar is no accident at all, that the underworld is his inevitable home, that given the social facts of America, both invisibility and what he now calls his 'hibernation' are his permanent condition." Marcus Klein, "Ralph Ellison," *After Alienation* (Cleveland and New York: World Publishing Co., 1964), p. 73.

16. Klein, in ibid., p. 62, interprets the meaning of the central character's accident differently: "An earnest yea-saying young man reluctant to be a saboteur explores the typical relationships between Negroes and whites and finds them charged with incipient violence, needing but the slightest accident to set them off."

17. It is significant that these responses are thought and not vocalized. His resistance is therefore on a level with the grandfather's resistance as expressed in his deathbed utterance.

18. That the dynamics of the central character's relation to the Brotherhood are the same as to the general society and its components may well underlie Ellison's otherwise enigmatic remark that the Brotherhood is not to be identified with the Communist party (*Shadow and Act*, p. 179), for were it otherwise, the relation among Bledsoe, Norton, and Jack, for example, is obscured. In other words Northern industry would use him for its ends no less than the Communist party, and to interpret the novel, therefore, as being essentially anti-Communist misses the point.

19. Robert Bone, *The Negro Novel*, p. 209, sees an analogy between the name *Ras* and the word race. That works out reasonably well for analytical purposes, but the fact is that Ellison must have intended to establish the connection between his character and the Rastafarians of Jamaica, a black nationalist group with which Marcus Garvey was involved prior to his coming to the United States. The name of the group is derived from Haile Salassie's name before his coronation as emperor of Ethiopia, Ras Tafarius. *Ras* in Ethiopic means "prince." Garvey became a great hero of black nationalism to the Rastafarians; hence, the name *Ras* is intended to evoke the image of Marcus Garvey. Compare Lloyd W. Brown, "Black Entitles: Names as Symbols in Afro-American Literature," *Studies in Black Literature* 1 (Spring): 42. "The Exhorter's name echoes the ancient Ethiopian title and the black aggressiveness of Jamaica's Rastafarians. And on a phonetic level, 'ras' is the popular West Indian expletive which usually accompanies a denunciatory style like that of the Exhorter."

20. James Alan McPherson, "Indivisible Man," *Atlantic Monthly* 226: 45-46.

21. Ralph Ellison, "Stormy Weather," *New Masses*, September 24, 1940, p. 20.

22. Ralph Ellison, "Recent Negro Fiction," *New Masses*, August 5, 1941, p. 26.

23. Ellison, *Shadow and Act*, p. 169.

24. See n. 6.

25. "By minimizing obstacles and limits Ellison's essays leave the impression that free will is axiomatic, that 'discipline' is not only a personal opportunity but a sufficient condition for civility in general. We might all be free if we would. From this position the most important question to be asked about any individual's situation is 'How well does he cope with it?' The importance ascribed to identity problems tends to equalize all

circumstances. What really counts is the quality of the perspective."
Lawrence W. Chisolm, "Signifying Everything," *Yale Review* 54: 454.

Susan Blake, "Black Folklore in the Works of Ralph Ellison," *PMLA* 94, makes the point as explicitly as I do through her study of Ellison's use of folklore. She writes that Ellison's fictions "suggest that the nature of the relationship [between black and white] can be changed by changing the perspective from which it is viewed and thus, implicitly, that the relationship exists only in the minds of the victims, as the invisible man's exists in his mind. This shift in perspective shifts the burden of change from the racist society to the oppressed race" (p. 135).

3

James Baldwin:
The Anatomy
of Space

"The only space which means anything to
me," I said, "is the space between myself
and other people."
—Leo Proudhammer in *Tell Me How Long
the Train's Been Gone*

THROUGH THE COURSE of his career, James Baldwin has come
closer to engaging in political affairs than have most other American writers. He has not, as have some European writers, actually
participated in affairs of state; American writers almost never do.
He has written, however, a good deal of social commentary in
which he has indicated support of certain political ideals and
disdain for others. On at least one notable occasion he met with the
attorney general, then Robert Kennedy, with the intention of
participating in discussion relating to the solution of the racial
problem.[1] He has as well given many speeches about race in which
he has advocated certain political positions and denigrated others.

This chapter is a revised version of the author's essay that originally appeared in
James Baldwin: A Critical Evaluation, ed. Therman B. O'Daniel, pp. 3–18 (Washington, D.C.: Howard University Press, 1977), © 1977 by Donald Gibson.

The expression of attitudes of a political character has not been limited to his essays, speeches, and public dialogues. His novels have also been vehicles for the expression of his thinking, his values, his general social orientation. They are a clear record of the development of his thought about social matters, as clear a record as any available.

Baldwin's outspokenness, his unwillingness to bite his tongue when speaking out on racial matters, the seriousness of his tone, and his tendency to speak in apocalyptic terms have probably convinced many that he is a political radical. This is by no means the case. Essentially a moralist, Baldwin has continually spoken about racism as a moral problem and has rarely related it, until very recently, to social forces of other kinds.[2] He is primarily an institutionalist who has been critical of the society almost exclusively in moral terms. He has only recently begun to speak at all about the relation of racism to other social phenomena, having assigned it in his mind to the realm of morality.[3] In this regard he has distinguished himself from black nationalists and socialists who have tended to see the problem and its solution far more in economic and cultural terms than he. For the most part he has remained traditional in his orientation. His fiction traces modifications in his basic outlook, significant modifications, but not essential changes. His progress from a roundly conservative outlook to one considerably less so is recorded in his fiction from *Go Tell It on the Mountain* to *If Beale Street Could Talk*.

Go Tell It on the Mountain is not only Baldwin's most coherent and unified novel, it is as well an apt testament of Baldwin's basic sense of the way things are. An autobiographical novel, it describes the life of a young boy, John Grimes, from his early years to his adolescence, its focus being on his status within the family and his relation to his father, Gabriel. John is the innocent victim of his father, a religious man steeped in hatred, narrowness, and self-righteousness; he is sadistic and inordinately authoritarian. Although John is powerless to deal with his father except to acquiesce to his demands, he finally reaches adolescence and rebels in the only way psychically available to him—through successfully competing with his father within the church. The novel describes the progress of John's maturation and the background out of which his life situation proceeds.

The terms in which the story is told suggest something of the scope of the action. Whereas the actual events are somewhat commonplace and not uncharacteristic of the lives of poor people, they are invested with significance far beyond their actuality. The novel is intended to be cosmic in scope, the interaction in ordinary terms between conflicting ultimates. John is the force of love, Gabriel of evil. The plot affirms the victory of love over evil and its working out the unwinding of historical necessity. That Baldwin has been known to think in terms of historical necessity is not strange to readers generally familiar with his work. His reference, for example, to the idea of cosmic vengeance suggested at the end of "Down at the Cross: Letter from a Region of My Mind" is a case in point:

> If we do not now dare everything, the fulfillment of that prophecy, recreated from the Bible in song by a slave, is upon us: *God gave Noah the rainbow sign, No more water, the fire next time!*[4]

This is not intended to be hyperbolic or mere rhetoric. It reflects what seems to be Baldwin's basic belief that outside the natural world exist forces to which human beings are accountable and that their lack of accountability will evoke punishment. The above quotation appeared originally in 1962, but Baldwin has made similar comments in more recent times. In his recorded conversation with Margaret Mead, *A Rap on Race*, in 1971, he reiterated the notion of retributive justice in stating that slavery is a crime which demands atonement, as does all other sin. The context in which he puts this—"Maybe I am an Old New England, Old Testament prophet," and slavery "is the crime which is spoken of in the Bible"—makes it clear that he is not speaking in sociological terms.[5] Although Baldwin does not explicitly speak here of vengeance being visited upon the perpetrator of crime, the implication is clear. Crime or sin affects the course of events in nature. The commission of evil so influences history as to determine that its course will run in such a way as to bring about retribution. This is all reflected in the plot of *Go Tell It on the Mountain*. The pasts of the individuals described there have all moved toward the time on the threshing floor during which John's problem is worked out, suggesting the operation of forces that exist beyond the province of the natural.

The cosmic scope of the novel is reflected in its style and in the large-scale religious framework within which the story is conceived and executed. The quality of the style, its biblical intonations, its authority, are specifically rooted in Christian tradition. The rhetoric of the novel, its parallel constructions and repetitions of words and phrases, its frequently archaic character and high seriousness all point toward the author's sense of a level of reality beyond the natural. Such passages as the following are common throughout the novel, and they serve, by style alone, to indicate something of the author's sense of the great weight brought to bear on the events of the novel by the tradition to which it refers:

> And he began to shout for help, seeing before him the lash, the fire, and the depthless water, seeing his head bowed down forever, he, John, the lowest among the lowly. And he looked for his mother, but her eyes were fixed on this dark army—she was claimed by this army. And his father would not help him, his father did not see him, and Roy lay dead.[6]

> But he could never go through this darkness, through this fire and this wrath. He never could go through. His strength was finished, and he could not move. He belonged to the darkness—the darkness from which he had thought to flee had claimed him. And he moaned again, weeping, and lifted up his hands. [P. 275]

Through their style, especially their tone, these typical passages reveal the writer's attitude toward the cosmic context in which the events of the story transpire. It would be one thing if the religiosity

of the novel were confined to the outlooks of the characters themselves. If that were the case, then we should expect to find some
distance indicated between the perspectives of the author and
characters. As it is, however, the supernatural dimension of the
novel is never questioned. No disparity exists between the author's
view and his characters' views in this regard. This observation is
significant because it bears directly on the plot of the novel and on
the novel's ultimate philosophical (perhaps better, "theological,")
meaning.

The resolution of the plot comes about when John achieves his
salvation on the threshing floor. What is resolved? All the fears,
anxieties, and tensions of John's life up to that point are washed
away. John finally sees his father in "proper" perspective; that is,
he has changed his relation to Gabriel and will no longer be
dominated by him. He has divested Gabriel of authority by trans-
ferring his allegiance from his earthly to his heavenly father. The
salient point in the threshing floor episode is the lack of distance
between the author and the main character. Another writer might
have seen the dynamics of the scene as indicating the resolution of
the relation between father and son and the particular mode it takes
as being simply the vehicle through which the transformation
occurs. As it is, the author believes as much as the character in the
scheme through which the transformation occurs. Hence no irony
or ambiguity is present in the scene. John's religious experience is
not seen as a subterfuge for dealing with a difficult and not unusual
psychic phenomenon—the tension between fathers and sons during
adolescence—but rather as true and real in itself. This means that
John's experience is a truly Christian one, that the novel is a
Christian novel and points to what Baldwin conceives to be a
sphere of reality beyond the experiential.

The style and plot resolution are only two facets of the novel
pointing to the writer's commitment to the scheme of Christianity
described there. In addition, the title of the novel, its section titles,
and the epigraphs (to the book, to the sections, and to the inter-
chapters) are quotations from the King James Bible or from
spirituals or gospel songs. The text is heavily interlarded with
similar quotations, with words, phrases, and sentences from the

same contexts. Here again the matter of tone is important because
a novel could conceivably be written that would rely heavily upon
the Christian tradition yet would view that tradition with varying
degrees of skepticism, irony, or ambivalence. But, as noted above
in relation to Baldwin's handling of John, no such attitude distinguishing or even qualifying the author's perspective exists.

Baldwin's commitment to a religious scheme accounts for the
conservative temper of *Go Tell It on the Mountain*. Although such
a commitment does not in itself bespeak conservatism (it is possible
that an individual's other views and values might counterbalance
these), such a thoroughgoing, pervasive commitment as his does
indeed indicate a rather rigid conservatism. The perspective put
forth in the book tells us, without qualification, that the chief
institution of the society is religion and that all others are subsumed beneath it; human action and interaction are to be seen
against the background of Christian values, and the significance of
human action is derived from this context. This view is conservative
because of its implied definition of human nature and the individual's relation to society. It suggests that authority does and
should reside in that particular institution and that human nature is
such that it must be contained, defined, and restrained within its
framework. It suggests further that one's relation to society ought
to be determined by one's attempt to mold oneself to the imperatives dictated by the institution.

These implications are borne out by the novel; their corollaries
are part and parcel of its plot, characterization, and theme. They
indeed are the basic premises from which the novel is written.
Consequently it is not surprising to find the brief foreword to the
Grosset and Dunlap edition of the novel hailing it as a "milestone
in the development of American literature" because it is "the first
novel about Negroes to be written from a non-racial point of
view." The point of view is indeed nonracial because Baldwin's
premises are such that they minimize the importance of the impingement upon the lives of his characters of social, of racial
realities. The book gives no indication that the nature of the lives of
its characters is largely determined by poverty and racial oppression
in general. I am not implying that Baldwin must have written a

book about characters whose lives are entirely the result of the impingement on them of social circumstance, but to exclude that factor to the extent that Baldwin does in this novel constitutes a distortion.

The omission from the novel of the realities of race is responsible for the emphasis on individual responsibility in Baldwin's judgment of his characters. The characters seem who or what they are because they have willed themselves to be or because of some flaw in their personality. Admittedly the fate of Richard—his arrest, incarceration, and suicide—points to racial injustice and to the social dimension. Even so, the emphasis is on the fate of that particular individual and on his relation with Elizabeth and not on Richard's life and death as in any way representative or not unlike the lives and deaths of many other black people. In any case, the focus of the novel is on a private, personal matter, and the resolution of the plot reflects the basic premises from which it is written in that the resolution takes place within the psyche of a particular individual. "The Threshing Floor," the apogee of the plot line, describes the change that takes place in John's character and is the most subjective episode within the novel. Consonant with the lack of emphasis on the social dimension, the action of the novel moves toward the subjective and private, away from external reality. Again this reflects Baldwin's conviction in this novel that true reality exists elsewhere than in the facts of human social experience. From this perspective any accolades that the book has received for being written from a nonracial point of view seem something other than literary judgments.

The step from *Go Tell It on the Mountain* to *Giovanni's Room*, Baldwin's second novel, is not a long one if we are aware that some of the basic assumptions of the first novel are operative in the second. The scope of the action of *Giovanni's Room* is smaller in not being cosmic. That dimension is missing. Like the first novel, however, the second is focused on the subjective inner experience of a single individual, a focus far more limited and intense because of the technical point of view, the events being circumscribed by their filtration through a single consciousness. The implication is, as in the previous novel, that the unique experience of the specific individual is per se of great consequence, greater consequence indeed than his experience as a member of a social group on any but the smallest scale. Again, as in the earlier novel, the social framework in which the action takes place is of minimal significance and at most in this novel adds local color. The central character of *Giovanni's Room*, David, has a social identity—he is an American in Paris—but that national identity is so broad and general as to be less meaningful than the author probably thinks. He, like the other characters, is far more individualized than representative of national origin.

It is here, in Baldwin's conservative assumptions about the character and significance of individual experience, that one should look for the reasons for his choosing to write about characters who are white or who are, more precisely, not black.[7] If one feels as Baldwin did at the time of this novel that the inner experience of the unique individual is of greater import than that deriving from or dependent upon race or socioeconomic class, then it stands to reason that a black writer should write "raceless" novels. The key to the question of race in *Giovanni's Room*, in other words, is not to be sought in race psychology (identification with the aggressor, Baldwin's wish to be white, and so on) but in the author's politics, a conservative politics whose nature leads him to take the least ostensibly political road and to withdraw into the "normality" and tensionlessness of the status quo.

The treatment of homosexuality in the novel, however, seems radical because of its apparent relation to received social standards of conduct and morality regarding homosexuality. The novel's standards, simply, seem contradictory to commonly accepted norms in Western society. How, then, does one reconcile the apparent radicalism of the book with the conservativism of its basic assumptions? The fact is that Baldwin's attitude toward homosexuality is decidedly negative. Whereas a great deal in the novel implies acceptance of homosexuality, the overwhelming evidence is negative, not positive or supportive, in character. On the one hand, the initial descriptions of the actual physical relationships between David and Giovanni are created in such a way as to indicate complete sympathy on the part of the author with their legitimacy and beauty. We are led to believe that the general relation between Giovanni and David is a true love relation on a par with true heterosexual relations. Their love for each other, we are told, goes beyond the physical, for they are said to be emotionally involved also. They are contrasted with lesser homosexuals who seek only physical gratification. So much for the positive side.

On the other hand, the resolution of the plot of the novel itself stems from Baldwin's analysis of the nature and character of homosexuality—at least as its nature and character are exhibited through David. The murder responsible for sending Giovanni to the guillotine comes about because David has abandoned him. He abandons him out of his preference for a heterosexual relationship and because, as he implies in his question to Giovanni, "What kind of life can two men have together, anyway?" the possibilities contained in an extended homosexual relationship are limited.[8] "What," David asks again, "do you think can happen between us?" (p. 189). Although David does indeed feel morally responsible for Giovanni's fate, his response in leaving Giovanni comes about because of the claims of an older, prior sense of morality, the same sense of morality operative in his first homosexual affair, which causes him to flee his friend Joey. In both cases David is acutely aware of moral imperatives stemming from his sense of masculine identity.

The distinction between David and Giovanni and other homosexuals in the book stems from the masculinity of both and the imputed resulting character. The novel makes clear the author's disgust with males who are not at least bisexual. (Both David and Giovanni are.) David's commitment to Hella—and his resulting abandonment of Giovanni's little, dirty, disorderly room—is again a function of the claims of character. Hence the plot's resolution stems from the character of the central figure, and his character itself constitutes a judgment of homosexuality.

Other elements of the plot constitute severely negative judgments of homosexuality, for example, the episode in which David briefly encounters a sailor walking along a boulevard:

> I was staring at him, though I did not know it, and
> wishing I were he. He seemed—somehow—younger
> than I had ever been, and blonder and more beautiful,
> and he wore his masculinity as unequivocally as he wore
> his skin. [P. 121]

The sailor passes and, seeing a certain look in David's eyes, gives
him in return "a look contemptuously lewd and knowing":

> I knew that what the sailor had seen in my unguarded
> eyes was envy and desire: I had seen it often in Jacques'
> eyes and my reaction and the sailor's had been the same.
> But if I were still able to feel affection and if he had seen
> it in my eyes, it would not have helped, for affection,
> for the boys I was doomed to look at, was vastly more
> frightening than lust. [Pp. 122-23]

David's escapades after he leaves Hella and goes to Nice, where
he picks up a sailor, are hardly a glorification of homosexuality
but are rather a description of its sordidness, a revelation of the
depths to which he has sunk, and a harbinger of his future life.
His leaving Hella is itself tragic in that it suggests his inability to
sustain any human relationship, heterosexual or homosexual. All
in all the book is about descent and is heavily weighted, understanding and sympathetic as the author might be, against homosexuality in subtler but as vividly negative terms as any religious
sermon might be. Hence the apparently radical morality of the
novel turns out to be not radical at all but far more deeply negative
about homosexuality than the most sanguinely liberal view might
be.[9]

Another Country reveals a liberalizing of Baldwin's attitudes but
is by no means an abdication of basically conservative values. The
context of the novel is social, not cosmological; it focuses on
problems related to racial interaction; it contains far more social
protest than any of the preceding novels; its morality is less stringent
though no less imperative than heretofore. At the same time, however, its assumptions about the basic nature of the social problems
it confronts give rise to a social analysis essentially conservative in

character. It assumes that large-scale social problems, such as racial oppression and its resulting social manifestations, are the result of limitations within the psyches of individuals rather than of the dynamics of contending social forces. Hence, the responsibility for social problems lies with the individual, be he oppressed or oppressor, victimizer or victim.[10] In the terms of the novel, this means that black people are shown oppressing whites, as well as conversely, and no clear distinction is made between the one act of oppression and the other. In *Another Country* race does not matter in the sense that every individual has the capacity, regardless of color, to be victim or victimizer, equal opportunity suffering indeed! I do not wish to argue the problem of the responsibility of the victim in his victimization. I would contend, however, that equating the two roles as a general premise serves more to justify oppressors, whether groups or individuals, than to condemn them.

The problem exists in the novel because of Baldwin's assumptions about individual responsibility. More particularly Baldwin believes that the injustices committed by groups against other groups and individuals against other individuals come about because individuals do not know themselves, cannot be honest with themselves or others, and therefore do not possess the capacity to love. The idea of love is central to Baldwin's thinking and lies at the heart of his system of values.[11] We noted its role in *Go Tell It on the Mountain*; its role in *Giovanni's Room* is also central. *Another Country* can be analyzed in terms of what it says about love, given the relations that Baldwin sees between love and the rest of life, given the politics involved when love is seen as more nearly basic to societal life than factors having to do with the dynamics of complex, industrial society.

The key to the understanding of *Another Country* lies in the antithetical relation in which its two chief characters, Rufus and Eric, stand. Rufus is black and a Northerner. He is incapable of sustaining relations of any kind with other people because he neither understands nor accepts himself. His desperate plight is precipitated when his desire for self-destruction is projected outward onto Leona, his mistress, whom he drives to insanity before himself committing suicide. Before his suicide he has exiled himself

from family and friends, and we see him at the nadir of his life—
hungry, filthy, homeless, and alone. Seeing no possibility of
changing the essential quality of his life, he climbs atop the George
Washington Bridge and piteously addressing God, "Ain't I your
baby too?" leaps to his death. His first sexual experience with
Leona is described in such a way as to define their developing
relationship, to indicate his character and something of the influence of race on his personality, to present the racial basis of his
sadomasochistic relation to her and others:

> He wanted her to remember him the longest day she
> lived. And, shortly, nothing could have stopped him,
> not the white God himself or a lynch mob arriving on
> wings. Under his breath he cursed the milk-white bitch
> and groaned and rode his weapon between her thighs.
> She began to cry. *I told you*, he moaned, *I'd give you
> something to cry about*, and at once, he felt himself
> strangling, about to explode or die. A moan and a curse
> tore through him while he beat her with all the strength
> he had and felt the venom shoot out of him, enough for
> a hundred black-white babies.[12]

Thereafter their relationship, strained by his self-annihilating
impulse and his simultaneous desire to punish the white race
through her, advances toward its bitter, destructive end, an end
ostensibly avoidable had he the capacity to understand and accept
himself and hence to love and be loved.

Eric is diametrically opposite Rufus in most ways. If we compare
the first chapter of book 1 with the first chapter of book 2, the
former dealing with Rufus and the latter with Eric, the point is
clear. The structure of the book and the content of the parallel
sections require that we make the comparison between the two
chief characters. Whereas Rufus is in hell, Eric is in paradise. We
need only compare Rufus's state throughout the first chapter of the
book with Eric's as we first meet him sitting in a garden over-
looking the sea. His situation—his place of residence as well as his
relation with his lover, Yves—is idyllic. Despite the peculiarity of

the relation—Yves is another male—it stands in contrast with Rufus's supreme isolation. Throughout the scene, we are led to believe that the relation exists with its particular quality because Eric is honest, open, and self-accepting. His personality is such that people, male and female, are drawn to him, and he feels no tension between himself and the rest of the world. His sexual preferences produce no shame or guilt for him. On the contrary, his bisexuality seems to allow him to avoid the normal conflict of the sexes. Other characters in the book experience difficulty because of the tensions they discover between themselves and others of the opposite sex, men or women; Eric, whose character leads him away from distinctions among people concerning sexual identity, has no tensions emanating from that source.

In that the attitudes Baldwin expresses about homosexuality (or more accurately bisexuality) in this novel are completely positive, the novel, in regard to that subject, is radical because they stand in total opposition to accepted norms of behavior. There is some suggestion that the bisexual male is the apogee of human development for Baldwin. That is, if we ask why Eric is created in the novel as the most understanding, best adjusted character, it would seem that the novel would answer that Eric does not observe the usual distinctions and categories of sex and race (in Baldwin's thinking) observed by others. He is therefore freer. Baldwin's stance here, however, implies some standard of judgment extraordinarily personal and private as well as sexist in nature. Nonetheless, it is consistent with the subjectivity of the love theme in the novel. Since bisexuality is hardly a matter of free choice, since it does not represent a cultural norm, its presentation as a viable alternative to generally existing modes of social behavior is hardly realistic. On the other hand, if Baldwin meant to suggest by his bisexual male characters an attitude less rigidly bound by standard categories of social differentiation, then he would have done well to show us a male who might possess the good qualities of an Eric without imposing the necessity of his being bisexual. The implication, however, that Rufus's life might have been saved had Vivaldo made some sexual gesture toward him (Baldwin would say a "loving" gesture) simply suggests an option not generally available in this culture and therefore more expressive of Baldwin's utterly private sense of values and little else.

The novel's theme of love is again pertinent here.[13] The assumption that the chief problem among the characters in the novel (and in the world) is the incapacity to love generated by whatever the psychic condition that keeps them out of touch with their basic selves leads to a basic contradiction in the novel. On the one hand, the novel contains more social protest than any of Baldwin's previous novels. Rufus and Leona constantly encounter racist reaction to their being on the street together and living together. So do Ida and Vivaldo. The novel on many occasions shows policemen at the ready to enforce the uncodified laws regarding what is considered proper relations between the black and white sexes. Hence a real and actual social dimension to racial relations is shown in the book. We see even that the interaction between Rufus and Leona is determined by social attitudes, which they act out. Yet in implying that the imperative to love is the responsibility of the discrete individual, the novel contradicts itself in that its assessment of the root of the problem of racial relations allows the author to blame his characters regardless of race and to ignore many considerations of race. What, for example, does a black writer mean when the best adjusted character in his novel is white and the worst black? What does he mean when he is unable or unwilling to show a single good relationship, homosexual or heterosexual, between two black people? What does he mean when he requires a black woman, Ida, to confess her infidelity to white Vivaldo but does not require her white lover to confess his infidelity to her? At worst these considerations could suggest a writer who has a great deal of spite for himself and his race. At best, and I choose to favor this explanation, his basic assumption involving the primacy of love minimizes racial considerations. The hero is he who has the capacity to love; the villain is he who lacks the capacity. Although whites seem favored in possessing that capacity, not all whites in the novel have it—Richard, for example—and at least one black character, Ida, is on her way to achieving it.

Another Country demonstrates the limitations of Baldwin's greatest strength as a writer of fiction and nonfiction: his ability to

express the innermost, deepest longings of his psyche. He comes
closer to putting himself on the printed page than do most other
contemporary novelists and than do any other contemporary
essayists. The problem, however, is that his analysis of his own
personal needs is indistinguishable in his mind from his analysis
of the world and its society. Admittedly the subjectivism of his
work has decreased with the passage of time, but even at his most
objective, in *Another Country*, in the novels thus far considered,
his basic presuppositions remain highly subjective reflections of
personal need and desire. Hence the accuracy and relevance of his
social analysis can be but of limited scope. His next novel, *Tell Me
How Long the Train's Been Gone*, further bears out this assessment despite the fact that it is still more politically liberal than
Another Country—more liberal yet ultimately conservative in that
the author's initial social assumptions remain constant.

Tell Me How Long the Train's Been Gone is Baldwin's most
directly political novel in that the issues regarding the question of
the relation of people to society and to one another are more
dramatically and explicitly posed than in any of the preceding
fiction. In this novel Baldwin pushes his liberalism to its extreme
limit, stating finally his great sympathy for radicalism (for the
radicalism of black youth during the 1960s) but ultimately rejecting
it for himself and claiming a spot on the political spectrum to the
left of center but far inward from the limit. A measure of the
degree of Baldwin's political shift may be established by comparing
this novel to the earliest, *Go Tell It on the Mountain*, in terms of
their expression of attitudes toward religion, their relative evaluation of the significance of private and public experience, and, as a
corollary, their sense of the relation of the fate of the individual to
social dynamics.

The conception of religion revealed in *Tell Me How Long the
Train's Been Gone* seems essentially atheistic, although Baldwin's
earlier Christian commitment remains, however obversely stated
and redefined. It goes without saying that the central character of
the novel, Leo Proudhammer, is the character most nearly representative of the perspective of the author, so much so, the tone
indicates, that no disparity exists between Leo's thoughts and

values and James Baldwin's. Nowhere in the book is there the
slightest suggestion of disjunction between their outlooks. Obviously Leo is not Baldwin himself—Baldwin has not of course
achieved success as an actor—but the biographical parallels are so
many as to suggest some degree of autobiography. Hence we may
infer that Leo's rather consistent attitudes toward God and the
church and toward his brother after Caleb becomes a minister—
especially given the tone in which these attitudes are expressed—
are not inconsistent with the author's own attitudes at the time the
novel was written. Leo says, "I cursed God from the bottom of my
heart, the very bottom of my balls. I called Him the greatest
coward in the universe because He did not dare to show Himself
and fight me like a man."[14] And later during the course of sexual
interplay between him and his brother, he says further, "I'll love
you, Caleb, I'll love you forever, and in the sight of the Father and
the Son and the fucking Holy Ghost and all the filthy hosts, and in
the sight of all the world, and I'll sing hallelujahs to my love for
you in hell" (p. 211). Leo is quite young at this time, and one might
read his bitter diatribe as a kind of obverse confession of faith, a
reading suggested by an impression, an insight that Leo has much
later when as a young man he again has bitter thoughts about
God:

> I had had quite enough of God—more than enough,
> more than enough, the horror filled my nostrils, I
> gagged on the blood-drenched name; and yet was forced
> to see that this horror, precisely, accomplished His
> reality and undid my belief. [P. 98]

We may, then, infer the writer's belief when he later curses God in
the presence of Caleb, by this time a minister:

> That God you talk about, that miserable white cock-
> sucker—look at His handiwork, look! . . . I curse your
> God, Caleb, I curse Him, from the bottom of my heart I
> *curse* Him. And now let Him strike me down. Like you
> just tried to do. [P. 425]

The disparity between the denotation of the words and their actual meaning puts Leo in the paradoxical position of the apparent atheist whose disbelief is so strong that it means the contrary. Who or what, after all, is there for the atheist to curse? No such attitude exists in the first novel, nor could it have existed as an expression of the view of the writer himself. If the strongly negative exhortations against God are indeed to be taken as testaments of faith, the point remains that no such ambiguous assertions on the part of the author appear in the earlier novel. Hence his position has shifted but not changed; his commitment to the institution is in any case a far lesser one. Nonetheless the implication is, especially given the conception indicated above of the role of God in human affairs, that for Leo (and for Baldwin) the universe is essentially God centered, however difficult that idea has become for the older Baldwin.

The relative value that Baldwin through the course of the novel places on inner experience as opposed to outer, public experience is, as said before, a measure of the relative value he places on social existence. One way of interpreting Baldwin's novel is in these terms. From the earliest novel to the latest, we can trace a clear and definite shift of emphasis on Baldwin's part from interest in the "inner space" in determining the nature, character, and quality of human experience.[15] *Tell Me How Long the Train's Been Gone* does not focus exclusively on the public space; there is in fact a tension in the novel between the complex of values associated with the one emphasis and those associated with the other. Just as the whole body of his novels may profitably be analyzed in these terms, so may this particular novel.

It is indeed interesting and more than happenstance that Leo Proudhammer, who so closely resembles Baldwin, should be an actor and not a writer. A writer may practice his craft in privacy, and his work may be presented without the requirement of his presence. An actor, however, usually must be present in order to practice his craft. The actor's role is the more public one and usually at a lesser remove from his audience. Leo Proudhammer does not like to be around people, and hence there is a certain tension between the requirements of his vocation and his personal feelings. At the time of his first meeting with Black Christopher, Leo says to him, "The only space which means anything to me is the space between myself and other people. May it never diminish" (p. 448). The tension suggested here between the desire for privacy and the necessity of public involvement—a tension inherent in the character and vocation of Leo—reflects the basic theme of the novel. The biography of Leo as described in the novel is a history of his achievement of isolation and a description of his rejection of those around him. He rejects his brother, Caleb, to whom he has been inordinately close, and his father and mother. Although he does not totally reject Barbara and Christopher, the people ostensibly closest to him, he maintains a certain distance from both through his acknowledgment to each that he is emotionally and sexually committed to the other. After his heart attack he goes to Europe alone, thus maintaining his isolation.

His commitments to Barbara and to Christopher are of a somewhat differing order, the antagonism between his two lovers mirroring this most significant inner conflict. His commitment to Barbara is to racelessness (whiteness?), to art, to privacy, to respectability, to fame, to wealth and social status, to prestige, to high culture, to individualism, to sexual orthodoxy, to status quo politics, to the privileges reserved by society for the wealthy and successful. His early dream of being an actor has meant not only leading a life different from that of his family but rejecting that life entirely, along with all the suffering and humiliation attendant upon it. Barbara represents for him all that his early life had not been. She is the "princess" (as she is actually called) and he the "prince" (as he is once referred to) who has won her, who has transferred a fairy-tale reality into actuality.[16]

His commitment to Black Christopher, on the other hand, is to specific racial identity, to revolutionary politics, to social involvement, to sexual aberration, to repudiation of the value of wealth and social status, to identification with the underprivileged, to reconciliation with his family and with his personal and racial pasts. He knows that the world does not in some sense honor the distinctions he makes, that from certain perspectives he and Christopher are indistinguishable. Yet they are truly not bound by a common racial identity, for socioeconomic class creates between them a significant distinction. Christopher himself recognizes this: "But, naturally, a whole lot of black cats think you [Leo] might be one of them, and in a way, you know, you stand to lose just as much as white people stand to lose" (p. 480).

The whole novel, with its unprecedented emphasis (in Baldwin's work) on its main character as a social person, in a sense is a justification of the values underlying the resolution of the plot. The forces that have been responsible for Leo's success have been the same forces that have sought to destroy him. There is ample apology for the necessity of escaping the circumstances of Leo's youth and young manhood. Yet the problem lies heavy on his soul, so heavy that he has a heart attack, not from overwork but from the impingement on his psyche of the problem made clear in a conversation with Christopher near the end of the novel:

> "If you don't want me to keep going under the feet of horses," Christopher said . . . "then I think you got to agree that we need us some guns. Right?"
> "Yes," I said. "I see that." He parked the car. I looked out over the water. There was a terrible weight on my heart—for a moment I was afraid that I was about to collapse again. I watched his black, proud profile. "But we're outnumbered, you know."
> He laughed and turned off the motor. "Shit. So were the early Christians." [P. 483]

The resolution of the plot has Leo leaving the country alone, the intended implication being that he makes no choice, that he leaves the dilemma lying. That, however, is not in fact the case, for he returns and resumes his career and the complex of values associated with it. A choice is made by default, and Leo (and Baldwin) opts for the one value cluster over the other.

For the first time Baldwin has come to see that love, the personal feelings of individuals for each other, is not enough. His response, to flee, is likewise not enough, for the problem awaits to greet him at his disembarkation every time he returns to America. His problem has no solution in the framework of his politics. He is American to the core and a liberal democrat. Liberal democratic politics has not successfully solved the problems that Baldwin addresses, explaining his towering rage. He knows that saying, "Be good! Be good!" is not enough, but his political vision allows no reaction beyond moral suasion. The intensity of his moralizing rhetoric is in direct proportion to the degree of his frustration with the country that has, fate of fates, given him his success. Baldwin's next novel expresses a lot of frustration and anger.

If Beale Street Could Talk explores racial oppression from a broader social perspective than any of the preceding novels. Baldwin's analysis of the source of oppression remains the same; it emanates from the human heart. The racism inherent in the functioning of institutions is the expression of racism in the hearts of individuals. In the novel, for example, the racism of policemen is reflected in the personal racism of the policeman Bell. If Bell understood his true relation to his antagonist, Fonny, he would not be a racist. Bell simply does not know enough. Solutions rest upon the oppressor's having some vision or insight into the nature of his actions and attitudes. Baldwin's intention is to supply, to create the vehicle by means of which that insight is to occur. *If Beale Street Could Talk*, his fifth novel, is such a vehicle.

Once again, as in most of Baldwin's preceding novels, religion plays a prominent role. The Christian religious referent is far less central than in *Go Tell It on the Mountain*, but it is nonetheless central, especially if the meaning of the referent in *Beale Street* is compared to its meaning in the immediately preceding novel. *Tell Me How Long the Train's Been Gone* presents Baldwin in his most blasphemous stance. What then is the meaning of the strongly positive, Christian referents of *Beale Street*? The question emerges directly from Baldwin's text. The novel's epigraph and subsection titles bespeak strong, positive Christian sentiment; the most hypocritical and least worthy character in the novel is the character closest to the church. If we can resolve this paradox, we might have some insight into the meaning of religion and Christianity—at least as that is implied in this context—and we can see the place of religion in his structure of values, at least insofar as that structure is expressed in the novel.

The epigraph of the novel, the lyric from an old spiritual asks, "Mary, Mary/What you going to name/That pretty little baby?" Since the narrator and central character, Tish, is pregnant throughout most of the time of the novel and goes into labor at the end, we might infer that the epigraph has some relation to her and her child to be. The comparison draws a likeness of some kind between Mary and Tish and between the unborn child and Christ. I do not think the analogy is intended to have specific meaning; rather it attempts to surround the chief character with whatever aura of positive association surrounds the image of Mary and baby Jesus. A similarly unspecific comparison is suggested when Tish notes that she and Fonny were known at school and in the neighborhood as Romeo and Juliet. Baldwin wishes to evoke with the comparison whatever romantic associations will be aroused, but the Shakespearean reference does not have the thoroughgoing implications of the analogy to Christian myth since the Mary-Christ reference is intended to suggest some meaning more basic to the whole of the novel than the other.

The first of the novel's two subsections is titled "Troubled about My Soul," and the second, "Zion." Both titles have religious meaning. The first refers to the action of the first section, which describes the development of the main complication of the novel. The concept of soul places the events of the subsection in metaphysical perspective. The title of the second subsection, "Zion," bears on the ambiguous conclusion of the novel. There is a question as to whether the final scene, which sees the baby born and its unjustly imprisoned father freed, is real, fantasy, or a combination of these. "Zion," with its strongly positive implications of being the place where a successful journey ends, suggests that the efforts of Tish and her family to free Fonny have been fruitful, that he is in fact free.

Less positive in meaning is the scene depicting Tish, Fonny, and Mrs. Hunt in church. It is quite humorous, but the humor expresses the hypocrisy of Mrs. Hunt and others and is not used to express disdain for the church as institution. I draw this inference because the few lines describing Tish's experience in her own church are entirely positive in tone, and one has no reason to suppose that any disparity exists between her sentiments and the author's:

Of course I was (more or less) used to Abyssinia Baptist
Church. It was brighter, and had a balcony. I used to sit
in that balcony, on Mama's knees. Every time I think of
a certain song, "Uncloudy Day," I'm back in that
balcony again, on Mama's knees.[17]

When Tish goes to visit Fonny in jail and describes entering the
building as "like walking into church," she is talking about walking into Mrs. Hunt's fundamentalist church about which Tish has
observed, "Whoever loved us was not here" (p. 32).

The novel sets up an ironic contrast, however obvious, between
Tish's family and Fonny's (exclusive of Fonny's father, Frank).
The one family functions as a small community based on its members' mutual love, support, respect, and understanding. Pooling
their meager economic resources, they expend endless energy doing
whatever is necessary to keep the family intact and to protect its
members from a hostile and constantly threatening social environment. They are the true Christians as opposed to those (Mrs. Hunt
and, by association, her daughters) who merely participate in the
weekly rituals of the institution. The Hunt women are preoccupied
with form and appearance and give little regard to true emotion,
especially love. The Rivers family, in contrast, do not merely
profess righteousness, they live it through the daily expression of
love, through constantly caring for one another. Relations within
the Hunt family are destructive because they are devoid of feeling.
The scenes describing sexual relations between Mr. and Mrs. Hunt
contrast sharply with those describing sexual relations between Tish
and Fonny. For the Hunts, sex is a grim and sadistic parody of a
religious rite and as ugly as the relation between them. For Tish and
Fonny the contrary prevails. Their sexual relations are perfect,
without ugliness or pain, even to the point of being highly roman-
ticized. Although Tish is sexually innocent, a virgin, her initiation
is perfectly achieved, so perfectly that the couple experience mutual
orgasm.

Quite clearly Baldwin's interest is in the behavior of individuals
toward each other, and he believes that those who are capable of
love interact more humanely than those who are not. Religion, in

Baldwin's thinking, has no necessary relation to love in that the capacity to love is not correlated to institutional religious commitment. Religion has such a prominent place in *Beale Street* and elsewhere because it provides a preexistent system of mythology that Baldwin may call upon to express far more than a language without that dimension.

Probably religion is also important in Baldwin's consciousness because it expresses such a significant element of black culture. In his fiction Baldwin often raises certain religious questions, theological points, for example, involving the relation of God to humans, or the meaning of God's sacrifice of his son, or the role of God in history or human affairs. But whereas Baldwin might conceivably question the virgin birth as a theological issue, he would never question its truth as folk expression. That is, he may express the most outrageous blasphemy, but invariably when he does, it expresses some mood, facet, or component of an individual's personality. The blasphemous utterances that occur in *Beale Street* express the depth and intensity of the characters' emotions. That Baldwin would choose to express the most intense feelings possible through blasphemy says something about his beliefs, for one must surely believe deeply if one feels that the most intense expression possible is cursing God or Christ. Again, as in earlier work, his embracement of Christian belief is measured by the intensity of his rejection of it.

The turmoil and suffering undergone by the characters in *Beale Street* is framed within a religious context. That is, some basic, universal meaning underlies their experience as social beings, as members of an oppressed minority. Thus Tish says at the beginning of the narrative, "I'm beginning to think that maybe everything that happens makes sense. Like, if it didn't make sense, how could it happen" (p. 3). This, along with the constant religious allusion, suggests that beneath the racism of the judicial system, the penal system, the educational system, there is meaning. The universe is not chaotic and the extent to which it seems so merely reflects the inability of humans to love each other. In this regard Baldwin has never strayed very far from where he began. Although *Beale Street* goes to greater lengths than any previous novel in depicting the extent of racism in the society, it still identifies the source of that racism and indeed of all evil as "that inward sphere," as Nathaniel Hawthorne would put it, the human heart.

NOTES

1. Arthur Schlesinger, *A Thousand Days* (Boston: Houghton Mifflin, 1963), pp. 962-63.

2. "Power is the arena in which racism is acted out." James Baldwin, *No Name in the Street* (New York: Dial Press, 1972), p. 93. "And that battle [school decentralization] is what is really the crucial battle going on now in the world: to get out of the hands of the people who have the means of production and the money, to get it out of their hands and into the hands of the people at various local levels so that they can control their own lives." James Baldwin and Margaret Mead, *A Rap on Race: Margaret Mead/James Baldwin* (Philadelphia: J. B. Lippincott, 1971), p. 134.

3. Baldwin is in a long line of black interpreters of racism who have seen it as a moral problem and whose chief strategy has been to point out the disparity between American ideals and American practices. I think it fair to say that most black critical commentators on the problem from the nineteenth century to the present have so interpreted it.

4. James Baldwin, *The Fire Next Time* (New York: Dial Press, 1963), pp. 119-20.

5. Baldwin and Mead, *Rap on Race*, pp. 174-75.

6. James Baldwin, *Go Tell It on the Mountain* (New York: Alfred A. Knopf, 1953), p. 274. Subsequent quotations are from this edition.

7. Compare an alternative explanation in Colin MacInnes's "The Dark Angel: The Writings of James Baldwin," in Gibson, *Five Black Writers*, pp. 127-28. MacInnes believes the characters are white because the story takes place in a predominantly white milieu.

8. James Baldwin, *Giovanni's Room* (New York: Dial Press, 1956), p. 208.

9. MacInnes, "Dark Angel," pp. 128-29, agrees.

10. Mead and Baldwin argue this point in *Rap on Race*, pp. 222-26.

11. Baldwin has discussed the idea of love countless times. In his fictional analysis of human relationships, the capacity to love is always central. *Another Country* is fraught with references to characters wanting love, lacking love, capable or incapable of loving. Baldwin discusses the idea of love in Baldwin and Mead, *Rap on Race*, p. 184, where he says, "I think love is the only wisdom."

12. James Baldwin, *Another Country* (New York: Dial Press, 1962), p. 22. Subsequent quotations are from this edition.

13. "The only significant realities in [*Another Country*] are individuals and love, and . . . anything which is permitted to interfere with the free operation of this fact is evil and should be done away with." Norman Podhoretz, "In Defense of James Baldwin," in Gibson, *Five Black Writers*, p. 145.

14. James Baldwin, *Tell Me How Long the Train's Been Gone* (New York: Dial Press, 1968), p. 210. Subsequent quotations are from this edition.

15. These terms, "inner" and "outer space," originally from W. H. Auden's *New Year Letter*, are used as critical terms in the way I have used them here in Nathan Scott, "The Dark and Haunted Tower of Richard Wright," in Gibson, *Five Black Writers*, pp. 17-18.

16. I would not insist on this point, but the frequent instances of self-abnegation on Leo's part, derogation of a racial character referring to blackness, would suggest the relation of race to this cluster of values.

17. James Baldwin, *If Beale Street Could Talk* (New York: New American Library, 1975), p. 27. Subsequent quotations are from this edition.

4

Charles W. Chesnutt:
The Anatomy
of a Dream

CHARLES WADDELL CHESNUTT (1858-1932),[1] the first widely published and read black[2] novelist, was in many respects among the most conventional of writers in technique and style, if not in subject matter. Technically his two collections of short stories and his three novels differ little from hundreds of other novels published during the late nineteenth and early twentieth centuries. His formal, urbane, objective style is characteristic of the time. His subject matter and his unique perspective on his subject matter, however, distinguish him from his contemporaries. Nearly all his writing concerns racial issues in some way or another, but from the perspective of a nonwhite man, which means he has a certain understanding and certain sympathies that others might lack. Along with this inside perspective, he possessed a certain complex intellectual habit of mind and an unyielding moral honesty and intensity that produced a rather complicated and thoroughly engaging fiction for those free enough from traditional bias to apprehend it.[3]

In his diary on July 31, 1875, Chesnutt made the following observation:

> Twice today, or oftener, I have been taken for "white."
> At the pond this morning one fellow said he'd "be
> damned if there was any nigger blood in me." At Cole-
> man's I passed. On the road an old chap, seeing the
> trunks, took me for a student coming from school. I
> believe I'll leave here and pass anyhow, for I am as
> white as any of them. One old fellow said today, "Look
> here, Tom. Here's a black as white as you are."[4]

Chesnutt expresses a paradox here, a paradox touching upon the
essence of his self-conception.[5] He indicates the disparity between
illusion and reality, perception and knowledge. He deals with the
enigma of the thing that is what it is not, and is not what it is:
"Here's a black as white as you are." His "I am as white as any of
them" is only meaningful in context coming from a person who
does not conceive of himself as white. Although Chesnutt indicates
the attitude that it is better to be white than black, his own personal
decision when he confronted the possibility of passing was not to
pass. His decision was not so much to be black as not to become
known as white, for throughout his life he seems to have distinguished between himself as mulatto and individuals more purely
Negro. Speaking at the time of his reception of the NAACP's
Spingarn Medal in 1928, Chesnutt says,

> . . . substantially all of my writings, with the exception
> of *The Conjure Woman*, have dealt with the problems
> of people of mixed blood, which, while in the main the
> same as those of the true Negro, are in some instances
> and in some respects more complex and difficult of
> treatment, in fiction as in life.[6]

He sometimes refers indirectly to himself as "Negro" or "colored"
but never directly. At one time he refers to himself as "an American
of acknowledged African descent," but he follows that with, "In
this case the infusion of African blood is very small—is not in fact
a visible admixture."[7]

At work in Chesnutt's paradoxical, multifaceted attitudes about his racial identity (and about his identity generally since race is an integral part of identity) is a particular habit of mind that allowed (or perhaps caused?) him to hold contradictory ideas at the same moment. It is what I would call the dialectical habit of mind, a way of perceiving the world in terms of ideas standing in opposing relation. In Chesnutt's case, opposing ideas may stand in diametrical opposition, but the opposing elements are not of equal weight; hence an idea or belief that Chesnutt strongly holds will be pitted against a contradictory idea, also within his scheme of values, of lesser weight or strength. Concretely expressed, Dr. Miller in *The Marrow of Tradition* embodies a great number of Chesnutt's own values, beliefs, and feelings, but Chesnutt's doubt about the validity of those values, beliefs, and feelings finds an objectification in the character of Josh Green. The two characters exist in thesis-antithesis relation.

Again to express concretely the dialectical character of his thought, we may take Chesnutt's expression of optimism and pessimism as an example. On the one hand, Chesnutt's characters (and the man himself as the diary indicates) are usually optimistic and hopeful of the accomplishment of some desired end. On the other, they are thwarted so frequently and so completely as to suggest the impossibility of achieving anything resembling human happiness. A third turn of the screw suggests that some force, some agency outside human experience, in some measure rights things. Hence murderers are usually punished; evil is frequently revenged as the imbalance caused by the commission of wrongdoing is frequently restored, betokening an ordered world. These attitudes, the optimistic and the pessimistic, find expression within the same contexts. At the end of his darkest tale, "The Web of Circumstance," Chesnutt attempts to relieve the gloom by appending a paragraph in which he, as author, speaks:

> Some time, we are told, when the cycle of years has rolled around, there is to be another golden age, when all men will dwell together in love and harmony, and when peace and righteousness shall prevail for a thousand years. God speed the day and . . . give us here and

>   there, and now and then, some little foretaste of this
>   golden age, that we may the more patiently and hope-
>   fully await its coming![8]

This paragraph was necessary in order to counteract the meaning of
the tale itself. Although inclined to believe that life as lived is
essentially tragic, Chesnutt never intends to go so far as to suggest
that life (and ultimately history) is without meaning, as the tale
indeed suggests. No "foretaste of a golden age" is visible there; so
Chesnutt, in the final passage of the tale and of the book, makes a
statement entirely contrary to the meaning of this particular tale,
as well as to the implications of some of the others. Once again
in his fiction, antithesis undercuts and hence qualifies thesis.

The tension resulting from opposing elements forms the center of
nearly all his fiction. Irony, paradox (of character and situation,
not language or style), and ambivalence are his stock in trade. In
his most complex work, theses, countertheses, subtheses, and
countersubtheses play off against one another, revealing a subtlety
of mind easily obscured by his formal style, diction, and traditional
technique. This subtle play of mind, the awareness and expression
of myriad gradations of thought and feeling, is another element
distinguishing Chesnutt from the majority of his contemporaries.[9]

The Conjure Woman (1899), Chesnutt's first published collection of tales, is written in the plantation tradition, a post-Civil
War mode that had as its end to sing of a glorious, golden,
and prosperous antebellum South.[10] Joel Chandler Harris and
Thomas Nelson Page are probably the best remembered of a group
of writers who were largely responsible for creating the myth of the
antebellum South, a myth expressing general contentment and
happiness unsullied by poverty, disease, and strife. Chesnutt in part
supports the values inherent in the tradition; this cannot be denied.[11]
But he differs from the others in that he does not depict slavery as
an entirely humane system. Throughout the course of Uncle Julius's
various narratives, the cruelty and inhumanity of slavery are shown
to be no less than that. At the same time, however, he does not
depict slavery as entirely inhumane. Some slaves are not unhappy;
some suffer untold misery.[12]

In *The Conjure Woman* it is clear enough that Chesnutt has a good deal of sympathetic feeling for old Uncle Julius, the black retainer, but his closer identification is with the primary narrator and his wife, who are the property owners, the landed gentry, the well-mannered aristocrats.[13] They are Northerners in this case (for the sake of probability in their relation with Uncle Julius), although in later works the quality of their characters is represented by Southerners. Chesnutt feels a mild condescension toward Uncle Julius; the tone indicates this. It is no accident of situation or character that allows us without difficulty to identify the "superior" persons. The employers of Uncle Julius are not shown to be better people simply because he works for them or because they are considerably better off economically and speak better English. The difference is a class difference; they are superior by dint of their superior class. At first Uncle Julius might appear to be of superior wit, but even this is not true.[14] He escapes with his pranks because of the indulgence of his employers; the things he gets away with are great gains to him but hardly of consequence to his employers. It would have been possible for Chesnutt, had he so chosen, to make master and servant equals—if not economically, certainly in other ways. Chesnutt chose not to do so because in his eyes the real distinctions among individuals are class distinctions, and class distinctions are real distinctions. (Later Chesnutt in part repudiates this notion.)

The question remains, Why did Chesnutt choose to utilize a tradition so blatantly dedicated to the support of interests not entirely his own? The writers of the plantation tradition preceding Chesnutt had demonstrated the availability of a market for a reactionary literature about the South. Many authors have, of course, written literature they felt would sell even at the expense of violating their own principles. Something of this motivation may have influenced Chesnutt's choice. I believe, however, that he was too principled a man to have written as he did solely out of a desire to sell work. An answer to the question more in keeping with Chesnutt's character and with his later work is that he found a great number of elements of the plantation tradition not incompatible with his own values: not slavery—he did not approve of that—but the orderly, harmonious social structure portrayed in the literature of the plantation and the imagined life of a socially responsible, moral, and chivalrous aristocracy.

The dialectical character of *The Conjure Woman* rests specifically in the tension between Chesnutt's allegiance to two sets of conflicting values. On the one hand, he identifies with the landed gentry; on the other, he sympathizes, for many reasons, with the black, landless, powerless peasant. Although the primary narrator of the tales is a Northerner and Uncle Julius is not in fact a slave, we are unquestionably intended to equate their relation to that of master and slave during antebellum times. It is no accident that the tales have been compared to Joel Chandler Harris's Uncle Remus tales, so frequently in fact that Chesnutt found it necessary to assert their originality.[15] The dichotomy is not a true one, for Chesnutt's greater sympathies are with the aristocratic class. For a multiplicity of reasons, he did not see the relation between class values and racism in the situation set up in *The Conjure Woman* or in similar situations in other works. He either did not see, or chose not to see, that the class he valued so highly depended for its existence upon a base of either peasants or slaves. The effect of the stories, finally, is to support in the main the values generally expressed by works in the plantation tradition. Had he not been so very much attached to the aristocratic idea, he might have been able to view more critically the relation between Uncle Julius and his employers. The most salient point here is that Chesnutt's class values and his morality are at odds, and this dialectic continues throughout his writing career until finally, in his last novel, *The Colonel's Dream*, he tries, though unsuccessfully, to unite them.

The title story of *The Wife of His Youth*, the second collection of tales, reveals more directly a dialectical relation between class values and morality.[16] The engaged reader of "The Wife of His Youth" will certainly feel a twinge of sympathetic regret for the central character, Mr. Ryder, who, in scrupulously following the dictates of a high code of morality, must accept as his wife an old, toothless, unlettered, and uncultured woman while relinquishing his social position and marriage to a young, refined, beautiful lady. Not only is the older woman culturally unlike Mr. Ryder,

but, contrary to the standards of beauty of the near white bourgeoisie of Groveland, she is physically black. The situation is intended to be ironic. The true meaning of the tale, however, lies in
its paradoxical nature.[17] The interpretation of the tale that sees Mr.
Ryder give up all for honor is true, but it is also true that Mr.
Ryder gets what he wants: in recognizing the claim of "the wife of
his youth," he rescues himself from a far worse fate—marriage. He
gains a housekeeper, for the distance between Mr. Ryder and "the
wife of his youth" in nearly all things is so great as to suggest that
their reunion will hardly resolve itself into an at all usual marital
relation.

Mr. Ryder's Blue Vein Society is committed to two sets of values
that come into conflict during the course of the narrative—one set
social, the other moral. On the one hand, they, and especially he as
"custodian of its standards" and "preserver of its traditions," are
committed to the exclusive values of an elite group designed to
protect itself from social involvement with the masses of black
people. They are strongly enough committed to these values to
weave a whole life-style around them, and they see duty not only to
themselves but to succeeding generations of "blue veins." "Self
preservation," Mr. Ryder holds, "is the first law of nature."
These values are a little silly to people outside those circles, but as
Chesnutt knew, and as he shows humorously in "A Matter of Principle," another tale in this volume, they are of the utmost consequence to those holding them.

On the other hand the blue veins are committed to traditional
moral values, and their claim to superiority over the mass of black
people resides in part in their claim to higher morality. We may
infer from their concurrence with Mr. Ryder's great decision, and
from their reaction to his references to such moral values as fidelity,
devotion, honor, and justice, that they too hold these values.
Everyone who hears Mr. Ryder's outline of his situation knows the
cost of following the course that morality advocates. Given the
conflicting moral and social values, Mr. Ryder chooses the one
course rather than the other. Why?

The obvious reason is a true one. Chesnutt wishes to show, as he
demonstrates in "A Matter of Principle," that such false and

superficial social standards as those held by the group he describes may have disastrous consequences. Here, as is the Clayton family in "A Matter of Principle," Mr. Ryder is caught within a snare inherent within his value scheme. In order to be true to his claim to be a gentleman, a man of honor whose morals are "above suspicion," he must honor his earlier commitment and involve himself in a relation that will be extremely disadvantageous socially. At the same time, however, he might have made the opposite decision and still not have received the opprobrium of the blue veins: "We must do the best we can for ourselves and those who are to follow us. Self-preservation is the first law of nature" (p. 7). He does not make the opposite decision, however, and he may have had a less conscious motivation than either he ascribes to himself or we are likely to ascribe to him. His life and character as described in the story suggest he is not really very anxious to marry. We do not know his age exactly, but the evidence suggests he is between forty-five and fifty.[18] Somewhat rigid in his attitudes and highly moral in the traditional sense, he has undoubtedly lived in celibacy for at least twenty-five years. The details we are given about his tastes suggest he has given himself over to the aesthetic life, to poetry, music, art, and nothing suggests that he experiences bodily passions. His favorite poet is Tennyson,[19] whose lines he is reading when, ironically, he first hears the approach of his "wife": "She looked like a bit of the old plantation life, summoned up from the past by the wave of a magician's wand, as the poet's fancy had called into being the gracious shapes of which Mr. Ryder had just been reading" (p. 12). By recognizing the claims of "the wife of his youth," Mr. Ryder obtains a housekeeper and companion, satisfies his scrupulous sense of morality, and avoids the necessity ever of having to deal with the question of marriage and sexuality. He makes the ostensibly moral choice, and the tension between class and moral values seems resolved only to be undercut by the impurity of his motives. In this case Chesnutt's critical view of the class he characterizes prevents his usual sympathetic attachment to the group possessing wealth, culture, and power. It must be remembered, though, that this group is a black bourgeoisie with aristocratic pretensions, and Chesnutt seems to have viewed it far more realistically and objectively than he did the Southern antebellum aristocracy.

In *The House behind the Cedars* (1900), as in other works, Chesnutt organizes a multiplicity of conflicting elements. He relies on the tension among them rather than subtle plot or more fully developed character to carry the novel. This is the reason his novels tend to have so many people in them; each character represents some attitude, emotion, or idea—the major characters representing central attitudes, emotions, and ideas, and the minor ones variations or shadings. In the main Chesnutt again sets up a rather complex dialectic. In broad outline, clearly identifiable is a thesis and its antithesis, a subthesis and a subantithesis, and a conclusion (not a synthesis). The broad outline of opposing elements is a function of plot; the lesser opposing elements are functions of character.

The thesis of the story, implicit within the narrative, is stated and its immediate results described in the first ten chapters, wherein Rena decides to pass into the white world and is established in her new position at her brother John's house. What I have called antithesis begins with chapter 11 (or at the end of chapter 10), after Rena has left the security of John's house in order to return to visit her mother in Patesville, and ends with chapter 15 where encountering her fiancé on the street, she falls fainting. The subthesis consists of her life thereafter until she leaves home again, having decided to claim a black racial identity and to aid in the uplift of her people (chapters 16-24). The subantithesis begins with her new life in Sampson County, climaxes with her unwilling encounter with Tryon and Wain in the woods, and ends with the resulting illness (chapters 24-31). The conclusion of the total action follows. It is consistent with the character of Chesnutt's thinking that his materials should be organized in this way. Out of a simple, melodramatic plot, a multitude of complexities arises.

First is the question posed by the subject of the novel: passing, racial identity itself. Through the character of John, Chesnutt presents the question in something of the same way he considered it in his diary (quoted above). The laws and customs that define him racially conflict with the evidence of his eyes and with his own knowledge of the total arbitrariness of racial definitions. This is apparent in chapter 18 during his interview as a boy with Judge Straight:

> "You want to be a lawyer. . . . You are aware, of course that you are a Negro?"
>
> "I am white," replied the lad, turning back his sleeve and holding out his arm, "and I am free, as all my people were before me. . . ."
>
> "You are black, my lad, and you are not free. . . ."
>
> "A Negro is black; I am white, and not black."
>
> "Black as ink, my lad. . . . One drop of black blood makes the whole man black."[20]

Judge Straight then tells John that the laws of the neighboring state, South Carolina, define "Negro" differently:

> "Then I need not be black," the boy cried, with sparkling eyes.
>
> "No," replied the lawyer, "You need not be black, away from Patesville. . . ."
>
> "From this time on," said the boy, "I am white."
>
> "Softly, softly, my Caucasian fellow citizen," returned the judge, chuckling with quiet amusement. [P. 172]

Rena's sense of racial identity stands in contrast to John's. Whereas he conceives of himself as white, she does not, instead believing she is essentially Negro. She accepts the definition of race given by law and custom in their area; he refuses to. Whereas she believes the secret she holds prior to her encountering Tryon in Patesville is that she is black, John believes the secret to be that somewhere in his past he had a black ancestor. Because she believes herself to be black, she tests Tryon by asking him if he would marry her if she were little Albert's black nurse, and she has no difficulty after the affair with Tryon is concluded in resuming a black identity. "Are you really colored?" asks Mrs. Tryon,

George's mother. "Yes, ma'am, I am colored" (p. 240). The affair with Tryon has the effect, in fact, of solidly confirming her racial identity in her own eyes.

While they live in South Carolina, John and Rena are constantly threatened with being overwhelmed by a social identity different from their assumed one. Pressure from the society threatens them ceaselessly, although John, described as being of a more pragmatic turn of mind, is less affected than Rena. Such pressure produces, obviously, a tension between the social and private perspectives. Since George Tryon knows the secret and is rather conventional, it is within his mind that the two opposing views come into dramatic conflict. He has had a sense of the character of Rena not entirely different from her concept of herself. Yet he is unable to reconcile his original sense of her as a person with his knowledge that by social definition she is black:

> He dreamed of her sweet smile, her soft touch, her gentle voice. In all her fair young beauty she stood before him, and then by some hellish magic she was slowly transformed into a hideous black hag. With agonized eyes he watched her beautiful tresses become mere wisps of coarse wool wrapped round with dingy cotton strings; he saw her clear eyes grow bloodshot, her ivory teeth turn to unwholesome fangs. [Pp. 146-47]

He vacillates between the two images until finally (at least during our last view of him in the novel) he decides to marry her at any cost: "Custom was tyranny. Love was the only law" (p. 292). We may infer that if he still believes with Dr. Green that "the Negro is an inferior creature; God has marked him with the badge of servitude, and has adjusted his intellect to a servile condition" (p. 136), he at least holds the notion less firmly. In any case the conflict focused in the character of George (objectified in the characters of Dr. Green and Judge Straight) is a microcosmic depiction of the major conflict of the novel.

The complexities of race as delineated in the novel are complicated further by Chesnutt's own far-from-simple attitudes.

Among the nonwhites in the novel, Chesnutt distinguishes four social levels: a dependent, serving group (including servants and others without skills); skilled tradesmen, independent and capable of supporting themselves through their craft; a third group of uncertain occupation in the novel's context, freemen before the war and clearly of higher social status than the preceding (and also mulatto); and a fourth level, to which Rena and John belong, physically and in manner indistinguishable from whites and with access (if they wish to pass) to the society of the white landholding, professional or leisure group. Such distinctions are based both upon color and economic class. What is significant here, however, is the attitude that Chesnutt, through tone, manifests toward these social levels. He prefers, and identifies most closely with, Rena and John, believing them to be among, as he puts it, the "best people."

Although from my perspective Chesnutt's values were misplaced, he was not unaware of some of the more obvious implications of his class bias. He must have known from logic and experience that frequently the "best people" are not the best but among the worst. He must also have known that "good blood" does not necessarily mean good manners and morals and that morality is by no means a direct function of social and economic class, to say nothing of color. For the sake of indicating his knowledge that things are not quite so simple, he makes the most devoted, loyal, and honest character in the novel a black man (racially and physically); the most villainous a mulatto; and the most bigoted a member of the class of "best people." His basic preference, however, for rigid class structure at the top of which exists a cultured, privileged few remains unchanged.

Behind this preference, and serving as a wide backdrop against which the melodrama of *The House behind the Cedars* unfolds, is a kind of fatalism and pessimism, the force of which seems finally to say that ultimately race and class do not matter anyway. Time and nature render human concerns negligible; the very nature of things is such as to guarantee human suffering. This is suggested by the opening lines of the novel:

> Time touches all things with destroying hand; and if he
> seems now and then to bestow the bloom of youth, the

sap of spring, it is but a brief mockery, to be surely and swiftly followed by the wrinkles of old age, the dry leaves and bare branches of winter. [P. 1]

At the conclusion of the novel when Frank discovers Rena deathly ill and raving and he declares his love for her,

> . . . the sun shone on as brightly as before, the mockingbird sang yet more joyously. A gentle breeze sprang up and wafted the odor of bay and jessamine past them on its wings. The grand triumphal sweep of nature's onward march recked nothing of life's little tragedies. [P. 289]

Rena suffers when she passes into the white world; she suffers when she tries to remain among her acknowledged people. Such, Chesnutt seems to feel, is our lot, and a melodrama of passing seeks to delve beneath that concern in order to make a broader and more universal statement than the kinds of statements we usually believe melodrama capable of making.

Chesnutt's second novel, *The Marrow of Tradition* (1901), is built upon a complex union of oppositions in much the same way as *The House behind the Cedars*, but the later novel is a far more complicated structure and indeed the most complex of Chesnutt's works. Its complexity lies in the presentation of a wide range of conflicting and complementary attitudes, ideas, and feelings, which Chesnutt as author presents and in the act of presenting weighs and judges. Hence it is extremely important to the comprehension of the novel that the reader give close attention to the novel's tone; otherwise the subtlety of the novel, its extremely careful modulation of tone, will be missed.[21] It is not unlikely that the novel's subtlety will be missed by the uninvolved, impatient reader who finds difficulty following the strands of the plot or who cannot remember the identities of the many characters.

The dialectical nature of the novel lies in its myriad contrasts and countercontrasts of character. One character in the novel, Old

Delamere, is an ideal type of the antebellum aristocrat, a type nearly died out (we are told) and a person with whom all others with aristocratic pretensions are to be compared. His opposite is McBane, formerly a poor white whose father had been a slave driver and who has unscrupulously attained wealth during Reconstruction. Having no redeeming qualities, he is the prototype of evil, and he is a standard by which we are to ascertain the degrees to which other characters are responsible for exerting depraved or pernicious influence.

Delamere and McBane are products of their social classes, their characters having been fixed as the direct result of the influence on them of the values of the particular social classes from which they derive. Delamere has had strongly ingrained within his personality a system of values identified in the novel with an aristocracy, so thoroughly ingrained, indeed, that the personality of the man is a clear reflection of the ideals of his class:

> Old Mr. Delamere, who might be taken as the apex of an ideal aristocratic development, had been distinguished, during his active life . . . for courage and strength of will, courtliness of bearing, deference to his superiors, of whom there had been few, courtesy to his equals, kindness and consideration for those less highly favored, and above all, a scrupulous sense of honor.[22]

McBane may expect never to rise above the limitations prescribed by the circumstances of his birth. He "had sprung from the poor white class" and was "foremost in negro-baiting and election frauds, had done the dirty work of politics, as [his father] had done that of slavery." His captaincy is "merely a polite fiction" (p. 34), and he has realized a fortune from the corrupt convict lease system. He "was an upstart, a product of the democratic idea operating upon the poor white man, the descendant of the indentured bond-servant and the socially unfit" (pp. 86-87).

The opposition of Delamere and McBane reflects the basic opposition in the novel of good and evil, each of which abstractions finds embodiment within the various characters. If we were to schematize the novel from this perspective (though such schematization might give the impression that it is more static than it is in actuality), we might set up a continuum and arrange the characters on it in terms of their distance from either pole. A primary consideration in judging the characters' relation to good and evil is their position in regard to racial matters, for Chesnutt, in dealing with race in the novel, saw himself as dealing with a problem that is essentially moral. Hence, the most favored people are those who are humane, tolerant, and unprejudiced. The worst are bigots and extreme racists. Most of those who people the novel are in between, tending in varying degrees, and even at various times, toward one pole or the other.

As is implied above, Chesnutt did not believe it possible that an honest man could also be a bigot. Everywhere he indicates his conclusion that racial attitudes and morality are inextricably intertwined, that bigotry is one of the varieties of immorality. For this reason he is able to deal with a wide range of moral problems with the assurance that he will not be very far distant from his concern with racial matters. Tom Delamere's murder of his aunt, his cheating at cards, his general dissolution, and his racism are all interrelated in that they stem from the same source. At the same time, Old Delamere's honesty, openmindedness, and tolerance in racial matters are linked to his aristocratic heritage. He is one "whose ideals not even slavery had been able to spoil" (p. 197), whose aristocratic ideals have made him incapable of immorality.

The general dialectic of the novel is sustained in regard to the author's handling of social class. Here, as in *The House behind the Cedars*, social classes are sharply delineated. The predominating class is white aristocratic, descended from old, Southern, slaveholding families, professionals in vocation. The comparable group of black citizens are professionals and are like the other group in manners and general outlook. A newly emergent class of whites, formerly poor, is represented by McBane, a class that after the war used politics and trade to rise above its former position. A black servant class, black workers, and a black peasantry also exist in the society of the novel. Although Chesnutt does not question the basic structure of the society, he is critical of it for failing to live up to its ideals as they are represented in Old Delamere. The dialectic of class exists in the discrepancy between the way things are, as described in the novel, and the way they ought to be and, even according to the novel, once were: "Time was, sir, when the law was enforced in this state in a manner to command the respect of the world! Our lawyers, our judges, our courts, were a credit to humanity and civilization" (p. 211). The dialectic is dramatized in the contrasting characters of Tom Delamere and Old Delamere.

Chesnutt's allegiance to the aristocratic values described in the novel stems from his conviction that the evil he sees would not exist if these values were faithfully adhered to. He feels that the problems of the world of the novel are the result of degeneration, a falling away from an ideal code of conduct. Tom Delamere murders his old aunt; Carteret and General Belmont, although offended by the manners of McBane, find themselves acting in a manner consonant with the values of a man whose father had been a slave driver, and ultimately they cause a bloody riot. Yet Chesnutt, idealizing out of historical experience an aristocratic code of conduct, is never critical of the basis of the code. He does not recognize the relation between the code and the structure of the society, for if he did, he would obviously have seen that an aristocratic society in the Southern American context could never have the fluidity necessary to accommodate a William and Janet Miller. He indicates that the aristocrats who stray from the responsibilities of their position are at fault, but not the society itself, which allows a privileged few to exercise unrestrained power. Despite the tacit admission on Chesnutt's part that a less moral and responsible generation of aristocrats has arisen, he nevertheless presents the group as the "best people." Despite the acknowledged limitations of their morality, Chesnutt finds them superior to the McBanes, the Ellises, and certainly to the Josh Greens, the Mammy James, and the Jerrys. The preference does not come as easily as it might, however, for Chesnutt presents a relatively strong case against his inclination to identify with this particular class.

We are led to believe that Dr. Miller and his wife, Janet, have every claim to membership in the aristocratic class but that the traditions of the class are responsible for excluding them. They are aristocrats in everything but color. Since Chesnutt's closest identification in the novel is with Dr. Miller, we might expect the doctor to be as exemplary a figure as Old Delamere. But the thoroughgoing dialectic of the novel and Chesnutt's tendency to be self-critical do not allow that. Miller has his flaws and Janet hers, flaws resulting from the influence of class values on them. Recognition of Janet by her white half-sister would have legitimized her claim to the highest social status. Chesnutt in part attributes Janet's desire to be recognized by her sister to a loving temperament, free from malice. Even so, he sees it as a "weakness" to be overcome:

> Janet would have worshiped this sister, even from afar off, had she received even the slightest encouragement. So strong was this weakness that she had been angry with herself for her lack of pride, or even of a decent self-respect. It was, she sometimes thought, the heritage of her mother's race, and she was ashamed of it as part of the taint of slavery. [P. 66]

In the novel's context Janet's overwhelming desire for the recognition of her sister does indeed indicate a "lack of pride . . . decent self respect." As presented in the novel, it is something she should be very ashamed of because it points to her sense of racial inferiority. I believe it fair to infer that she would not have been so anxious to claim the sisterly relation had her father been McBane or some low person without wealth or status. Eventually, through the most difficult of circumstances, the reader will recall, Janet gains the strength of character necessary to overcome this infirmity when she is able to say to Olivia, "I throw you back your father's name, your father's wealth, your sisterly recognition. I want none of them" (p. 329). It is not so clear, however, that her husband grows as much.

Chesnutt treats Dr. Miller with sympathy, but some of his basic assumptions, especially assumptions stemming from his class orientation, are scrutinized clearly and unapologetically. The dialectic inherent within the juxtaposition of Dr. Miller and Josh

Green makes this apparent. During their first encounter Dr. Miller attempts to convince Josh Green that he should not be vengeful, that he should suffer wrong, endure injustice. Josh counters every argument forcefully and convincingly:

> "The Bible says that we should 'forgive our enemies, bless them that curse us, and do good to them that despitefully use us'."
>
> "Yas, suh, I've l'arnt all dat in Sunday-school an' I've hered do preachers say it time an' time ag'in. But it 'pears ter me dat dis fergitfulniss an' fergivniss is might one-sided. De w'ite folks don' fergive nothin' de niggers does. . . . De niggers is be'n train' ter fergiveniss' an' fer fear dey might fergit how ter fergive, de w'ite folks gives 'em somethin' new ev'y now an' den, ter practice on." [P. 113]

During this scene Miller, noting Josh's willingness to die for a cause, asks whether he himself would be equally willing to give up his life. He does not answer the question, but as Chesnutt hints, he will have a chance soon enough. During his second encounter with Josh Green, Miller, suffering the limitations of the careful, middle-class man, again attempts, relying on reason and good sense, to resolve a situation already beyond the bounds of rationality. He tries to persuade Josh Green and his followers that they should not arm themselves for self-protection in a case of clear provocation by local whites bent on random lynching of blacks. He uses every argument he can think of: going to the sheriff, the president of the country, responsible white citizens of the town. Again his arguments and his efforts to enlist the aid of whites fail, and though he ultimately prevents the lynching of Sandy Campbell, he does not prevent the occurrence of the bloody riot. And finally, when Dr. Miller is asked to serve as leader of a group of blacks in their effort to protect themselves, he again argues against resistance, his main point being, "We would only be throwing our lives away" (p. 282). Again Josh counters every argument as forcefully and as effectively as before. His final words during this scene tell heavily against the character of Dr. Miller (and the lawyer Watson and presumably the whole class to which they belong): "Dese gentlemen may have somethin' ter live fer; but ez fer my pa't, I'd rather be a dead nigger any day dan a live dog!" (p. 284).[23] Because Miller senses the full negative implications of his refusal to lead the militants, yet by temperament is unable to engage in violent action, he is somewhat torn:

> Miller, while entirely convinced that he had acted wisely in declining to accompany them, was yet conscious of a distinct feeling of shame and envy that he, too, did not feel impelled to throw away his life in a hopeless struggle. [P. 285]

In the novel's context of values General Belmont's defense of Miller is less than complimentary: "He's a good sort of negro, doesn't meddle with politics, nor tread on any one else's toes" (pp. 251-52). Although Miller is clearly distinguished from Mammy Jane and Jerry, it is significant that neither of them "treads on anyone else's toes" either; yet they are not spared:

> Mammy Jane had gone to join the old mistress upon whose memory her heart was fixed; and yet not all her reverence for her old mistress, nor all her deference to the whites, nor all their friendship for her, had been able to save her from this raging devil of race hatred which momentarily possessed the town. [P. 297]

The doctor is not equated to these two, but something of the opprobrium attached to them attaches to him as well. Are we not to relate this statement in somewhat modified form to the situation of Dr. Miller, whose only child is killed during the riot? The balance between Josh Green and Jerry is a delicate one to maintain, and although Miller lies between them, Chesnutt suggests that the doctor, however justified his position, inclines more toward the one side than the other in his attitudes and actions relating to getting along with whites in Wellington.[24]

In the scale of contrasts Dr. Miller's counterpart from the perspective of social bearing in relating to whites is Old Delamere's servant, Sandy. We are intended to see Sandy as possessing a certain dignity derived from his intimate association with true aristocracy. His manners are impeccable, as are his morals, and his mode of interaction with whites around him indicates alternatives different from the practices of Jerry and Mammy Jane. His dignity in the face of insult, his sense of self, are comparable to Miller's. Both maintain their dignity through allegiance to the values, we are told, of the aristocratic class.

In his careful delineation of attitudes pertaining to relations between white and black and in his scrupulously honest expression of contrast and comparison, Chesnutt presents yet another attitude, however briefly, different from those possessed by the black characters considered above. The attitude of the black nurse in chapter 4 forms one pole of a subdialectic in the novel. The tone of the few paragraphs relating to her is interesting and revealing insofar as it suggests something of Chesnutt's rather complex habit of mind. Her attitudes contrast, of course, with those of Mammy Jane in the scene in which they appear. Note the interweaving in the following passages of Chesnutt's approval and disapproval, his praise and condemnation, his criticism and defense of an attitude representative of that belonging "to the younger generation of colored people":

> Standing, like most young people of her race, on the border line between two irreconcilable states of life, she had neither the picturesqueness of the slave, nor the unconscious dignity of those of whom freedom has been the immemorial birthright; she was in what might be called the chip-on-the-shoulder stage, through which races as well as individuals must pass in climbing the ladder of life,—not an interesting, at least not an agreeable stage, but an inevitable one, and for that reason entitled to a paragraph in a story of Southern life. . . . Had this old woman [Mammy Jane], who had no au-

thority over her, been a little more polite, or a little less offensive, the nurse might have returned her a pleasant answer. These old time negroes, she said to herself, made her sick with their slavering over the white folks, who, she supposed, favored them and made much of them because they had once belonged to them,—much the same reason why they fondled their cats and dogs. For her own part, they gave her nothing but her wages, and small wages at that, and she owed them nothing more than equivalent service. It was purely a matter of business; she sold her time for their money. There was no question of love between them. [P. 42]

Clearly the nurse's way of thinking, not only in terms of Chesnutt's tone here but in comparison to his later statement at the time of the death of Mammy Jane, is a viable alternative to Mammy Jane's, and though Chesnutt says she lacks the "unconscious dignity of those of whom freedom has been the immemorial birthright," she is not without dignity, and this the author admires. But most significantly the nurse's sense of self, as ambivalently presented as it is, does not derive from an aristocratic heritage. Dr. Miller's more accommodating racial attitudes must be measured against the nurse's, as well as against the attitudinal stances of others regarding social interaction.

Despite the seemingly endless contrasts and countercontrasts in the novel,[25] despite the complex dialectic the novel expresses, Chesnutt's deepest allegiances in *The Marrow of Tradition* are to Dr. Miller and to the style and mode of life and values that he represents. His conclusions are not held lightly, however, nor were they come by easily, for at the core of the value structure of the novel lies a host of unresolved questions, insurmountable questions. At the end of the novel is an overwhelming sense of what I have described earlier as a tragic dimension. Certain wrongs are righted, but nobody emerges from the experience described in the novel unscarred. Chesnutt's third and last published novel, *The Colonel's Dream*, is written out of considerably more certainty in that the values put forth in the novel, which seem to represent the author's own beliefs, are presented with far less ambivalence. That tragic dimension, however, the implication of humanity's final defeat in attempting to realize significant goals, remains.

The Colonel's Dream (1905) has little of the complexity of The Marrow of Tradition. The issues it raises are far more clear-cut, the lines distinguishing good and evil more sharply drawn. The villains are clearly known, their motivations exposed, and their characters lacking redemptive qualities. Class lines are delineated although they are under great stress as a rising middle class (formally poor whites) wrests political and economic power from the old aristocracy. The dialectical character of Chesnutt's earlier novels is maintained here, although in simpler form. Chesnutt seems far less certain in this novel than in earlier ones that a rigidly structured society with a benevolent aristocracy at its head (given the realities of the Southern political, economic, and social situation) is the best possible societal arrangement. In fact The Colonel's Dream makes a case for the desirability of egalitarian democracy.

Colonel French, the protagonist, is the source of good, of benevolence and right thinking in Clarendon. His antagonist, who seems in his capacity for evildoing the devil incarnate, is William Fetters. The conflict between them forms the core of the novel. In describing their interaction, Chesnutt intends to make a statement about the nature of things, and for this reason Fetters, whose pernicious influence pervades all of Clarendon and its environs, seems as much a force as a person. Fetters controls the town and has managed so to extend his influence as to have every person of means except Colonel French and the lawyer Caxton under his control. Faulkner's Flem Snopes is his more modern counterpart— Flem, who by a shrewd, animal cunning manages to corrupt a whole community by undercutting the power of the aristocracy and seizing control himself. Fetters is concerned with garnering wealth and power, and he will do anything, we are led to believe, to accomplish his ends. Likewise, he embodies the forces of racism and exploitation since these are shown in the novel to be so closely intertwined with and so necessary to the achievement of his ends.

The colonel's dream, a plan to make the town of Clarendon into a model of democracy and prosperity, means considerably more than this in the novel's context. As it is described in the novel, the fulfillment of the dream will signify the potentiality of the imposition of pattern and coherence in life itself. If the ethical actions of people have any broad significance at all, the premise of the novel runs, then one free to do good and bent on doing good will accomplish his end. The colonel's business career is behind him, and with his great wealth and his relative freedom from responsibilities, he is free to attempt to fulfill himself as a human. On the outcome of the conflict of the novel is staked the meaning of things. As Colonel French left New York for Clarendon, he "was entering upon a new life of his own, from which he was to look back upon his business career as a mere period of preparation for the real end and purpose of his earthly existence."[26]

In his uncritical, undeviating sympathy for Colonel French, Chesnutt seems inclined, as in his earlier novels, to favor the claims of an aristocratic class over those of all others, but in *The Colonel's Dream* a distinct difference is to be observed. The earlier novel gives the impression that the aristocrats need only live up to their responsibilities as members of the class. In Chesnutt's eyes they seem to be in fact the "best people" and of "good blood." Something of that attitude remains in this novel, but finally it is repudiated. Colonel French's son, Phil, is described by the colonel as "a born gentleman." The voice of the author tells us that Phil "had inherited the characteristics attributed to good blood. Features, expressions, bearing, were marked by the signs of race" (pp. 16-17).[27] Some ambivalence, however, attaches to Chesnutt's attitudes toward the aristocratic class, a more nearly basic ambivalence than previously expressed:

> The colonel was himself a gentleman, and the descendant of a long line of gentlemen. But he had lived too many years among those who judged the tree by its fruit, to think that blood alone entitled him to any special privileges. The consciousness of honourable ancestry might make one clean of life, gentle of manner, and just in one's dealings. In so far as it did this it was something

to be cherished, but scarcely to be boasted of, for
democracy is impatient of any excellence not born of
personal effort, of any pride save that of achievement.
[P. 37]

In the following passage where Chesnutt distinguishes between
the colonel's feelings and principles—really a conflict between
Chesnutt's necessary commitment to egalitarian democracy[28] and
his strong identification with an aristocracy—Chesnutt's ambivalent
emotions are even more obvious:

> In principle the colonel was an ardent democrat; he
> believed in the rights of man, and extended the doctrine
> to include all who bore the human form. But in feeling
> he was an equally pronounced aristocrat. A servant's
> rights he would have defended to the last ditch; famil-
> iarity he would have resented with equal positiveness.
> Something of this ancestral feeling stirred within him
> now. [P. 81]

Out of this conflict emerges the theme of the novel, and it is
ultimately resolved in its social, if not in its private, implications.
The colonel at the conclusion of the novel is firmly convinced that
an irresponsible aristocracy functions to the detriment of the social
body, although there is no reason to believe that the colonel has
altered his private feelings about the meaningfulness of his aristocratic heritage insofar as his personal system of values is concerned. He will continue to be an aristocrat in feeling, but he will
no longer rely upon the possibility of an aristocratic class's functioning as a viable, positive force, whose benevolent influence will
shape the destiny of the South:

> "The best people, Laura," he said with a weary smile,
> "are an abstraction. When any deviltry is on foot they
> are never there to prevent it—they vanish into thin air at
> its approach. When it is done, they excuse it; and they
> make no effort to punish it. So it is not too much to say

that what they permit they justify, and they cannot shirk the responsibility." [P. 283]

Nothing in the novel suggests the possibility of solutions to the problems posed. On the contrary, the suggestion seems to be that no significant correctives exist. The novel ultimately focuses on the response of the colonel to his experience, and his response is the primary clue to the meaning of the novel from the author's perspective. The colonel's leaving, his removal of his son's and old Peter's bodies to a Northern cemetery, the burning of the ancestral mansion, signify a break with his Southern past and a total failure to implement a set of moral and political values incompatible with the realities of the Southern situation. The novel, then, as a commentary on the capacity of people to act reasonably and well and to be successful in encouraging others to do the same, is indeed bleak.

The colonel's conclusion that "the best people . . . are an abstraction" signals, in view of Chesnutt's frequent and unambiguous use of the term *best people* throughout his fiction, a marked change in attitude and thinking, a final synthesis. His whole manner of thinking about society had been based on assumptions derived from the hypothesis that a rigidly structured society led by a benevolent, responsible aristocracy is the best social scheme. By means of the dialectical exploration and testing of this hypothesis, by measuring his own preference for an aristocracy against the realities of Southern economic, political, and racial experience, he finally worked out the problem, concluding that the Southern aristocracy was at once essentially powerless and irresponsible. Having got that far in his thinking, considering alternatives, he opted, momentarily and in principle, for egalitarian democracy, only to discover that such a principle does not work necessarily in and of itself nor will it work when opposed by powerful enough antagonists. His next step, and a short step it was since this possibility had lurked in the background for years, was to conclude with some finality that life is essentially tragic anyway, so nothing matters in the end. Both *The House behind the Cedars* and *The Marrow of Tradition* indicate his thinking in this direction. In *The Colonel's Dream* this notion is reflected in the colonel's withdrawal after his experience in Clarendon into private life and his implicit pessimism about the potential of humans to do good for themselves or others.

The Colonel's Dream is Chesnutt's last published novel. It represents his having finally come to terms with an unrealistic and mythical conception of an antebellum Southern aristocracy, a conception probably derived from the same sources that fed the imaginations of Thomas Nelson Page, Joel Chandler Harris, and other writers of the plantation school. I believe he was taken in entirely by the myth of the antebellum South and that the only area of the myth he viewed critically at all was slavery. He identified with the aristocratic class until he began to be convinced that there was no glory in identifying with the powerless, irresponsible remnants of the class left after the Civil War, especially after he began to see some of the political implications of such identification. Thereafter he became an aristocrat of the mind, never repudiating the myth but recognizing the distance between his aristocratic ideas and actuality. "The best people are an abstraction" is his concession to the reality that currently no Old Delameres exist—they have been replaced by his sons. The sons of Delamere he repudiates —but not the father, not the ideal. The end of The Colonel's Dream signifies that the ideal aristocratic heritage has assumed its existence at a further remove from reality, from history. Hence the tension between that ideal and Chesnutt's awareness of the reality around him is slackened and for all practical purposes the problem is solved. No longer does he feel the pressure that had caused him twenty-five years earlier to feel, "I think I must write a book."[29] He has written his book—five books—and is finally freed from (or firmly chained to?) an idea that obsessed him.

NOTES

1. His first biography, Charles Waddell Chesnutt: Pioneer of the Color Line, was written by his daughter, Helen M. Chesnutt (Chapel Hill: University of North Carolina Press, 1952). A definitive biography has yet to be written. Frances Richardson Keller has put forth An American Crusade: The Life of Charles Waddell Chesnutt (Provo, Utah: Brigham Young University Press, 1978), but that work is limited by the biographer's

thesis and by her limited knowledge of literature. It is a thoroughly re-searched doctoral dissertation but not a definitive biography.

2. I use the adjective *black* here hesitatingly since Chesnutt did not precisely consider himself black, neither literally nor figuratively, a subject discussed in the following paragraph.

3. Chesnutt's critics have not always been free from bias. Paul Elmer More found that "Chesnutt had done everything he could to humiliate whites" in *The Marrow of Tradition* (see Chesnutt, *Charles W. Chesnutt*, p. 179). Earl Schenck Miers in the introduction to *The Wife of His Youth* (Ann Arbor: University of Michigan Press, 1968), pp. x-xi, finds a reviewer to be correct who sees Chesnutt as "a brother to Uncle Remus."

4. Chesnutt, *Charles W. Chesnutt*, p. 13.

5. A more pertinent observation about his sense of self is contained in a journal entry omitted from his daughter's biography but quoted in an article detailing the effects of her editorial practices on the image of Chesnutt projected by the biography. Chesnutt comments, "I am neither fish, flesh, nor fowl—neither 'nigger,' white, nor 'buckrah.' Too 'stuck-up' for the colored folks, and, of course, not recognized by the whites." William L. Andrews, "A Reconsideration of *Charles Waddell Chesnutt: Pioneer of the Color Line*," *CLA Journal* 19: 142. A detailed discussion of Chesnutt's "conflict over his own racial identity" is contained in Michael Flusche's excellent article, "On the Color Line: Charles Waddell Chesnutt," *North Carolina Historical Review* 53: 17-19. Flusche believes Chesnutt's problem of racial identity may have been "the major obstacle Chesnutt encountered as a writer." I, on the contrary, see it as chiefly responsible for his particular intellectual habit of mind, the impetus for his writing.

6. Charles Chesnutt, "Post-Bellum—Pre-Harlem," *Crisis* 38: 194.

7. Chesnutt, *Charles W. Chesnutt*, pp. 68-69.

8. Chesnutt, *Wife of His Youth*, pp. 322-23.

9. John M. Reilly, "The Dilemma in Chesnutt's *The Marrow of Tradition*," *Phylon* 32: 31-38, has observed the same phenomenon although he describes it differently, as "a complex of subtly graded inclinations and conceptions which are continuously modifying and canceling each other."

10. See Francis Pendleton Gaines, *The Southern Plantation* (New York: Columbia University Press, 1925), pp. 62-94. See also Hugh M. Gloster, *Negro Voices in American Fiction* (Chapel Hill: University of North Carolina Press, 1948), pp. 7-10.

11. Chesnutt comments specifically on the limitations of some writers of the plantation tradition in his diary; see Chesnutt, *Charles W. Chesnutt*, pp. 58-59. Sylvia Lyons Render does not agree that Chesnutt shared

anything of the vision of the old South put forth by plantation-tradition writers. She believes Chesnutt's concept of the old South to be "realistic rather than romantic." See her introduction to *The Short Fiction of Charles W. Chesnutt* (Washington, D.C.: Howard University Press, 1974), pp. 24-25.

12. Compare Flusche's commentary, "On the Color Line," pp. 11-12, on the similarity of Chesnutt's tales to other tales in the same tradition. Flusche comments further, "By writing fiction akin to the plantation genre, Chesnutt chose to do battle on unfavorable terrain. . . . There was no way he could be heard so long as he remained on his opponents' territory. His own imagination was shackled by the character types common in the plantation literature."

13. The sympathetic distance between Chesnutt and Uncle Julius can be measured by the extent to which Julius is a stereotypical character, and that is clearly delineated in Render, introduction to *Short Fiction*, pp. 24-25.

14. This perspective is confirmed by David Britt, "Chesnutt's Conjure Tales: What You See Is What You Get," *CLA Journal* 15: 274: "Since in only one of the seven stories is Julius able to gain something of value to himself personally, he is either singularly unsuccessful as a hustler, or presented by Chesnutt as a 'darky entertainer' in the minstrel tradition, or the stories are not about financial matters at all. My contention is that Julius's tales are not aimed at manipulating John in the way the surface narrative implies."

15. Chesnutt, "Post-Bellum—Pre-Harlem," p. 193.

16. The other stories in *The Wife of His Youth* reveal the same dialectical character as the title story.

17. Render, introduction to *Short Fiction*, p. 30, reads the story as reflecting a lack of color prejudice on Chesnutt's part, meaning that she sees the story's implications as being more straightforward than I do.

18. He is less than twenty-one at the time he runs away from the plantation. The "wife of his youth" has been searching for him for twenty-five years. Mrs. Dixon, his intended, is twenty-five, and he is "old enough to have been her father" (p. 5).

19. Recall Faulkner's use of Tennyson as a means of characterizing Hightower in *Light in August* (New York: Random House, Modern Library, 1950): "One wall of the study is lined with books. He pauses before them, seeking, until he finds the one which he wants. It is Tennyson. It is dogeared. He has had it ever since the seminary. He sits beneath the lamp and opens it. It does not take long. Soon the fine galloping language, the gutless swooning full of sapless trees and dehydrated lusts begins to

swim smooth and swift and peaceful. . . . It is like listening in a cathedral to a eunuch chanting in a language which he does not even need to not understand" (p. 278).

20. Charles Chesnutt, *The House behind the Cedars* (Ridgewood, N.J.: Gregg Press, 1968), pp. 169-70. Subsequent quotations are from this edition.

21. By *tone* I mean the attitude of the author as expressed in the work.

22. Charles Chesnutt, *The Marrow of Tradition* (Ann Arbor: University of Michigan Press, 1969), p. 96. Subsequent quotations are from this edition.

23. For a full description and discussion of the character of Josh, and especially of Chesnutt's complex attitude toward him, see J. Noel Heermance, *Charles W. Chesnutt: America's First Great Black Novelist* (Hamden, Conn.: Shoe String Press, 1974), pp. 214-17.

24. Compare John M. Reilly's treatment of the contrast between Dr. Miller and Josh Green and, hence, Chesnutt's judgment of Miller's character. I do not believe Chesnutt is as condemning of Miller as Reilly says. The irony that Reilly observes at work in the novel extends to Chesnutt's perspective on his chief character. See Reilly, "The Dilemma in Chesnutt's *The Marrow of Tradition*," *Phylon* 32: 36-37.

25. For example, the following one large area invites contrast. Every character in the novel, white and black, possesses different racial attitudes. The attitude of each invites comparison with every other one. Clusters of characters possess similar attitudes, and each cluster may be compared with every other cluster.

26. Charles Chesnutt, *The Colonel's Dream* (Upper Saddle River, N.J.: Gregg Press, 1968), p. 14. Subsequent quotations are from this edition.

27. Flusche, "On the Color Line," observes that "Chesnutt's use of blood to designate race or lineage also indicated his inability to break from the concepts he detested. He had once written to Cable that he disliked Albion Tourgée's cultivated white Negroes who were always bewailing their fate and cursing the drop of black blood which 'taints' . . . their otherwise pure race" (p. 19). The extent and character of my disagreement with Flusche is contained in my discussion of this topic. In general I believe Chesnutt's reliance on old traditions concerning blood and lineage is more complex than Flusche says, although he must certainly be given credit for making the observation.

28. This point has not been developed in my analysis although it is abundantly evident in the novel. Faced with an economically and morally bankrupt aristocracy and an amoral, rising bourgeoisie, the colonel seeks

to effect economic equality among black and white workers and other kinds of equality as well. Although his final goals are not spelled out, we may infer, given his concern with the convict lease system, with improving the education of blacks, and his opposition to segregation, that his ideal is full equality in all areas of life. These seem to be his principles, although not necessarily reflective of his feelings. It is clear, as is pointed out above, that he will always feel superior to those who are, from his perspective, his social inferiors. He would prefer the leadership of a benevolent aristocracy, but since the aristocracy is powerless, he is forced to support egalitarian principles.

29. Chesnutt, *Charles W. Chesnutt*, p. 21.

5

Jean Toomer:
The Politics
of Denial

"Time and space have no meaning in a canefield." —*Cane*[1]

THE KEY TO THE meaning of Jean Toomer's *Cane* is contained in the book's final section, "Kabnis," in which the central character, the narrator of most of the preceding tales and the person who comes closest to expressing the attitudes, ideals, and feelings of the author, presents a critical commentary on himself and on all that has gone before. Viewed from this perspective, "Kabnis" becomes far less obscure than it has frequently been interpreted as being, the unity of the whole book, its novelistic quality, is revealed, and the novel is shown to be less a revelation of the essence of black life than generally claimed. *Cane* finally turns out to be, more accurately, an index of the orientation of its author than of the nature of black history and character.[2] This is demonstrated in the stories, poems, and vignettes preceding "Kabnis," so clearly demonstrated that it is difficult to believe that critics who have seen *Cane* as in some sense a revelation of the essential black soul are not talking about something other than Toomer's book.[3]

The character Kabnis has been described as a "languishing idealist,"[4] as indeed he is. The significant aspect, however, is the nature of his idealism, its extent and its implications. Kabnis is a thoroughgoing philosophical idealist who scorns the world of actuality (as commonly conceived) and embraces an imaginary world, ideal and more real than the ephemeral and evanescent world of materiality, of the senses. Truth and beauty reside for him outside ordinary experience, in a sphere beyond the experiential. The narrator(s?) or male protagonists of the tales and sketches leading up to "Kabnis" are either Kabnis himself or characters so like him in orientation that the distinction is insignificant.[5] All of them are inclined to translate sense experience into more "acceptable" terms, to filter out ugliness, harshness, unpleasantness, and to recoil from the recognition of things as they are. Their inmost desire is to step out of history, out of time, and to exist in some unchanging realm, some lotus land of perfect being. This analysis is entirely in keeping with Toomer's own statement about his intentions in his writings:

> As for writing—I am not a romanticist. I am not a classicist or a realist, in the usual sense of the terms. I am an essentialist. Or, to put it in other words, I am a spiritualizer, a poetic realist. This means two things. I try to lift facts, things, happenings to the planes of rhythm, feeling and significance. I try to clothe and give body to potentialities.[6]

The narrator of "Karintha," the first section of *Cane*, whether Toomer or Kabnis, is just such a person. His perspective on Karintha creates and controls the sense we get of her from the sketch. Who is she? What is she like? The sketch provides certain information about her, information such as that which might comprise a clinical description. She is sexually precocious and eventually promiscuous. She feels contemptuous of the men with whom she has sexual relations, an attitude said to be typical of prostitutes. She commits infanticide after her child is born, burying it in a smoldering pile of sawdust. When she is young, she sings (or screams?) in a high-pitched voice that "would put one's ears to itching," and she stones the cows, beats her dog, and fights other children, behavior not very unusual for a child.

How does one interpret such an individual? What are we to think of her? This is determined by the narrator, and as long as we stay within the frame of reference he sets up for us, we will see what he sees. What he sees is a pagan earth goddess, human, yet not of the earth; a principle of femaleness in nature, an object of worship and adoration, but beyond external nature: "Her skin is like dusk on the eastern horizon, O cant you see it, O cant you see it, Her skin is like dusk on the eastern horizon . . . When the sun goes down" (p. 5). The figures of speech that Toomer uses to describe Karintha have the effect of minimizing her actuality. She is compared not with things but with qualities or states of things. We are told not that she is beautiful but that she carries beauty, as though she bears the abstraction itself. At twelve she was "a wild flash," and "her sudden darting past you was a bit of vivid color, like a black bird that flashes light." Her running is a quality of sound, a "whir," which has the nonexistent "sound of the red dust that sometimes makes a spiral in the road." The figures used to describe her are one aspect of the narrator's tone through which he reveals his attitude toward her. She is described caressingly, as though he himself is one of those men who brings her money. The narrator himself places her outside of time and reality, seeing her as something of a saint, a goddess scornful of her suppliants. Above morality, beyond judgment, Karintha has attributed to her a purity and innocence deriving from the narrator's preference for idealization.

Becky, the titular character of the second sketch, seems real enough until we consider what happens to her—not in actuality but in the eyes of the narrator of the sketch. The movement of the piece is condensed in a few lines at the beginning: "Her eyes were sunken, her neck stringy, her breasts fallen, til then. Taking their works, they filled her, like a bubble rising—then she broke." Her situation as described evokes the harshest reality, caught as she is between the intolerance of the two races, cast out, though secretly supported by both. "No one ever saw her," including the reader.

During the course of the vignette she recedes farther and farther from the narrative until (like the bursting bubble) she disappears, and we do not know whether she is buried under the mound of fallen brick or whether she had died before: "Through the dust we saw the bricks in a mound upon the floor. Becky, if she was there, lay under them" (p. 12). In any case she becomes spirit, and as spirit she is more alive to the townspeople than when she lived. As Becky the living person recedes from the sight and knowing of the townspeople, the spiritualized Becky grows apace. Her reality is transformed into idea, and the idea of her eventually subsumes and displaces her reality.

Again, as in "Karintha," the perspective of the narrator accounts for the otherworldly orientation of "Becky." The straightforwardness of the tone, the lack of irony indicates that the narrator participates in the values and beliefs of the world projected there, a world in which, as of old, the supernatural makes its presence felt in overt ways. As the narrative progresses and Becky recedes from the world, the element of the supernatural becomes more evident. The form that the supernatural takes is Christian in part, pagan in part; the orthodox Christ ("O pines, whisper to Jesus . . .") and unorthodox superstition (". . . the ground trembled as a ghost train rumbled by"). Becky's recession is indeed paralleled by the increasing emphasis on the supernatural. The sordid, ugly brutishness of her life and of her sons' lives (of so much actuality) disappears as she moves outside of time, outside of a historical framework, a transformation wrought by the imagination of the narrator of the tale.

"Carma," "Fern," and "Esther" tell similar tales, different in detail but each in its manner confirming (in various ways) an overall ahistorical, otherworldly orientation. In "Carma" the point is made through the style (as in others of the sketches), through the voice of the narrator (whose voice is the style), and through plot and character. The style of the long parenthetical description of the setting strains beyond the actuality suggested as its basis, through the sound and echo of music, through reflections and emanations of light, toward the purity of idea (in the Platonic sense). This is not to say that a sense of actuality is not evoked in

the tale but rather that Toomer strives to mute actuality by trans-
forming it through metaphor to something less real and substantial
than it would be were it commonly experienced:

> The sun is hammered to a band of gold. Pine-needles,
> like mazda, are brilliantly aglow. . . . Smoke curls up.
> Marvelous web spun by the spider sawdust pile. . . .
> From far away, a sad strong song. Pungent and com-
> posite, the smell of farmyards is the fragrance of the
> woman. She does not sing; her body is a song. She is the
> forest, dancing. Torches flare . . . juju men, greegree,
> witch-doctors. . . . The Dixie Pike has grown from a
> goat path in Africa. [Pp. 17-18]

The description leads to the final statement above and suggests
finally that some kind of magical transformation has occurred, a
transformation giving special significance to the narrator's statement shortly afterward: "Time and space have no meaning in a
canefield."

The setting of the tale reflects upon the scant plot. Carma (whose
name means "fate" or "destiny") is responsible for her husband's
being on the chain gang. It is in her role as fate that she is "strong
as any man," even "stronger." Her husband becomes then her
victim, not simply because of the operation of circumstance—
more than simply a domestic quarrel is involved—but because of
their roles in the very nature of things. Carma, like other females in
Cane, plays out the role assigned her in the universal scheme: the
bitch-goddess, and "should she not take others, this Carma, strong
as a man, whose tale as I have told it is the crudest melodrama?"
The setting, moving as it does away from actuality, supplies the
unrealistic dimension to "Carma," to a tale of "crudest melodrama."

"Fern" is essentially like "Karintha," although the otherworldly
orientation of "Fern" is more explicitly drawn out. We are invited
to share with the narrator of the tale, almost certainly Kabnis here
if not elsewhere, his particular vision of the titular character, Fern.
Fern is described as having some special quality deriving in part
from her femaleness, a quality that represents an inverted sexuality

or an idealization of the sexual response. Men desire her sexually, but in possession of her they derive "no joy from it." Yet they become inexplicably bound to her; they become, indeed, suppliants:

> Fern's eyes desired nothing that you could give her; there was no reason why they should withhold. Men saw her eyes and fooled themselves. Fern's eyes said to them that she was easy. When she was young, a few men took her, but got no joy from it. And then, once done, felt bound to her (quite unlike their hit and run with other girls), felt as though it would take a lifetime to fulfill an obligation which they could find no name for. They became attached to her, and hungered after finding the barest trace of what she might desire. [Pp. 24-25]

Toomer is of course describing a habit of mind perennial in Western civilization, a tendency manifested in Platonism but more specifically in the medieval cults devoted to the worship of the Virgin.[7] The psychology of the phenomenon is explained by Toomer in terms of superstition, although I see it as an abhorrence for, contempt for, and fear of the natural and ephemeral and a preference for the purity and timelessness of the ideal:

> As you know, men are apt to idolize or fear that which they cannot understand, especially if it be a woman. She did not deny them, yet the fact was that they were denied. A sort of superstition crept into their consciousness of her being somehow above them. Being above them meant that she was not to be approached by anyone. She *became* a virgin. [My emphasis] [P. 26]

We are told that "men were everlastingly bringing her their bodies" but that eventually "she began to turn them off." The implication is that men who come within her purview worship her even though they do not have sexual contact with her. So far does she become removed from actuality in the view of the narrator that he feels on the verge of a mystical experience when he is alone with her at the creek. It is here, despite my reluctance to interpret it in this way, that we are invited to make the comparison with the Virgin:

> I felt strange, as I always do in Georgia, particularly at dusk. I felt that things unseen to men were tangibly immediate. It would not have surprised me had I had a vision. People have them in Georgia more often than you would suppose. A black woman once saw the mother of Christ and drew her in charcoal on the courthouse wall. [P. 31]

Hence, in perceiving his experience from an unnatural perspective, the narrator intends to take it out of time, out of history.

In "Esther" the central character is like the narrator-participant of "Fern" in that she too tends through her imagination to transmute the world of actuality into a world corresponding to her own psychological needs. Esther stands essentially in the same relation to King Barlo as the narrator to Fern in the preceding story. A state of mind, a particular psychological orientation, interests Toomer here as throughout *Cane*, and Esther is another variation on that theme. The narrator himself does not appear in "Esther," but it is clear enough that his interest and sympathy lie with the perspective of the central character.

Esther differs from Karintha, Becky, Carma, and Fern in that she is in fact a virgin and does not simply have virginal qualities attributed to her by the narrator of the tale or by those around her. Nothing of the whore-saint duality is present in her character, although a duality of a different sort does exist. Esther is sexually frustrated; her thinly veiled dreams reveal intense sexual need and pent-up, unreleased sexual energy. In opposition to her natural drive toward sexual release stands an equally strong, or stronger, resistance to participation in nature and in the world around her. For her the world of imagination is preferable to the reality of her life; so she forgets the names of the people who come into her father's store and "her eyes hardly see the people to whom she gives change." The image of Barlo, whom she saw when he was in a religious trance when she was nine years old, becomes fixed in her mind—Barlo, "a clean-muscled, magnificent, black-skinned Negro" (p. 36). Barlo appeals to her in part because of his physical appearance and known sexual prowess, in part because he is a holy man and of another world. When she was nine and had seen him entranced and had heard of the events surrounding his mystical experience and departure from town, "he became the starting point of the only living patterns that her mind was to know" (p. 40). Associated with him in Esther's mind are the events surrounding Barlo's vision that

> . . . a great, heavy, rumbling voice actually was heard. That hosts of angels and of demons paraded up and down the streets all night. That King Barlo rode out of town astride a pitch-black bull that had a glowing gold ring in its nose. And that old Limp Underwood, who hated niggers, woke up next morning to find that he held a black man in his arms. This much is certain: an inspired Negress, of wide reputation for being sanctified, drew a portrait of a black madonna on the courthouse wall. [Pp. 39-40]

To Esther this becomes not only the reality of this particular event but the reality of life itself. The unworldly, supernatural element of that early experience defines for her true and essential reality, turns her mind away from things as they are to a world behind the world perceived with the senses, from the world of shadows to a world of true being. In this sense Barlo becomes "the starting point of the only living patterns that her mind was to know."

At twenty-two, when she "decides that she loves him," she has fallen in love with an image, with an object of her imagination, a sensuous yet pure creature not unlike herself. She has eventually decided, her sexual desire having surfaced to consciousness, to unite with Barlo and to conceive a child, though in the purity of idea. When she actually confronts Barlo in Nat Bowle's place, the inevitable happens. The man himself cannot possibly conform to her idea of him:

> She sees a smile, ugly and repulsive to her, working
> upward through thick licker fumes. Barlo seems hideous.
> The thought comes suddenly, that conception with a
> drunken man must be a mighty sin. She draws away,
> frozen. Like a somnambulist she wheels around and
> walks stiffly to the stairs. Down them. Jeers and hoots
> pelter bluntly upon her back. She steps out. There is no
> air, no street, and the town has completely disappeared.
> [P. 48]

These are the final lines of the tale. Esther, like so many others in
Toomer's world, has retreated from time and space, having been
forced into the recesses of her mind by a reality too gross, too
impure to be endured. Since Barlo has been so central to the
development of her otherworldly orientation, we might expect that
she will never again risk bringing her imagination into conjunction
with the world.

"Blood-Burning Moon," with its emphasis on sexual passion
and its vivid portrayal of violence and bloodshed, seemingly stands
in contrast to most of the sketches preceding and following it.
However, the context of the events of the tale elevates those
events out of a (philosophically) naturalistic scheme and into the
realm of the supernatural. This is not, then, precisely a denial of
history on Toomer's part as much as a particular interpretation of
history that has the effect of locating historical causation outside
time and space. The relation of human, natural, and supernatural
events is close. Indeed nature, natural process, is so intertwined
with human destiny as to presage it, and the supernatural manifests itself through nature.

The narrator of "Blood-Burning Moon" presents the supernatural element of the story in such a way as to leave no room for
doubt on the reader's part of its reality and authenticity in the
world created there. Nothing in his tone indicates that he has the
least skepticism about the role of the supernatural:

> Up from the dusk the full moon came. Glowing like a
> fired pine-knot it illumined the great door and soft

showered the Negro shanties aligned along the single
street of factory town. The full moon in the great door
was an omen. Negro women improvised songs against
its spell. [P. 51]

It is within this framework (repeated at the end of the tale) that
the events of the narrative transpire. Tom Burwell and Bob Stone
are realistic enough in their portraiture, their motives firmly and
realistically established. Nonetheless the tale's supernatural referent
cannot but give the impression that the two vying males are acting
out roles determined in a context far larger than either knows.
When Louisa thinks of the two men and gazes at the rising moon,
the two figures become jumbled in her mind. A resulting "strange
stir" within her is reflected in the agitation and restlessness of her
singing. This is sensed by the animals around her: Dogs "began
plaintively to yelp and howl. Chickens woke up and cackled.
Intermittently, all over the countryside dogs barked and roosters
crowed as if heralding a weird dawn or some ungodly awakening"
(p. 53). The eventual confrontation between Bob and Tom ultimately
seems to arise out of some supernatural necessity rather than out
of their characters and situation. Hence the orientation of the tale
is unworldly since its events point away from the natural world
toward forces outside time and history, as is likely to happen when
any religious or otherwise supernatural presuppositions are involved in the interpretation of natural events.
    Of the stories preceding it, "Avey" is most like "Karintha" and
"Fern" in that the narrator idealizes the titular character to such an
extent as to render her invulnerable to his advances. He is a devotee,
an acolyte, whose vision of Avey and commitment to the idea of
her are such that he cannot free himself from her or accomplish his
will to have sexual relations with her (two perhaps not unrelated
disabilities). It is not insignificant that Avey is as sexually free as
she is, for theoretically she should be available to the narrator. His
psychological makeup is such, however, that in his heart of hearts
he does not wish to profane the purity Avey possesses as the result
of being transformed in his mind from a sensuous passionate being,

even primitively so, to a disembodied ideal. Although she is not compared to the Virgin Mary as Fern is, she has something about her of the mythical archetypal female, thoroughly feminine, non-aggressive, and naturally, uninhibited sexually in a passive sort of way. Instinctively she recognizes the quality of the narrator's psychology, which causes him to relate to her in a Platonic manner, and she loves him as he really wants to be loved, as she must love him in order to bind him to her: She kisses his forehead, cradles him in her lap, and loves him "in her own way."

Consciously he wishes to engage her physically, as when they are alone during the summer excursion. His actual response, however, never quite seems to match his conscious desires: "I should have taken her in my arms the minute we were stowed in that old life-boat. I dallied, dreaming" (p. 80). Later, as on a quest, he makes his way with difficulty to New York where he walks the streets "hoping to meet her." Subsequently he meets her in Washington and takes her, he tells us, to "a spot in Soldier's Home to which I always go when I want the simple beauty of another's soul" (p. 85). He tells the watchman there why he comes: "I come there to find the truth that people bury in their hearts. . . . I do not come there with a girl to do the thing he's paid to watch out for" (pp. 85-86). Later she falls asleep lying against him, and when a sexual urge passes through his body, he is afraid to move, "lest," he says, "I disturb her." He lies still until his body numbs and grows cold. Although he does not apparently idealize all females—"Giving themselves [girls in Wisconsin] completely was tame beside just the holding of Avey's hand"—his tendency to idealize is called forth in relation to Avey. And insofar as he idealizes her, trans-forming her into an intangible entity, he shrinks from things as they are; he removes her from time and reality.

"Theater" and "Box Seat" appear quite different from most of the other sketches in *Cane*, but they are essentially variations on the same theme. Both stories are about people whose fantasies about themselves and others create such disparity between themselves and the world as to cause frustration in fulfilling their hopes and desires. The one story, "Theater," is a miniature of the other in that the inability of the protagonist to distinguish between his fantasy and

reality is in minute, simplified context in "Theater" and in larger
context in "Box Seat." John, in "Theater," is, like Dan in the
other story, a dreamer, a fantasizer, a poet. As he watches the girls
dance and physically responds to the sensuous atmosphere of the
theater, "he wills thought to rid his mind of passion." Dorris
dances and radiates passion and sensuousness, yet, though she is
before his very eyes, he transforms the experience, at the moment
of its occurrence, into fantasy:

> Glorious songs are the muscles of her limbs.
> And her singing is of canebrake loves and mangrove
> feastings.
> The walls press in, singing. Flesh of a throbbing
> body, they press close to John and Dorris. They close
> them in. John's heart beats tensely against her dancing
> body. Walls press his mind within his heart. And then,
> the shaft of light goes out the window high above him.
> John's mind sweeps up to follow it. Mind pulls him
> upward into dream. Dorris dances . . . John dreams.
> [P. 98]

He fantasizes about a relationship with her, about meeting her after
a performance, about being alone with her and having a life with
her. When the dance to which everyone in the theater has responded
is finished, Dorris looks at his face, "seeks for her dance in it. She
finds it a dead thing in the shadow which is his dream." In the
story Toomer goes to great lengths to distinguish clearly between
mind and body, thought and action, idea and reality. Dorris, who
thinks of John as a sexual partner, stands in contrast to him, for
she gives herself up to physical expression as much as he withdraws
from the world into dream. The tone of the story indicates that
whereas the author views Dorris sympathetically, his greater
sympathy is with John:

> John is the manager's brother. He is seated at the center
> of the theater, just before rehearsal. Light streaks down
> upon him from a window high above. One half his face

is orange in it. One half his face is in shadow. The soft
glow of the house rushes to, and compacts about, the
shaft of light. Thoughts rush to, and compact about it.
Life of the house and of the slowly awakening stage
swirls to the body of John, and thrills it. John's body is
separate from the thoughts that pack his mind. [Pp. 91-92]

John's orientation away from reality is described with sympathy
and understanding.

The proximity of the narrator of "Box Seat" to Dan Moore, the
protagonist, is indicated by the similarity between the opening
paragraph of the story and Dan's metaphorical interpretation of
what he sees before him as he walks down the street toward Muriel's
house. The voice of the first paragraph is the narrator's:

Houses are shy girls whose eyes shine reticently upon
the dusky body of the street. Upon the gleaming limbs
and asphalt torso of a dreaming nigger. Shake your
curled woolblossoms, nigger. Open your liver lips to the
lean, white spring. Stir the root-life of a withered people.
Call them from their houses, and teach them to dream.
[P. 104]

It is Dan and the narrator and the author who wish to "call them
from their houses, and teach them to dream." "To teach them to
dream" in this context means to teach ordinary, middle-class-
oriented people to recognize possibilities for life beyond those
sanctioned by middle-class society. Dan's idea of himself and of
possibility is exaggerated to such an extent that his fantasies are
clearly neurotic in character (although the tone indicates that
Toomer makes no negative judgment of him on that score):

"Look into my eyes. I am Dan Moore. I was born in a
cane field. The hands of Jesus touched me. I am come
to a sick world to heal it. Only the other day, a dope
fiend brushed against me." [Pp. 105-6]

> A passing street car and something vibrant from the
> earth sends a rumble to him. That rumble comes from
> the earth's deep core. It is the mutter of powerful under-
> ground races. . . . The next world-savior is coming up
> that way. Coming up. A continent sinks down. The
> new-world Christ will need consummate skill to walk
> upon the waters where huge bubbles burst. [P. 106]

Dan is a prophet and a seer, a nonconformist whose vision is at
odds with the perspective of the rest of the world. His image of
himself is of mythic proportion:

> Dan: I am going to reach up and grab the girders of this
> building and pull them down. The crash will be a signal.
> Hid by the smoke and dust Dan Moore will arise. In his
> right hand will be a dynamo. In his left, a god's face
> that will flash white light from ebony. I'll grab a girder
> and swing it like a walking stick. Lightning will flash.
> I'll grab its black knob and swing it like a crippled cane.
> Lightning. . . [Pp. 126-27]

During the course of the narrative, Dan's attention wavers back
and forth between his huge fantasy and the ordered, middle-class-
oriented world around him. Given the tone of the story, the critical
attitude toward a world that does not know how to dream and the
positive attitude toward Dan and his fantasies, it would seem that
the author values the visionary perspective presented through Dan
over the gross and grotesque quality (for example, the vicious
boxing match between the two dwarfs) of social reality. Dan's
words as he stands up in the theater and shouts, "JESUS WAS ONCE
A LEPER," are to be read as a true perspective upon the situation he
is witnessing. We are not intended to see him as deranged; on the
contrary, he sees more truly and more clearly than do ordinary
people. Dan, the poet and the prophet, possesses a vision more real
than actuality, intangible and ideational as that dream may be.

"Bona and Paul" is hardly more than a repetition of the same
attitudes and ideas contained in the sketches preceding it, the dif-

ference between it and others resulting from the particularity of the circumstances. Paul is indistinguishable from the many characters preceding him who, unable to bear the world as it is, transform it psychologically into more acceptable terms. This is precisely his response when he goes with Bona, Art, and Helen to the Crimson Gardens. The patrons there stare at him, wondering about his racial or national identity. Their staring and whispering drive him into himself. Art, noticing the attention directed toward his group and sensing its cause, responds in anger: "What are *you* looking at, you godam pack of owl-eyed hyenas?" Paul responds differently:

> A strange thing happened to Paul. Suddenly he knew that he was apart from the people around him. Apart from the pain which they had unconsciously caused. Suddenly he knew that people saw, not attractiveness in his dark skin, but difference. Their stares, giving him to himself, filled something long empty within him, and were like green blades sprouting in his consciousness. There was fullness, and strength and peace about it all. He saw the faces of the people at the tables around him. White lights, or as now, the pink lights of the Crimson Gardens gave a glow and immediacy to white faces. The pleasure of it, equal to that of love or dream, of seeing this. [P. 145]

As the passage continues, it becomes clear that Paul's distance from actuality waxes:

> Art and Bona and Helen? He'd look. They were wonderfully flushed and beautiful. . . . Who were they, anyway? God, if he knew them. He'd come in with them. Of that he was sure. Come where? Into life? Yes. No. Into the Crimson Gardens. A part of life. A carbon bubble. Would it look purple if he went out into the night and looked at it? His sudden starting to rise almost upset the table. [Pp. 145-146]

Eventually, after they have begun dancing, an aroused sexual passion leads them by "instinct" to leave the Crimson Gardens alone. Something happens, however, as they leave. Paul sees the face of the black doorman as leering at them, the implication being that he knows why Bona and Paul are leaving and by leering expresses a too-knowing and too-familiar attitude. The leer calls into doubt for Paul the validity of his waking dream-vision and threatens thereby to force him back to an awareness of things as they are. (This includes his past, his black Southern heritage, his actual social position.) He needs must, therefore, draw the black doorman into his world by explaining things as he sees them. His speech, like that of some Andersonian grotesque, must seem gibberish to the doorman:

> I came back to tell you, brother, that white faces are petals of roses. That dark faces are petals of dusk. That I am going out and gathering petals. That I am going out and know her whom I brought here with me to these gardens which are purple like a bed of roses would be at dusk. [P. 153]

When he returns to the place where he had left Bona, he finds she has gone. Thus Paul's withdrawal from the world is the first hint we have from the author of any very significant critical view of the tendency of his hero, poet, idealist to turn toward some "reality" different from that commonly conceived in the world. In the final section of "Kabnis," that tension grows more acute, and it is in relation to that section that the meaning of all that has gone before is to be assessed.

"Kabnis" has the function that most endings of works of narrative literature have—to shape, to define, to interpret, to judge what has preceded. Along with internal elements of coherence (stylistic and thematic elements), the final section of *Cane* is in large measure responsible for the sense of unity the whole work has engendered in readers since its publication, for despite its obscurity it is the only piece in the whole that could conceivably have imparted to readers the feeling of finality, of ending, that it does.

"Kabnis" is the longest section, it contains the most characters, it is the broadest in its scope and implications, and it is the most complex. It examines the implications of what has preceded it and hence becomes a critique of philosophical idealism, of belief that locates essential reality outside time and history, of perspective that transforms reality into idea or image. Its quality as critique accounts for its inordinately odd tone. Its hero, Kabnis, comes closest to representing the values of the writer; yet Kabnis is weak, ineffectual, cowardly, and in many ways inept.[8] The writer in effect compares himself with every other character in the tale and in each case comes off poorly. He nonetheless clings to his vision and despite the evidence to the contrary (supplied by himself in the writing itself) is unable to yield to reality, to adjust to the world of fact.

The Kabnis at the beginning of the tale is nervous, irritable, and frightened, an alien in a strange land that he does not entirely understand except in its physical, natural aspect. The beauty of the land, of the night, of nature he comprehends very well; but the people—their customs and mores, their personalities and habits of interaction—are entirely foreign to him and extremely threatening. He feels in fact that his very life is in danger because he is nothing but a poet who has only the capacity to transform reality. On other levels of existence, he is incompetent and ineffectual. But even his capacity to transform experience or matter into metaphor sometimes betrays him, for it is in the very exercise of his imaginative capabilities that he transforms his environment into one far more hostile and threatening than it is in reality. The tension between actuality and idea is the central conflict in the story, a conflict first dramatized by its existence within the personality of Kabnis and then projected into the relationships between Kabnis and the people around him.

Kabnis is a poet, a dreamer. He is not, however, so distant from the world that he cannot recognize the claims made on him by the world of actuality even though he prefers "poetic" reality to actuality. The juxtaposition is posed by Kabnis himself early in the story as he lies in bed, restless and unable to sleep. The impingement of the world on him is the cause of his discomfort, a discomfort represented initially in his inability to sleep, but later as we learn of his general situation, we find that great claims are made on him by the demands of his situation. The school requires that he follow rather strict rules of deportment—that he not smoke or drink, that he attend church regularly and in general behave in a rigidly defined fashion. Certain factors pertinent to racial relations in the South impinge on him (though less so, apparently, than he thinks), as well as factors stemming from his being a Northerner among Southerners. The common element uniting these and the more specific facets of his relation to his environment is the social nature of the impinging factors. His difficulty in dealing with the world is closely related to his unwillingness to define himself in social terms or to accept social relationship as in any way related to essential identity. The conception suggested frequently in the tale that his identity rests in his "soul" bespeaks the problem. He recognizes the claims on him of actuality—they do exist—but he resists those claims, and the degree of his resistance is an index to the degree of his location of reality out of geographical space, out of time, and out of history.

He fantasizes early in the tale and thus sets up the terms of the story's concern. He is alone at this point:

> Near me. Now. Whoever you are, my warm glowing sweetheart, do not think that the face that rests beside you is the real Kabnis. Ralph Kabnis is a dream. And dreams are faces with large eyes and weak chins and broad brows that get smashed by the fists of square faces. The body of the world is bull-necked. A dream is a soft face that fits uncertainly upon it. . . . God, if I could develop that in words. Give what I know a bull-neck and a heaving body, all would go well with me, wouldn't it, sweetheart? If I could feel that I came to the South to face it. If I, the dream (not what is afraid in me) could become the face of the South. How my lips would sing for it, my songs being the lips of its soul. Soul. Soul hell. There ain't no such thing. [P. 158]

Here he sets up a dichotomy, although he clearly favors one pole above the other. The dream, not the man as he exists, is the "real" Kabnis, and he wishes that the dream of what the South is could replace the actuality of the place. His sense of the oppressiveness of the actuality of the place and his doubt about the validity of his perspective call him back, however: "Soul. Soul hell. There ain't no such thing." With the expression of this sentiment his perspective shifts, and he focuses on his physical environment, hearing first a rat running across the ceiling and the dust sift down through a crack. He translates the physical phenomenon into idea: "Dust of slavefields, dried and scattered" (p. 159). Soon afterward he hears a chicken settling on a perch in the next room. His response is excessive. In a desperate but futile attempt to exert some control over his environment (even the poultry is hostile), he rushes out, catches the chicken, and wrings its neck, wiping the blood from his hands on the grass. "That's done. Old Chromo in the big house there will wonder what has become of her pet hen. Well, it'll teach her a lesson: not to make a hen-coop of my quarters" (p. 161). Immersed as he is in the world—fresh blood on his hands—Kabnis, angered by his situation, raises his fist to curse God but "the night's beauty strikes him dumb. He falls to his knees . . ."

> "God almighty, dear God, dear Jesus, do not torture me with beauty. Take it away. Give me an ugly world. Ha, ugly. Stinking like unwashed niggers. Dear Jesus, do not chain me to myself and set these hills and valleys, heaving with folk-songs, so close to me that I cannot reach them. There is a radiant beauty in the night that touches and . . . tortures me." [Pp. 161-162]

Again, however, his sense of the actuality of the setting overwhelms him, changing his perspective:

> "Ugh. Hell. Get up, you damn fool. Look around. What's beautiful here? Hog pens and chicken yards.

> Dirty red mud. Stinking outhouse. What's beauty any-
> way but ugliness if it hurts you? God, he doesn't exist,
> but nevertheless He is ugly. Hence, what comes from
> Him is ugly. Lynchers and business men, and that cock-
> roach Hanby, especially. How come that he gets to be
> principal of a school? Of the school I'm driven to teach
> in? God's handiwork, doubtless. God and Hanby, they
> belong together. Two godam moral-spouters." [P. 162]

And again the mood shades into its opposite:

> "Oh, no, I won't let that emotion come up in me. Stay
> down. Stay down, I tell you. O Jesus, Thou art beauti-
> ful. . . . Come, Ralph, pull yourself together. Curses and
> adoration don't come from what is sane." [P. 162]

From this point to the end of the first section of "Kabnis" the
perspective alternates between the actuality of the environment and
its transformation into terms more desirable, less oppressive. As
the tale progresses from the first section, Kabnis becomes increasingly involved in the day-to-day lives of the townspeople,
participating in their daily (and nightly) affairs, even to the point of
engaging himself in the métier of wagoner, plunging more and
more deeply into his physical environment, into time and history
and at the same time sharpening the quality of his experience, the
division between idea and actuality. Everyone around him is better
able to function in the world than he. His involvement may be seen
in terms of descent (if we think in the traditional graphic terms
that describe spatially the relation between the material and the
nonmaterial, the physical and the spiritual, earth and air, fire and
water, history and eternity, the world and the heavens, and so on),
culminating in a quite literal descent into the basement of Fred
Halsey's workshop.

At the nadir of his descent he confronts Father John, who is the
physical embodiment, the incarnation of actuality, of history, time,
race, and of a whole complex cluster of associations Kabnis has.
The culmination of the story "Kabnis" and of the whole book is

mirrored in the confrontation between Kabnis and Father John, and the meaning of the whole is encapsuled in that confrontation. Kabnis forcefully and directly repudiates Father John and all that he represents and in so doing vindicates (though in nonrational terms) the values put forth in the preceding tales, poems, and sketches, those values upheld by the poet-narrators and protagonists and by the author himself insofar as his primary identification is with the narrators and protagonists and insofar as he himself is the poet who authors the poems contained in the work. The nature of these values, poetic values from Toomer's perspective, has been delineated throughout the essay.

This conclusion needs to be qualified somewhat in that the tone of "Kabnis" is not as unambivalent as the statement implies. First, in the tone of the tale is a certain objectivity, which stems from Toomer's dramatic technique (the speeches are rendered as dialogue, the descriptive and narrative materials are read as though they were stage directions, and the action is rendered in the present tense) and from the quality of the voice of the narrator whose tone gives the impression of a judicious impartiality because it does not clearly and openly support the values that ultimately emerge as the values of the author and the book as a whole. The author's tone is not entirely unsympathetic to the values of the poet-protagonist (it is sometimes impossible to separate Kabnis's voice from that of the author), but he admits through his tone something of the limitations of Kabnis's perspective and, by implication, his own as well. For example, he creates Kabnis as something of a bumbler, inept in handling tools and unduly awkward in dealing with people. Kabnis's ineptness in relation to females is made clear, as is his fear and incapacity to deal with authority (in his relation to Hanby, the principal). By comparison Lewis is an ideal figure, and Kabnis suffers in the comparison. Lewis is unafraid, at home in the world, capable of dealing with it, respected by others, strong of character, and certain of his identity on all levels. Nothing in Toomer's treatment of Lewis suggests that he—in so many ways a better person than Kabnis—is regarded with less than total sympathy. "But theres something t' yo th' others ain't got," Stella says of him, and there is no reason to believe that Toomer does not concur. Toomer's tone in relation to Father John is also respectful, and highly so. When Kabnis speaks to him so harshly, unkindly, and unfeelingly, it is obvious that he does not deserve such treatment. Kabnis's tirade against Father John (note too the respectfulness implied by the name given the character by the author) is more a negative reflection on Kabnis than on the object of his insult. Everyone else treats Father John with respect and veneration; he is cared for and revered as some delicate, fragile, and invaluable antique. Nevertheless, Kabnis violently and contemptuously rejects him and in so doing rejects identification with his racial past, racial identity generally, the past, his present social environment, and time. This accounts for the extremely antiblack nature of a good deal of Kabnis's speech during the tale:

> "Halsey! Halsey! Gone and left me. Just like a nigger. I thought he was a nigger all the time."

> "Your [Father John's] soul. Ha. Nigger soul. A gin soul that gets drunk on a preacher's words. . . . Ain't surprising the white folks hate y' so." [P. 232]

> Lewis: The old man as symbol, flesh and spirit of the past, what do you think he would say if he could see you? You look at him Kabnis.
> Kabnis: Just like any done-up preacher is what he looks t' me . . . blue-bloods. [P. 217]

Yet despite the limitations of Kabnis's poetic sensibility so clearly revealed, the writer finally vindicates Kabnis in the most subtle and indirect ways: by indicating that unconsciously Kabnis does not totally reject Father John ("Why I can already see you [Father John] toppled off that stool an stretched out on the floor beside me—not beside me, damn you, by yourself" [p. 233]); by Carrie Kate's sympathy for Kabnis, her sympathetic indulgence of his attitudes; and by the identification throughout the tale of the sensibilities of the author as poet with those of Kabnis as poet. Kabnis as poet, we are to infer, shares perceptions and a poetic vision not unlike that possessed by implication by the narrator of the tale. Thus the final paragraph, final in its style and its view of things, becomes a final comment—though not logically established —on Kabnis the poet, on the poetic vision, and on poets as they are defined in *Cane*:

> Outside, the sun arises from its cradle in the tree-tops of the forest. Shadows of pines are dreams the sun shakes from its eyes. The sun arises. Gold-glowing child, it steps into the sky and sends a birth-song slanting down gray dust streets and sleepy windows of the southern town. [P. 239]

Although a great deal is yet unknown about the details of Toomer's life, enough is known to suggest that he in fact held attitudes consistent with those claimed for him in this essay.[9] (That he held such attitudes is not in itself conclusive proof that they appear in *Cane*; yet it strengthens the likelihood of my reading of *Cane* as being correct.) His commitment (around the time of *Cane*'s publication in 1923) to the teachings of Gurdjieff is a case in point. The values and attitudes I have identified in *Cane* are by no means inconsistent with Gurdjieff's teachings. Gurdjieff taught that the world as perceived by the uninstructed, undeveloped consciousness is not the real world and that the real quality of being diminishes as it proceeds in stages from ultimate being. Such thinking diminishes the importance of the real world and directs attention elsewhere.

Toomer's lack of focus on social realities allowed him refuge from a difficult situation in regard to racial matters. It was easier for him to refuse to recognize common American definitions of race because he did not believe those definitions to be binding on his own sense of racial identity.[10] In a brief autobiographical sketch Toomer wrote the following in 1922:

> Racially, I seem to have (who knows for sure) seven blood mixtures: French, Dutch, Welsh, Negro, German, Jewish, and Indian. Because of these, my position

in America has been a curious one. I have lived equally amid the two race groups. Now white, now colored.[11]

He seemingly records a change in these sentiments a few lines later:

"my growing need for artistic expression has pulled me deeper into the Negro group. . . . I heard folksongs come from the lips of Negro peasants. I saw the rich dusk beauty that I had heard many false accents about, and which till then, I was somewhat skeptical."[12]

But this does not say he discovered racial identity in Georgia, for his interest in "the Negro group" is as an observer, not as a participant.[13] In *Cane* it is clear that the narrator of the tales and sketches occurring in the South is highly sympathetic toward the objects of his scrutiny, but his involvement is based upon his "need for artistic expression," and thus he is a stranger to the life of the region he describes. In his notes for an autobiography (never completed) he wrote:

Though I personally had experienced no prejudice or exclusion either from the whites or the colored people, I had seen enough to know that America viewed life as if it were divided into white and black. Having lived with colored people for the past five years, at Wisconsin the question might come up. What was I? I thought about it independently, and, on the basis of fact, concluded I was neither white nor black, but simply an American. I held this view and decided to live according to it. I would tell others if the occasion demanded it.[14]

He married twice during his life, and each time, consistent with his repudiation of a black racial identity, married white women, a fact important in this context only because it, along with his actual denial of relation to the race, reflects his disaffection.[15]

The implication of this discussion of Toomer's life is intended to suggest something of the degree to which he was oriented away from social and political reality.[16] His conscious sense of himself as neither black nor white but American, his immersion in Gurdjieff beliefs (suggesting his desire for values other than those available in the American historical context), bespeak his unwillingness to deal with his environment in any way but to escape and deny it. He retreated into idealism and mysticism and thus repudiated the world as it exists. Rather than a depiction of black life as it really is, *Cane* turns out instead to be the response of one for whom black life in its social, political, and historical dimension was too much to bear.

NOTES

1. Jean Toomer, *Cane* (New York: Boni and Liveright, 1923), p. 19. Subsequent quotations are from this edition.

2. See Susan L. Blake's excellent article, "The Spectatorial Artist and the Structure of *Cane*," *CLA Journal* 17: 534. Her point is not the same as mine, but her comment at the article's conclusion suggests she has noted the features of *Cane* that I interpret as pointing to a retreat from reality. She speaks of the novel as advocating a "retreat into mysticism."

3. Such critics are Alaine Locke, *Phylon* 14: 34; Robert Bone, *The Negro Novel in America* (New Haven: Yale University Press, 1958), p. 82; Arna Bontemps, introduction to *Cane* (New York: Harper & Row Perennial Classics, 1969), p. x; Sherwood Anderson as quoted in Darwin Turner, "An Intersection of Paths: Correspondence between Jean Toomer and Sherwood Anderson," *CLA Journal* 17: 455-67; Louise Blackwell, "Jean Toomer's *Cane* and Biblical Myth," *CLA Journal* 17: 535-42.

S. P. Fullinwider, "Jean Toomer, Lost Generation or Negro Renaissance," *Phylon* 28: 400, supports my contention that *Cane* expresses less than the essence of blackness or negritude. He observes, "Toomer had two points of view toward Negroes: one expressing his doubts, one expressing his hopes; one repelling him, the other attracting him." Darwin Turner says explicitly that Toomer did not interpret Southern black people: "He wrote lyrically about Southern women isolated or destroyed because they have ignored society's restrictions on sexual behavior." Turner, *In a Minor Chord: Three Afro-American Writers and Their Search for Identity* (Carbondale: Southern Illinois University Press, 1971), p. 27.

4. Bontemps, introduction to *Cane*, p. xii.

5. Blake, "Spectator Artist," pp. 516-34, points out that the narrative

voice of the whole of *Cane* is the same voice. She identifies that voice with a persona, the "spectatorial artist." I, as she ultimately does in her article, identify that voice as the voice of Toomer.

6. Jean Toomer, "Chapters from Earth-Being, An Unpublished Autobiography," *Black Scholar* 2: 12. David Littlejohn, *Black on White: A Critical Survey of Writing by American Negroes* (New York: Viking Press, 1969), p. 59, indicates that he sees the same characteristic of the novel, but he interprets it differently: "Common things are seen as if through a strangely neurotic vision, transformed into his own kind of nightmare."

7. I do not know whether Toomer intended Fern to be compared specifically to the Virgin Mary; I am not interested in pushing that comparison between the situation involving Fern—the reactions of men to her —and the constantly recurring tendency in Western civilization to idealize the female as being at once a virgin and a whore.

8. In a letter to Waldo Frank, Toomer said, "Kabnis is Me." See Charles W. Scruggs, "The Mark of Cain and the Redemption of Art: A Study in Theme and Structure of Jean Toomer's *Cane*," *American Literature* 44: 282. See also Victor A. Kramer, "The 'Mid-Kingdom' of Crane's 'Black Tambourine' and Toomer's *Cane*, *CLA Journal* 17: 492-97. Kramer discusses in detail the character of Kabnis and, by implication, the relation of character to author as does Blake, "Spectatorial Artist," pp. 529-34. Turner, *In a Minor Chord*, who has told us the most about Toomer, has this to say: "His [Toomer's] male figures are stereotypes, personifications, and reproductions of his satiric self-pitying, or idealized image of himself" (p. 27).

9. The fullest, most nearly complete biographical account to date is Turner's chapter on Toomer in *In a Minor Chord*, pp. 1-59.

10. Mabel Dillard discusses this matter in detail in "Jean Toomer: The Veil Replaced," *CLA Journal* 17: 468-73.

11. Bontemps, introduction to *Cane*, p. viii.

12. Ibid., pp. viii-ix.

13. Turner, *In a Minor Chord*, comments that since Toomer was a visitor to the South, "he could write sympathetically as one who feels kinship yet maintains artistic detachment. He desired merely to observe, to sense, and to reflect the milieu, not to change it" (pp. 28-29).

14. Bontemps, introduction to *Cane*, p. xv.

15. It is of interest to note Toomer's response, quoted in *Time* magazine in 1932, to a question about his marriage to his first wife, Margery Latimer: "Americans probably do not realize it, but there are no racial barriers any

more, because there are so many Americans with strains of Negro, Indian and Oriental blood." Quoted in Frank Durham, comp., *Studies in Cane* (Columbus, Ohio: Charles E. Merrill Publishing Co., 1971), p. 16. Turner, *In a Minor Chord*, reports Toomer's least ambiguous and most direct comment on his racial identity (1932): "Though I am interested in and deeply value the Negro, I am not a Negro" (p. 32).

16. Edward Margolies indicates his awareness of the point I raise here when he asks, "Is Toomer unconsciously saying that beauty resides in the pain and suffering of black men? Is the mother earth of Georgia to which he beckons his Negroes a death dream that brings ultimate release? . . . Are passivity and withdrawal from modern life ultimate fulfillment? The paradox is inexplicable in rational terms, but Toomer patterned his life on similar paradoxes." Margolies, *Native Sons: A Study of Twentieth-Century Black American Authors* (Philadelphia: J. B. Lippincott, 1968), p. 40. See also Charles Scruggs, "Jean Toomer: Fugitive," *American Literature* 47: 84-96. This meticulous and brilliantly conceived study of Toomer's struggle with identity reveals the extent of its complexity and, as I interpret it, supports my thesis about Toomer's orientation away from time and history.

Bibliography
of Secondary
Sources

GENERAL WORKS

"American Negro Novelists." *Studies in the Novel* (North Texas State University) 3, ii, Special Number.

Baker, Houston A., Jr. *Long Black Song: Essays in Black American Literature and Culture*. Charlottesville: University Press of Virginia, 1972.

Baldwin, James. "Everybody's Protest Novel." *Zero* 1: 54-58.

_____. "Many Thousands Gone." *Partisan Review* 18: 665-80.

Barksdale, Richard K. "Black America and the Mark of Comedy." In *The Comic Imagination in American Literature*, edited by Louis D. Rubin, Jr., pp. 349-60. New Brunswick, N.J.: Rutgers University Press, 1972.

Bigsby, C. W. E. *The Black American Writer*. Baltimore: Penguin Books, 1969.

Bone, Robert A. *The Negro Novel in America*. New Haven: Yale University Press, 1958.

Brooks, A. Russell. "The Comic Spirit and the Negro's New Love." *CLA Journal* 6: 35-43.

Bruck, Peter, ed. *The Black American Short Story in the Twentieth Century: A Collection of Critical Essays*. Amsterdam: Grüner, 1977.

Cartey, Wilfred. "I've Been Reading: The Realities of Four Negro Writers." *Columbia University Forum* 9 (Summer): 34-42.

Cook, Mercer G. *Modern Black Novelists: A Collection of Critical Essays.* Englewood Cliffs, N.J.: Prentice-Hall, 1971.

Cooke, Michael. "The Descent into the Underworld." *Iowa Review* 5: 72-90.

Cosgrove, William. "Modern Black Writers: The Divided Self." *Negro American Literature Forum* 7: 120-22.

Cruse, Harold. *The Crisis of the Negro Intellectual.* New York: William Morrow, 1977.

Davis, Arthur P. *From the Dark Tower.* Washington, D.C.: Howard University Press, 1974.

Dickstein, Morris. "Wright, Baldwin, Cleaver." *New Letters* 38: 117-24.

Ellison, Ralph. *Shadow and Act.* New York: Random House, 1964.

Ford, Nick Aaron. "Four Popular Negro Novelists." *Phylon* 15: 29-39.

Gayle, Addison, Jr. "A Defense of James Baldwin." *CLA Journal* 10: 201-8.

_____. *The Way of the New World.* New York: Doubleday, Anchor Books, 1976.

Gibson, Donald B. *Five Black Writers: Essays on Wright, Ellison, Baldwin, Hughes, and LeRoi Jones.* New York: New York University Press, 1970.

Glicksberg, Charles. "Negro Fiction in America." *South Atlantic Quarterly* 45: 478-88.

Gloster, Hugh M. *Negro Voices in American Fiction.* Chapel Hill: University of North Carolina Press, 1948.

Gross, Seymour, and Hardy, John E. *Images of the Negro in American Literature: Essays in Criticism.* Chicago: University of Chicago Press, 1966.

Hassan, Ihab. *Radical Innocence.* Princeton, N.J.: Princeton University Press, 1961.

Hemenway, Robert. *The Black Novelist.* Columbus, Ohio: Charles E. Merrill, 1970.

Hill, Herbert, ed. *Anger and Beyond.* New York: Harper & Row, 1966.

Howe, Irving. "Black Boys and Native Sons." In *A World More Attractive: A View of Modern Literature and Politics,* pp. 98-122. New York: Horizon Press, 1963.

Hughes, Carl Milton. *The Negro Novelist, 1940-1950.* New York: Citadel Press, 1953.

Hyman, Stanley Edgar. "American Negro Literature and the Folk Tradition." In *The Promised End: Essays and Reviews, 1942-1962*, pp. 295-315. Cleveland: World Publishing Co., 1963.

Inge, M. Thomas. *Black American Writers: Bibliographical Essays I: The Beginnings through the Harlem Renaissance and Langston Hughes.* New York: St. Martin's Press, 1977.

————; Duke, Maurice; and Bryer, Jackson R., eds. *Black American Writers: Bibliographical Essays II: Richard Wright, Ralph Ellison, James Baldwin, and Amiri Baraka.* New York: St. Martin's Press, 1975.

Isaacs, Harold. "Five Writers and Their African Ancestors." *Phylon* 21: 243-65.

Jackson, Blyden. "The Negro's Image of the Universe as Reflected in His Fiction." *CLA Journal* 4: 22-31.

Kent, George. *Blackness and the Adventure of Western Culture.* Chicago: Third World Press, 1972.

Klotman, Phyllis R. *Another Man Done Gone: The Black Runner in Contemporary Afro-American Literature.* Port Washington, N.Y.: Kennikat, 1975.

Knox, George. "The Negro Novelist's Sensibility and the Outsider Theme." *Western Humanities Review* 11: 137-48.

Lawson, Lewis. "Cross Damon: Kierkegaardian, Man of Dread." *CLA Journal* 14: 298-316.

Lehan, Richard. "Existentialism in Recent American Fiction." *Texas Studies in Literature and Language* 1:181-201.

Littlejohn, David. *Black on White: A Critical Survey of Writing by American Negroes.* New York: Viking, 1966.

McPherson, James M.; Holland, Lawrence B.; Banner, James M., Jr.; Weiss, Nancy J.; and Bell, Michael D. *Blacks in America: Bibliographical Essays.* Garden City, N.Y.: Doubleday, Anchor Books, 1972.

Major, Clarence. *The Dark Feeling: Black American Writers and Their Work.* New York: Third World Press, 1974.

Marcus, Steven. "The American Negro in Search of Identity, Three Novelists: Richard Wright, Ralph Ellison, James Baldwin." *Commentary* 16: 456-63.

Margolies, Edward. *Native Sons: A Critical Study of Twentieth-century Negro-American Authors.* Philadelphia: J. B. Lippincott, 1968.

Maund, Alfred. "The Negro Novelist and the Contemporary Scene." *Chicago Jewish Forum* 13: 28-34.

O'Daniel, Therman B. "James Baldwin: An Interpretive Study." *CLA Journal* 7: 37-47.

Riesman, David. "Marginality, Conformity, and Insight." *Phylon* 14: 241-57.

Rosenblatt, Roger. *Black Fiction.* Cambridge, Mass.: Harvard University Press, 1974.

Schraufnagel, Arthur. *From Apology to Protest: The Black American Novel.* Deland, Fla.: Everett/Edwards, 1973.

Scott, Nathan A., Jr. "Judgment Marked by a Cellar: The American Negro Writer and the Dialectic of Despair." *University of Denver Quarterly* 2: 5-35.

Turner, Darwin. *In a Minor Chord: Three Afro-American Writers and Their Search for Identity.* Carbondale: Southern Illinois University Press, 1971.

Williams, Shirley A. *Give Birth to Brightness: A Thematic Study in Neo-Black Literature.* New York: Dial Press, 1972.

RICHARD WRIGHT

Aaron, Daniel. "Richard Wright and the Communist Party." *New Letters* 38,ii (1971): 170-81.

Abcarian, Richard, ed. *Richard Wright's Native Son.* Belmont, Calif.: Wadsworth Publishing Co., 1970.

Amis, Lola J. "Richard Wright's *Native Son*: Notes." *Negro American Literature Forum* 8: 240-43.

Baker, Houston, ed. *Twentieth-century Interpretations of Native Son.* Englewood Cliffs, N.J.: Prentice-Hall, 1972.

Bakish, David. *Richard Wright.* New York: Ungar, 1973.

Baldwin, James. "Alas, Poor Richard." In *Nobody Knows My Name,* pp. 181-215. New York: Dial Press, 1961.

Baldwin, Richard E. "The Creative Vision of *Native Son*." *Massachusetts Review* 14: 378-90.

Baron, Dennis E. "The Syntax of Perception in Richard Wright's *Native Son*." *Language and Style* 9: 17-28.

Bayliss, John F. "*Native Son*: Protest or Psychological Study?" *Negro American Literature Forum* 1 (Fall): 5-6.

Berry, Faith. "Portrait of a Man as Outsider." *Negro Digest* 18 (December 1968): 27-37.

Bone, Robert. *Richard Wright.* Pamphlets on American Writers Series. Minneapolis: University of Minnesota Press, 1969.

Britt, David. "Native Son: Watershed of Negro Protest Literature." *Negro American Literature Forum* 1 (Fall): 4-5.

Brivic, Sheldon. "Conflict of Values: Richard Wright's *Native Son*." *Novel* 7: 231-45.

Brooks, Mary Ellen. "Behind Richard Wright's 'Artistic Conscience.' " *Literature and Ideology* (Montreal) 13: 21-30.

Brown, Cecil. "Richard Wright: Complexes and Black Writers Today." *Negro Digest* 18 (December 1968): 78-82.

Brown, Lloyd W. "Stereotypes in Black and White: The Nature of Perception in Wright's *Native Son*." *Black Academy Review* 1 (Fall): 35-44.

Brunette, Peter. "Two Wrights, One Wrong." In *The Modern American Novel and the Movies*, edited by Gerald Peary and Roger Shatzkin, pp. 131–42. New York: Ungar, 1978.

Bryant, Jerry H. "Wright, Ellison, Baldwin: Exorcising the Demon." *Phylon* 37: 174-88.

Bryer, Jackson R. "Richard Wright (1908-1960): A Selected Checklist of Criticism." *Wisconsin Studies in Contemporary Literature* 1: 22-33.

Burgum, Edwin Berry. "The Art of Richard Wright's Short Stories." *Quarterly Review of Literature* 1: 198-211.

————. "The Promise of Democracy in the Fiction of Richard Wright." *Science and Society* 7 (Fall 1943): 338-52.

Campbell, Finley C. "Prophet of the Storm: Richard Wright and the Radical Tradition." *Phylon* 38: 9-23.

Cauley, Arne O. "A Definition of Freedom in the Fiction of Richard Wright." *CLA Journal* 19: 327-46.

Cayton, Horace. "Frightened Children of Frightened Parents." *Twice a Year* 12-13: 262-69.

Charney, Maurice. "James Baldwin's Quarrel with Richard Wright." *American Quarterly* 15 (1963): 65-75.

Cleaver, Eldridge. "Notes on a Native Son." In *Soul on Ice*, pp. 97-111. New York: McGraw-Hill, 1967.

Cobb, Nina Kressner. "Richard Wright: Individualism Reconsidered." *CLA Journal* 21: 335-54.

Cohn, David L. "The Negro Novel: Richard Wright's *Native Son*." *Atlantic Monthly* 165: 659-61.

Creekmore, Herbert. "Social Factors in *Native Son*." *University Review* 8: 136-43.

Cruse, Harold. *The Crisis of the Negro Intellectual*. New York: William Morrow, 1967.

Curling, R. Maud. "Presentacion de Richard Wright y Bigger Thomas." *Anales del Departmento de Lenguas Modernas.* Universidad de Costa Rica. No. 1, Agosto 1972. San José: Universidad de Costa Rica, pp. 19-24.

Davis, Arthur P. *"The Outsider* as a Novel of Race." *Midwest Journal* 7: 320-26.

Davis, Vivian I. "The Genius of Fantastic Feebleness (with Apologies to Richard Wright)." *Proceedings of the Comparative Literature Symposium* (Texas Tech University) 8 (1975): 99-116.

De Arman, Charles. "Bigger Thomas: The Symbolic Negro and the Discrete Human Entity." *Black American Literature Forum* 12: 61-64.

Delmar, P. Jay. "Tragic Patterns in Richard Wright's *Uncle Tom's Children.*" *Negro American Literature Forum* 10: 3-12.

Demarest, David P., Jr. "Richard Wright: The Meaning of Violence." *Negro American Literature Forum* 8: 236-39.

Dickstein, Morris. "Wright, Baldwin, Cleaver." *New Letters* 38,ii: 117-24.

D'Itri, Patricia. "Richard Wright in Chicago: Three Novels That Represent a Black Spokesman's Quest for Self-Identity." *Midwestern Miscellany* (Society for the Study of Midwestern Literature Newsletter) 4: 26-33.

Ellison, Ralph. "Richard Wright's Blues." *Antioch Review* 5: 198-211.

_____. "The World and the Jug." *New Leader*, December 9, 1963, pp. 22-26.

_____. "A Rejoinder." *New Leader*, February 3, 1964, pp. 15-22.

Emanuel, James A. "Fever and Feeling: Notes on the Imagery in *Native Son.*" *Negro Digest* 18 (December 1968): 16-26.

Everette, Mildred W. "The Death of Richard Wright's American Dream: 'The Man Who Lived Underground.' " *CLA Journal* 17: 318-26.

Fabre, Michel. "The Richard Wright Archive: The Catalogue of an Exhibition." *Yale University Library Gazette* 53: 57-78.

_____. "Richard Wright: Beyond Naturalism?" In *American Literary Naturalism: A Reassessment*, edited by Yoshinoby Hakutani and Lewis Fried, pp. 136-53. Heidelberg: C. Winter, 1975.

_____. "Richard Wright's First Hundred Books." *CLA Journal* 16: 458-74.

_____. "Richard Wright and the French Existentialists." *MELUS* 5,ii: 39-51.

_____. "Richard Wright: The Man Who Lived Underground." *Studies in the Novel* (North Texas State University) 3: 165-79.

_____. *The Unfinished Quest of Richard Wright*. New York: William Morrow, 1973.

_____. "Wright's Exile." *New Letters* 38,ii(1971): 136-54.

Fabre, Michel, and Margolies, Edward. "Richard Wright (1908-1960): A Bibliography." *Bulletin of Bibliography* 24: 131-33, 137.

Felgar, Robert. " 'The Kingdom of the Beast': The Landscape of *Native Son*." *CLA Journal* 17: 333-37.

Feuser, Willfred F. "The Men Who Lived underground: Richard Wright and Ralph Ellison." In *A Celebration of Black and African Writing*, edited by Bruce King and Kolawold Ogangbesan. Oxford: Oxford University Press, 1975.

Fishburn, Katherine. *Richard Wright's Hero: The Faces of a Rebel-Victim*. Metuchen, N.J.: Scarecrow, 1977.

Fleissner, Robert. "How Bigger's Name Was Born." *SBL* 8,i: 4-5.

Ford, Nick Aaron. "The Ordeal of Richard Wright." *College English* 15: 87-94.

_____. "Richard Wright, a Profile." *Chicago Jewish Forum* 21: 26-30.

French, Warren. "Epilogue: Beginner's Luck." In *The Social Novel at the End of an Era*, pp. 171-88. Carbondale: Southern Illinois University Press, 1966.

_____. "The Lost Potential of Richard Wright." In *The Black American Writer*, edited by C. W. E. Bigsby, 1: 125-42. Deland, Fla.: Everett/Edwards, 1969.

Fuller, Hoyt. "On the Death of Richard Wright." *Southwest Review* 46: vi-vii, 334-37.

Gaskill, Gayle. "The Effect of Black/White Imagery in Richard Wright's *Black Boy*." *Negro American Literature Forum* 7: 46-48.

Gayle, Addison, Jr. "Richard Wright: Beyond Nihilism." *Negro Digest* 18 (December 1968): 5-10.

Gérard, Albert. "Vie et vocation de Richard Wright." *Revue générale belge* 98: 65-78.

Gibson, Donald B. "Richard Wright: A Bibliographical Essay." *CLA Journal* 12: 360-65.

_____. "Richard Wright's Invisible Native Son." *American Quarterly* 21: 728-38.

_____. "Richard Wright and the Tyranny of Convention." *CLA Journal* 12: 344-57.

Giles, James R. "Richard Wright's Successful Failure: A New Look at *Uncle Tom's Children*." *Phylon* 34: 256-66.

Glicksberg, Charles I. "Existentialism in *The Outsider*." *Four Quarters* 7: 17-26.

Goldman, Robert M., and Crane, William D. "*Black Boy* and *Manchild in the Promised Land*: Content Analysis in the Study of Value Change over Time." *Journal of Black Studies* 7: 169-80.

Gotoh, Tomokuni. "American Negro Writer, Wright and Africa—with Priority Given to Wright's African Sketches, *Black Power*." *Africa-Kenkyu* (Tokyo) 13 (1973): 10-21. [In Japanese]

Gounard, Jean François. La Carrière mouvementée de Richard Wright." *Review of the University of Ottawa* 46: 520-43.

_____. "Richard Wright as a Black Writer in Exile." *CLA Journal* 17: 307-17.

_____. "Richard Wright's 'The Man Who Lived Underground': A Literary Analysis." *Journal of Black Studies* 8: 381-96.

Graham, Don B. "*Lawd Today* and the Example of *The Waste Land*." *CLA Journal* 17: 327-32.

Graham, Louis. "The White Self-Image Conflict in *Native Son*." *Studies in Black Literature* 3,ii: 19-21.

Green, Gerald. "Back to Bigger." In *Proletarian Writers of the Thirties*, edited by David Madden. Carbondale: Southern Illinois University Press, 1968.

Grenander, M. E. "Criminal Responsibility in *Native Son* and *Knock on Any Door*." *American Literature* 49: 221-33.

Gross, Barry. "Art and Act: The Example of Richard Wright." *Obsidian* 2,ii: 5-19.

Gross, Seymour L. "Dalton and Color-Blindness in *Native Son*." *Mississippi Quarterly* 27: 75-77.

Hajek, Friederike. "American Tragedy—zwei Aspekte: Dargestellt in Richard Wright's *Native Son* und in Theodore Dreiser's *An American Tragedy*." *Zeitschrift für Anglistik und Amerikanistik* (East Berlin) 20: 262-79.

Hamalian, Linda Bearman. "Richard Wright's Use of Epigraphs in *The Long Dream*." *Black American Literature Forum* 10: 120-23.

Hand, Clifford. "The Struggle to Create Life in the Fiction of Richard Wright." In *The Thirties: Fiction, Poetry, Drama*, edited by Warren French, pp. 81-87. Deland, Fla.: Everett/Edwards, 1967.

Hill, Herbert, moderator. "Reflections on Richard Wright: A Symposium on an Exiled Native Son," with Horace Cayton, Arna Bontemps, and Saunders Redding. In *Anger and Beyond*, edited by Herbert Hill, pp. 196-212. New York: Harper & Row, 1966.

Hoeveler, Diane Long. "Oedipus Agonistes: Mothers and Sons in Richard Wright's Fiction." *Black American Literature Forum* 12: 65-68.

Hyman, Stanley Edgar. "Richard Wright Reappraised." *Atlantic Monthly* 225: 127-32.

Jackson, Blyden. "Richard Wright: Black Boy from America's Black Belt and Urban Ghettos." *CLA Journal* 12: 287-309.

————. "Richard Wright in a Moment of Truth." *The Southern Literary Journal* 3 (Spring 1971): 3-17.

Jordon, June. "On Richard Wright and Zora Neale Hurston: Notes toward a Balancing of Love and Hatred." *Black World* 23,x: 4-8.

Karrer, Wolfgang. "Richard Wright: 'Fire and Cloud' (1938)." In *The Black American Short Story: A Collection of Critical Essays*, edited by Peter Bruck, pp. 99-110. Amsterdam: Grüner, 1977.

Keady, Sylvia H. "Richard Wright's Women Characters and Inequality." *Black American Literature Forum* 10: 124-28.

Kearns, Edward. "The 'Fate' Section of *Native Son.*" *Contemporary Literature* 12: 146-55.

Kennedy, James G. "The Content and Form of *Native Son.*" *College English* 34: 269-83.

Kent, George E. "On the Future Study of Richard Wright." *CLA Journal* 12: 366-70.

————. "Richard Wright: Blackness and the Adventure of Western Culture." *CLA Journal* 12: 322-43.

Kim, Kichung. "Wright, the Protest Novel, and Baldwin's Faith." *CLA Journal* 17: 387-96.

King, James R. "Richard Wright: His Life and Writings." *Negro History Bulletin* 40: 738-43.

Kinnamon, Keneth. *The Emergence of Richard Wright: A Study in Literature and Society*. Urbana: University of Illinois Press, 1972.

————. "*Lawd Today*: Richard Wright's Apprentice Novel." *Studies in Black Literature* 2,ii: 16-18.

————. "*Native Son*: The Personal, Social, and Political Background." *Phylon* 30 (Spring 1969): 66-72.

————. "The Pastoral Impulse in Richard Wright." *Mid-Continent American Studies Journal* 10 (Spring 1969): 41-47.

————. "Richard Wright Items in the Fales Collection." *Bulletin of the Society for the Libraries of New York University* 66: 4.

————. "Richard Wright's Use of *Othello* in *Native Son.*" *CLA Journal* 12: 358-59.

Klotman, Phyllis R., and Yancey, Melville. "The Gift of Double Vision:

Possible Political Implications of Richard Wright's 'Self-Consciousness' Thesis." *CLA Journal* 16: 106-16.

_____. "Moral Distancing as a Rhetorical Technique in *Native Son*: A Note on 'Fate.' " *CLA Journal* 18: 284-91.

Knipp, Thomas, ed. *Richard Wright: Letters to Joe C. Brown*. Kent, Ohio: Kent State University Library Occasional Papers, 1968.

Knox, George. "The Negro Novelist's Sensibility and the Outsider Theme." *Western Humanities Review* 11: 137-48.

Kostelanetz, Richard. "The Politics of Unresolved Quests in the Novels of Richard Wright." *Xavier University Studies* 8 (1969): 31-64.

Larsen, R. B. V. "The Four Voices of Richard Wright's *Native Son*." *Negro American Literature Forum* 6 (1972): 105-9.

Lawson, Lewis A. "Cross Damon: Kierkegaardian Man of Dread." *CLA Journal* 14: 298-316.

Leary, Lewis. "*Lawd Today*: Notes on Richard Wright's First/Last Novel." *CLA Journal* 15: 411-20.

Le Clair, Thomas. "The Blind Leading the Blind: Wright's *Native Son* and a Brief Reference to Ellison's *Invisible Man*." *CLA Journal* 13: 315-20.

Lewis, Theophilus. "The Saga of Bigger Thomas." *Catholic World* 153: 201-6.

McBride, Rebecca, and McBride, David. "Corrections of a Richard Wright Bibliography." *CLA Journal* 20: 422-23.

McCall, Dan. *The Example of Richard Wright*. New York: Harcourt, Brace, and World, 1969.

McCarthy, Harold T. "Richard Wright: The Expatriate As Native Son." *American Literature* 44: 97-117.

McNallie, Robin. "Richard Wright's Allegory of the Cave: 'The Man Who Lived Underground.' " *South Atlantic Bulletin* 42,ii: 76-84.

Margolies, Edward. *The Art of Richard Wright*. Carbondale: Southern Illinois University Press, 1969.

_____, and Fabre, Michel. "Richard Wright (1908-1960): A Bibliography." *Bulletin of Bibliography* 24: 131-33, 137.

Miller, Eugene E. "Voodoo Parallels in *Native Son*." *CLA Journal* 16: 81-95.

Moore, Gerian Steve. "Richard Wright's *American Hunger*." *CLA Journal* 21: 79-89.

Nagel, James. "Images of 'Vision' in *Native Son*." *University Review* 36 (December 1969): 109-15.

Oleson, Carol. "The Symbolic Richness of Richard Wright's 'Bright and

Morning Star.'" *Negro American Literature Forum* 6 (1972): 110-12.

Ordova, R. "Richard Wright, Writer and Prophet." In *Twentieth Century American Literature: A Soviet View*, translated by Ronald Vroon, pp. 384-410. Moscow: Progress, 1976.

Paliwal, G. D. "Richard Wright and the Negro." *Rajasthan University Studies in English* 8 (1975): 72-83.

Primean, Ronald. "Imagination as Moral Bulwark and Creative Energy in Richard Wright's *Black Boy* and LeRoi Jones' *Home.*" *Studies in Black Literature* 3,ii: 12-18.

Rao, Vimala. "The Regionalism of Richard Wright's *Native Son.*" *Indian Journal of American Studies* 7,i: 94-102.

Ray, David, ed. *Richard Wright: Impressions and Perspectives*. Ann Arbor: University of Michigan Press, 1973.

Real, Willi. "Richard Wright, 'The Man Who Lived Underground' (1944)." In *Die Amerikanische Short Story der Gegenwart: Interpretationen*, edited by Peter Freese, pp. 54-63. Berlin: Schmidt, 1975.

————. "Richard Wright: *Native Son* (1940)." In *Der Roman im Englischunterricht der Sekundarstufe, II: Theorie und Praxis* (Informationen zur Sprach und Literaturdidaktic II), edited by Peter Freese and Liesel Hermes, pp. 169-84. Paderborn: Shöningh, 1977.

Redden, Dorothy S. "Richard Wright and *Native Son*: Not Guilty." *Black American Literature Forum* 10: 111-16.

Redding, Saunders. "The Alien Land of Richard Wright." In *Soon, One Morning: New Writing by American Negroes*, edited by Herbert Hill. New York: Alfred A. Knopf, 1963.

Reed, Kenneth T. "*Native Son*: An American *Crime and Punishment.*" *Studies in Black Literature* 1,ii: 33-34.

Reilly, John M. Afterword to Richard Wright, *Native Son*. New York: Perennial Classics, 1966.

————, editor. *Richard Wright: The Critical Reception*. New York: B. Franklin, 1978.

————. "Richard Wright." In *Black American Writers: Bibliographical Essays, II*, edited by Thomas M. Inge et al., pp. 1-46. New York: St. Martin's, 1978.

————. "Richard Wright's Apprenticeship." *Journal of Black Studies* 2, iv (1972): 439-60.

————. "Richard Wright's Curious Thriller, *Savage Holiday.*" *CLA Journal* 21: 218-23.

194 BIBLIOGRAPHY OF SECONDARY SOURCES

Ridenour, Ronald. " 'The Man Who Lived Underground': A Critique."
Phylon 31: 54-57.

Riley, Roberta. " 'The High White Empty Building with Black Windows':
Insights from the Work of Richard Wright." *Illinois School Journal*
55 (1975): 34-38.

Rubin, Steven J. "The Early Short Fiction of Richard Wright Reconsidered." *Studies in Short Fiction* 15: 405-10.

Sadler, Jeffrey. "Split Consciousness in Richard Wright's *Native Son*."
South Carolina Review 8,ii: 11-24.

Sander, Reinhard W. "Black Literature and the African Dream: Richard
Wright's *Lawd Today*." *Nsukka Studies in African Literature* 1,i:
91-107.

Sanders, Ronald. "Richard Wright Then and Now." *Negro Digest* 18
(December): 83-98.

Savory, Jerold J. "Descent and Baptism in *Native Son*, *Invisible Man*, and
Dutchman." *Christian Scholar's Review* 3: 33-37.

Scott, Nathan A., Jr. "The Dark and Haunted Tower of Richard Wright."
Graduate Comment (Wayne State University) 7 (July 1964): 93-99.

_____. "Search for Beliefs: The Fiction of Richard Wright." *University
of Kansas City Review* 23 (Autumn 1956): 19-24.

_____. "Search for Beliefs: Richard Wright." *University of Kansas City
Review* 23 (Winter 1956): 131-38.

Scruggs, Charles W. "The Importance of the City in *Native Son*." *Ariel:
A Review of International English Literature* 9,iii: 37-47.

Sherr, Paul C. "Richard Wright: The Expatriate Pattern." *Black Academy
Review* 2: 81-90.

Shimizu, Takeo. "Uncle Tom no Kodomo-tachi: Hairetsu no Gui." *Eigo
Seinan* (Tokyo, Japan) 124: 244-48.

Siegel, Paul N. "The Conclusion of Richard Wright's *Native Son*."
PMLA 89: 517-23.

Sillen, Samuel. "The Response to *Native Son*." *New Masses*, April 23,
1940, pp. 25-27.

_____. "The Meaning of Bigger Thomas." *New Masses*, April 30,
1940, pp. 26-28.

_____. "*Native Son*: Pros and Cons." *New Masses*, May 21, 1940, pp.
23-26.

Singh, Amritrag. "Misdirected Responses to Bigger Thomas." *Studies in
Black Literature* 5, ii: 5-8.

Smith, Sidonie A. "Richard Wright's *Black Boy*: The Creative Impulse as
Rebellion." *Southern Literary Journal* 5,i: 123-36.

Starr, Alvin. "Richard Wright and the Communist Party: The James T. Farrell Factor." *CLA Journal* 21: 41-50.

Stepto, Robert B. " 'I Thought I Knew These People': Richard Wright and the Afro-American Literary Tradition." *Massachusetts Review* 18: 525-41.

Stocking, Fred. "On Richard Wright and 'Almos' a Man.' " New York: Dell, 1976, pp. 275-81.

Sullivan, Richard. Afterword to Richard Wright, *Native Son.* New York: Signet, 1950.

Tate, Claudia C. *"Black Boy*: Richard Wright's Tragic Sense of Life." *Black American Literature Forum* 10: 117-19.

Tatham, Campbell. "Vision and Value in *Uncle Tom's Children.*" *Studies in Black Literature* 3, i: 14-23.

Turner, Darwin T. *"The Outsider*: Revision of an Idea." *CLA Journal* 12 (June 1969): 310-21.

Ward, Jerry W. "Richard Wright's Hunger." *Virginia Quarterly Review* 54: 148-53.

Wasserman, Jerry. "Embracing the Negative: *Native Son* and *Invisible Man.*" *Studies in American Fiction* 4: 93-104.

Webb, Constance. *Richard Wright: A Biography.* New York: George Putnam's Sons, 1968.

———. "What Next for Richard Wright?" *Phylon* 10 (Second Quarter 1949): 161-66.

Weiss, Adrian. "A Portrait of the Artist as a Black Boy." *Bulletin of the Rocky Mountain Modern Language Association* 28: 93-101.

Wertham, Frederic. "An Unconscious Determinant in *Native Son.*" In *Psychoanalysis and Literature*, edited by Hendrick M. Ruitenbeck, pp. 321-25. New York: E. P. Dutton, 1964.

White, Grace M. "Wright's Memphis." *New Letters* 38,ii: 105-16.

White, Ralph. "Black Boy: A Value Analysis." *Journal of Abnormal Psychology* 42: 440-61.

Widmer, Kingsley. "The Existential Darkness: Richard Wright's *The Outsider.*" *Wisconsin Studies in Contemporary Literature* 1 (Fall 1960): 13-21.

RALPH ELLISON

Abrams, Robert E. "The Ambiguities of Dreaming in Ellison's *Invisible Man.*" *American Literature* 49: 592-603.

Auguste, Yves L. "Du Nègre masqué de Stephen Alexis à l'Homme invisible de Ralph Ellison," *Présence Africaine* 101-2: 176-87.

Balet, S. "The Problem of Characterization in Ralph Ellison's *Invisible Man*." *La Française Moderne* 15: 277-81.

Bataille, Robert. "Ellison's *Invisible Man*: The Old Rhetoric and the New." *Black American Literature Forum* 12: 43-45.

Baumbach, Jonathan. "Nightmare of a Native Son: Ellison's *Invisible Man*." *Criticism* 6: 48-65.

Bell, J. D. "Ellison's *Invisible Man*." *Explicator* 29: item 19.

Bennett, John Z. "The Race and the Runner: Ellison's *Invisible Man*." *Xavier University Studies* 5: 12-26.

Benoit, Bernard, and Fabre, Michel. "A Bibliography of Ralph Ellison's Published Writings." *Studies in Black Literature* 2,iii: 25-28.

Bentson, Kimberly W. "Ellison, Baraka, and the Faces of Tradition." *Boundary* 6: 333-54.

Bloch, Alice. "Sight Imagery in *Invisible Man*." *English Journal* 55: 1019-21, 1024.

Bluestein, Gene. "The Blues as a Literary Theme." *Massachusetts Review* 8: 593-617.

Bone, Robert. "Ralph Ellison and the Uses of Imagination." In *Anger and Beyond: The Negro Writer in the United States*, edited by Herbert Hill. New York: Harper & Row, 1966.

Brown, Lloyd W. "Ralph Ellison's Exhorters: The Role of Rhetoric in *Invisible Man*." *CLA Journal* 13: 289-303.

Bucco, Martin. "Ellison's Invisible West." *Western American Literature* 10: 237-38.

Callahan, John F. "Chaos, Complexity and Possibility: The Historical Frequencies of Ralph Waldo Ellison." *Black American Literature Forum* 11: 130-38.

Cambon, Glauco. "Ralph Ellison della invisibla." *Aut Aut* 3: 135-44.

Cannon, Steve; Raphael, Lennox; and Thompson, James. "A Very Stern Discipline." *Harper's Magazine* 234, 1402 (March 1967): 76-95.

Carlson, David L. "Ralph Ellison: Twenty Years After." *Studies in American Fiction* 1: 1-23.

Cash, Earl A. "The Narrators in *Invisible Man* and Notes from Underground: Brothers in the Spirit." *CLA Journal* 16: 505-7.

Chaffee, Patricia. "Slippery Ground: Ralph Ellison's Bingo Player." *Negro American Literature Forum* 10: 23-24.

Cheshire, Ardner R., Jr. "*Invisible Man* and the Life of Dialogue." *CLA Journal* 20: 19-34.

Christadler, Martin. "Ellison: *The Invisible Man*." In *Der amerikanische Roman: Von den Anfängen bis zur Gegenwart*, edited by Hans-Joachim Lang, pp. 333-69. Düsseldorf: August Bagel, 1972.

Clarke, John H. "The Visible Dimensions of *Invisible Man*." *Black World* 20,ii: 27-30.

Clipper, Lawrence J. "Folkloric and Mythic Elements in *Invisible Man*." *CLA Journal* 13: 229-41.

Collier, Eugenia W. "The Nightmare Truth of an Invisible Man." *Black World* 20,ii: 12-19.

Corry, John. "An American Novelist Who Sometimes Teaches." *New York Times Sunday Magazine*, November 20, 1966, pp. 55, 179-85, 196.

———. "Profile of an American Novelist: A White View of Ralph Ellison." *Black World* 20,ii: 116-25.

Covo, Jaqueline. *The Blinking Eye: Ralph Waldo Ellison and His American, French, German, and Italian Critics, 1952-1971: Bibliographic Essays and a Checklist*. Metuchen, N.J.: Scarecrow Press.

———. "Ralph Waldo Ellison: Bibliographic Essays and Finding List of American Criticism, 1952-1964." *CLA Journal* 15: 171-96.

———. "Ralph Ellison in France: Bibliographic Essays and Checklist of French Criticism, 1954-1971." *CLA Journal* 16: 519-26.

Deutsch, Leonard J. "Ellison's Early Fiction." *Negro American Literature Forum* 7: 53-59.

———. "Ralph Waldo Ellison and Ralph Waldo Emerson: A Shared Moral Vision." *CLA Journal* 16: 159-78.

———. "The Waste Land in Ellison's *Invisible Man*." *Notes on Contemporary Literature* 7,vi: 5-6.

Doyle, Mary Ellen, S.C.N. "In Need of Folk: The Alienated Protagonists of Ralph Ellison's Short Fiction." *CLA Journal* 19: 165-72.

Ducornet, Guy. "Ralph Ellison: Homme invisible, pour qui chantes-tu? Grasset, 1969, traduction de Robert Merle." *Les Langues Modernes* 63 (1969): 394-401.

Ehlers, Leigh A. " 'Give Me the Ocular Proof': *Othello* and Ralph Ellison's *Invisible Man*." *Notes on Contemporary Literature* 6,v: 10-11.

Ellison, Ralph. "Light on *Invisible Man*." *Crisis* 60: 154-56.

Fass, Barbara. "Rejection of Paternalism: Hawthorne's 'My Kinsman Major Molineux' and Ellison's *Invisible Man*." *CLA Journal* 15: 317-23.

Fischer, Russell G. "*Invisible Man* as History." *CLA Journal* 17: 338-67.

Ford, Nick A. "The Ambivalence of Ralph Ellison." *Black World* 20, ii: 5-9.

Forrest, Leon. "A Conversation with Ralph Ellison." *Muhammad Speaks*, December 15, 1972, pp. 29-31.

_____. "Racial History as a Clue to the Action in *Invisible Man*." *Muhammad Speaks*, September 15, 1972, pp. 28, 30.

Foster, Frances S. "The Black and White Masks of Frantz Fanon and Ralph Ellison." *Black Academy Review* 1,iv (1970): 46-58.

Geller, Allen. "An Interview with Ralph Ellison." *Tamarack Review* 32: 3-24.

Gérard, Albert. "Ralph Ellison et le dilemme noir (Le Roman afro-américain)." *Revue générale belge* 97: 154-56.

Gibson, Donald B. "Ralph Ellison and James Baldwin." In *The Politics of Twentieth-Century Novelists*, edited by George A. Panichas, pp. 307-20. New York: Hawthorne Books, 1971.

Giza, Joanne. "Ralph Ellison." In *Black American Writers: Bibliographical Essays II*, edited by M. Thomas Inge, Maurice Duke, and Jackson R. Beyer, pp. 47-71. New York: St. Martin's Press, 1975.

Glicksberg, Charles. "The Symbolism of Vision." *Southwest Review* 39: 259-65.

Goede, William. "On Lower Frequencies: The Buried Men in Wright and Ellison." *Modern Fiction Studies* 15: 483-501.

Gottesman, Ronald, ed. *The Merrill Studies in "Invisible Man."* Columbus, Ohio: Merrill, 1971.

Greene, Maxine. "Against Invisibility." *College English* 30: 430-36.

Griffin, Wilford. "Ellison's *Invisible Man*." *Explicator* 36, ii: 28-29.

Grow, Lynn M. "The Dream Scenes of *Invisible Man*." *Wichita State University Bulletin* 50,iii: 3-12.

Guttmann, Allen. "Focus on Ralph Ellison's *Invisible Man*: American Nightmare." In *American Dreams, American Nightmares*, edited by David Madden, pp. 188-96. Carbondale: Southern Illinois University Press, 1969.

Gvereschi, Edward. "Anticipations of *Invisible Man*: Ralph Ellison's 'King of the Bingo Game.' " *Negro American Literature Forum* 6: 122-24.

Harris, Trudier. "Ellison's 'Peter Wheatstraw': His Basis in Black Folk Tradition." *Mississippi Folklore Register* 9: 117-26.

Haupt, Garry. "The Tragi-Comedy of the Unreal in Ralph Ellison's *Invisible Man* and Mark Twain's *Adventures of Huckleberry Finn*." *Interpretations* 4 (1972): 1-12.

Hays, Peter L. "The Incest Theme in *Invisible Man*." *Western Humanities Review* 23: 335-39.

Heller, Arno. "Ralph Ellison's *Invisible Man*: Das Rassenproblem als Analyse moderner Existenz." *Die Neueren Sprachen* 21: 2-9.

Hersey, John, ed. *Ralph Ellison: A Collection of Critical Essays*. Englewood Cliffs, N.J.: Prentice-Hall, 1974.

Horowitz, Floyd Ross. "The Enigma of Ellison's Intellectual Man." *CLA Journal* 7: 126-32.

————. "An Experimental Confession from a Reader of *Invisible Man*." *CLA Journal* 13,iii: 304-14.

————. "Ralph Ellison's Modern Version of Brer Bear and Brer Rabbit in *Invisible Man*." *Mid-Continent American Studies Journal* 4,ii: 21-27.

Howard, David C. "Points in Defense of Ellison's *Invisible Man*." *Notes on Contemporary Literature* 1,i: 13-14.

Johnson, Abby Arthur. "From Ranter to Writer: Ralph Ellison's *Invisible Man*." *South Atlantic Bulletin* 42,ii: 35-44.

Kaiser, Ernest. "A Critical Look at Ellison's Fiction and at Social and Literary Criticism by and about the Author." *Black World* 20,ii: 53-59, 81-97.

Kent, George E. "Ralph Ellison and Afro-American Folk and Cultural Tradition." *CLA Journal* 13: 265-76.

Kist, E. M. "A Langian Analysis of Blackness in Ralph Ellison's *Invisible Man*." *Studies in Black Literature* 7,ii: 19-23.

Klein, Marcus. "Ralph Ellison." *After Alienation*. Cleveland: World Publishing, 1964.

Klotman, Phyllis R. "The Running Man as Metaphor in Ellison's *Invisible Man*." *CLA Journal* 13: 277-88.

Knox, George. "The Totentanz in Ellison's *Invisible Man*." *Fabula* 12: 168-78.

Kostelanetz, Richard. "The Politics of Ellison's Booker: *Invisible Man* as Symbolic History." *Chicago Review* 19,ii: 5-26.

————. "Ralph Ellison: Novelist as Brown Skinned Aristocrat." *Shenandoah* 20,iv (1969): 56-77.

Lane, James B. "Underground to Manhood: Ralph Ellison's *Invisible Man*." *Negro American Literature Forum* 7: 64-72.

Langman, F. H. "Reconsidering *Invisible Man*." *Critical Review* (Melbourne, Sydney) 18: 114-27.

Lee, A. Robert. "Sight and Mask: Ralph Ellison's *Invisible Man*." *Negro American Literature Forum* 4: 22-33.

Lee, L. L. "The Proper Self: Ralph Ellison's *Invisible Man*." *Descant* 10 (Spring): 38-48.

Lehan, Richard. "The Strange Silence of Ralph Ellison." *California English Journal* 1,ii: 63-68.

Lewis, R. W. B. "Ellison's Essays." *New York Review of Books*, January 28, 1965.

Lieber, Todd M. "Ralph Ellison and the Metaphor of Invisibility in Black Literary Tradition." *American Quarterly* 24: 86-100.

Lieberman, Marcia R. "Moral Innocents: Ellison's *Invisible Man* and *Candide.*" *CLA Journal* 15: 64-79.

Ludington, Charles T., Jr. "Protest and Anti-Protest: Ralph Ellison." *Southern Humanities Review* 4: 31-39.

McDaniel, Barbara A. "John Steinbeck: Ralph Ellison's Invisible Source." *Pacific Coast Philology* 8: 28-33.

Maner, Robert. Quelques réflexions à propos de *Invisible Man* de R. W. Ellison." In *Yaorende: Equipe de Recherches en Lit. Afr. Comp.*, edited by Thomas Melone, pp. 482-504. N.d.

Mason, Clifford. "Ralph Ellison and the Underground Man." *Black World* 20,ii: 20-26.

Mengeling, Marvin E. "Whitman and Ellison: Older Symbols in a Modern Mainstream." *Walt Whitman Review* 12: 67-70.

Mitchell, Louis D. "Invisibility: Permanent or Resurrective." *CLA Journal* 17: 379-86.

Mitchell, Louis D., and Stauffenberg, Henry J. "Ellison's B. P. Rinehart: 'Spiritual Technologist.' " *Negro American Literature Forum* 9: 51-52.

Moore, Robert H., ed. "On Initiation Rites and Power: Ralph Ellison Speaks at West Point." *Contemporary Literature* 15: 165-86.

Moorer, Frank E., and Baily, Lugene. "A Selected Check List of Materials by and about Ralph Ellison." *Black World* 20,ii: 126-30.

Nash, R. W. "Stereotypes and Social Types in Ellison's *Invisible Man.*" *Sociological Quarterly* 6:349-60.

Neal, Larry. "Ellison's Zoot Suit." *Black World* 20,ii: 31-52.

Nettlebeck, C. W. "From Inside Destitution: Celine's *Bardamer* and Ellison's *Invisible Man.*" *Southern Review: An Australian Journal of Literary Studies* 7: 246-53.

Nichols, William W. "Ralph Ellison's Black American Scholar." *Phylon* 31: 70-75.

O'Daniel, Therman B. "The Image of Man Portrayed by Ralph Ellison." *CLA Journal* 10: 272-84.

Olderman, Raymond M. "Ralph Ellison's Blues and *Invisible Man.*" *Wisconsin Studies in Contemporary Literature* 8: 142-59.

Omans, Stuart E. "The Variations on a Masked Leader: A Study on the Literary Relationship of Ralph Ellison and Herman Melville." *South Atlantic Bulletin* 40,ii: 15-23.

Ostendorf, Bernhard. "Ralph Ellison, 'Flying Home' 1944." In *Die amerikanische Short Story der Gegenwart: Interpretationen*, edited by Peter Freese, pp. 64-76. Berlin: Schmidt, 1975.

————. "Ralph Ellison's 'Flying Home': From Folk Tale to Short Story." *Journal of the Folklore Institute* 13: 185-99.

Overmyer, Janet. "The Invisible Man and White Women." *Notes on Contemporary Literature* 6,iii: 13-15.

Parrish, Paul A. "Writing as Celebration: The Epilogue of *Invisible Man*." *Renascence* 26: 152-57.

Plessner, Monika. "Bildnis des Künstlers als Volksaufwiegler." *Merkur* 24: 629-43.

Powell, Grosvenor E. "Role and Identity in Ralph Ellison's *Invisible Man*." In *Private Dealings: Eight Modern American Writers*, edited by David Burrows et al., pp. 95-105. Stockholm: Almgrist and Wiksell, 1970.

Pryse, Marjorie. "Ralph Ellison's Heroic Fugitive." *American Literature* 46: 1-15.

Radford, Frederick L. "The Journey towards Castration: Interracial Sexual Stereotypes in Ellison's *Invisible Man*." *Journal of American Studies* 4: 227-31.

Randall, John H., III. "Ralph Ellison: Invisible Man." *Revue des Langues Vivantes* (Brussels) 31: 24-44.

Real, Willi. "Ralph Ellison: King of the Bingo Game (1944)." In *The Black American Short Story in the Twentieth Century: A Collection of Critical Essays*, edited by Peter Bruck, pp. 111-27. Amsterdam: Grüner, 1977.

Reilly, John M., ed. *Twentieth-Century Interpretations of Invisible Man: A Collection of Critical Essays*. Englewood Cliffs, N.J.: Prentice-Hall, 1969.

Rocard, Marcienne. "Homme Invisible, pour qui joues-tu?" *Caliban* 10: 67-76.

Rodnon, Stewart. "Ralph Ellison's 'Invisible Man': Six Tentative Approaches." *CLA Journal* 12: 244-56.

Rollins, Ronald G. "Ellison's *Invisible Man*." *Explicator* 30: item 22.

Rovit, Earl. "Ralph Ellison and the American Comic Tradition." *Wisconsin Studies in Contemporary Literature* 1: 34-42.

Sage, Howard. "An Interview with Ralph Ellison: Visible Man." *Pulp* (Flushing, N.Y.) 2,ii: 12.

Saito, Tadatoshi. "Ralph Ellison and James Baldwin in the 1950's." In *American Literature in the 1950's. Annual Report 1976*, pp. 32-40. Tokyo: Tokyo Chapter, American Literature Society of Japan.

Sale, Roger. "The Career of Ralph Ellison." *Hudson Review* 18: 124-28.

Sanders, Archie D. "Odysseus in Black: An Analysis of the Structure of *Invisible Man*." *CLA Journal* 13: 217-28.

Saunders, Pearl I. "Symbolism in Ralph Ellison's 'King of the Bingo Game.' " *CLA Journal* 20: 35-39.

Schafer, William J. "Irony from Underground—Satiric Elements in *Invisible Man*." *Satire Newsletter* 7: 22-29.

_____. "Ralph Ellison and the Birth of the Anti-Hero." *Critique* 10, ii: 81-93.

Scheer-Schäzler, Brigitte. "Aspekte der Raum—Zeitgestaltung in Ralph Ellison's *Invisible Man*." *Revue des Langues Vivantes* (Brussels) 38: 65-70.

_____. "Ralph Ellison." In *Amerikanische Literatur der Gegenwart*, edited by Martin Christadler, pp. 190-209. Stuttgart: Alfred Kröner, 1977.

Scruggs, Charles W. "Ralph Ellison's Use of *The Aeneid* in *Invisible Man*." *CLA Journal* 17: 368-78.

Sequeira, Isaac. "The Uncompleted Initiation of the Invisible Man." *Studies in Black Literature* 6:i: 9-13.

Singh, V. D. "*Invisible Man*: The Rhetoric of Colour, Chaos, and Blindness." *Rajasthan University Studies in English* 8: 54-61.

Singleton, M. K. "Leadership Mirages as Antagonists in *Invisible Man*." *Arizona Quarterly* 22: 157-71.

Tischler, Nancy. "Negro Literature and Classic Form." *Contemporary Literature* 10,iii: 352-65.

Skerrett, Joseph T., Jr. "Ralph Ellison and the Example of Richard Wright." *Studies in Short Fiction* 15: 145-53.

Spillers, Hortense. "Ellison's 'Usable Past': Toward a Theory of Myth." *Interpretations* 9: 53-69.

Stark, John. "*Invisible Man*: Ellison's Black Odyssey." *Negro American Literature Forum* 7: 60-63.

Steinbrink, Jeffrey. "Toward a Vision of Infinite Possibility: A Reading of *Invisible Man*." *Studies in Black Literature* 7,iii: 1-5.

Stepto, Robert B., and Harper, Michael S. " 'Study and Experience': An Interview with Ralph Ellison." *Massachusetts Review* 18: 417-35.

Sylvander, Carolyn W. "Ralph Ellison's *Invisible Man* and Female Stereotypes." *Negro American Literature Forum* 9: 77-79.

Thompson, James; Raphael, Lennox; and Cannon, Steve. "A Very Stern Discipline: An Interview with Ralph Ellison." *Harper's Magazine* 234 (March): 76-95.

Trimmer, Joseph F. "The Grandfather's Riddle in Ralph Ellison's *Invisible Man*." *Black American Literature Forum* 12: 46-50.

_____. "Ralph Ellison's 'Flying Home.' " *Studies in Short Fiction* 9: 175-82.

Turner, Darwin. "Sight in *Invisible Man.*" *CLA Journal* 13: 258-64.

Volger, Thomas A. "*Invisible Man*: Somebody's Protest Novel." *Iowa Review* 1: 64-82.

Walling, William. " 'Art' and 'Protest': Ralph Ellison's *Invisible Man* Twenty Years After." *Phylon* 34: 120-34.

———. "Ralph Ellison's *Invisible Man*: 'It Goes a Long Way Back Some Twenty Years.' " *Phylon* 34: 4-16.

Warren, Robert Penn. "The Unity of Experience." *Commentary* 39: 91-96.

Weinstein, Sharon R. "Comedy and the Absurd in Ralph Ellison's *Invisible Man.*" *Studies in Black Literature* 3,iii: 12-16.

Weixlmann, Joe, and O'Banion, John. "A Checklist of Ellison Criticism, 1972-1978." *Black American Literature Forum* 12: 51-55.

Williams, John A. "Ralph Ellison and *Invisible Man*: Their Place in American Letters." *Black World* 20,ii: 10-11.

Wilner, Eleanor R. "The Invisible Black Threads: Identity and Nonentity in *Invisible Man.*" *CLA Journal* 13: 242-57.

JAMES BALDWIN

Alexander, Charlotte A. *Baldwin's "Go Tell It on the Mountain," "Another Country," and Other Works: A Critical Commentary.* New York: Distributed by Monarch Press, 1966.

Allen, Shirley S. "The Ironic Voice in Baldwin's *Go Tell It on the Mountain.*" In *James Baldwin: A Critical Evaluation*, edited by Therman B. O'Daniel, pp. 30-37. Washington, D.C.: Howard University Press, 1977.

———. "Religious Symbolism and Psychic Reality in Baldwin's *Go Tell It on the Mountain.*" *CLA Journal* 19: 173-99.

Baker, Houston A., Jr. "The Embattled Craftsman: An Essay on James Baldwin." *Journal of African-Afro-American Affairs* 1,i: 28-51.

Barksdale, Richard K. " 'Temple of the Fire Baptized.' " *Phylon* 14: 326-27.

Bell, George E. "The Dilemma of Love in *Go Tell It on the Mountain* and *Giovanni's Room.*" *CLA Journal* 17: 397-406.

Berry, Boyd M. "Another Man Done Gone: Self Pity in Baldwin's *Another Country.*" *Michigan Quarterly Review* 5: 285-90.

Bhattacharya, Lokenath. "James Baldwin." *Quest*, no. 44: 60-66.

Bigsby, C. W. "The Committed Writer: James Baldwin as Dramatist." *Twentieth-Century Literature* 13: 39-48.

"The Black Scholar Interviews: James Baldwin." *Black Scholar* 5,iv (1973-1974): 33-42.

Blaisdel, Gus. "James Baldwin, the Writer." *Negro Digest* 13 (January): 61-68.

Blount, Trevor. "A Slight Error in Continuity in James Baldwin's *Another Country.*" *Notes and Queries* 13: 102-3.

Bluefarb, Sam. "James Baldwin's 'Previous Condition': A Problem of Identification." *Negro American Literature Forum* 3: 26-29.

Bone, Robert A. "The Novels of James Baldwin." *Tri-Quarterly*, no. 2 (1965): 3-20.

Bonosky, Phillip. "The Negro Writer and Commitment." *Mainstream* 15, ii: 16-22.

Boyle, Kay. "Introducing James Baldwin." In *Contemporary American Novelists*, edited by Harry T. Moore. Carbondale: Southern Illinois University Press, 1964.

Bradford, Melvin E. "Faulkner, James Baldwin, and the South." *Georgia Review* 20: 431-43.

Breit, Harvey. "James Baldwin and Two Footnotes." In *The Creative Present: Notes on Contemporary American Fiction*, edited by Nona Balakian and Charles Simmons. Garden City, N.Y.: Doubleday, 1967.

Britt, David D. "America: Another Country." *BaShiru* 4: 47-51.

Brooks, A. Russell. "James Baldwin as Poet-Prophet." In *James Baldwin: A Critical Evaluation*, edited by Therman B. O'Daniel, pp. 126-34. Washington, D.C.: Howard University Press, 1977.

Brooks, Hallie B. "Baldwin in Paperback." *Phylon* 21: 296-97.

Bruck, Peter. *Von der "Store Front Church" zum "American Dream."* (BAS 2) Amsterdam: Grüner, 1975.

Burks, Mary Fair. "James Baldwin's Protest Novel: *If Beale Street Could Talk.*" *Negro American Literature Forum* 10: 83-87, 95.

Charney, Maurice. "James Baldwin's Quarrel with Richard Wright." *American Quarterly* 15: 65-75.

Clarke, John Henrik. "The Alienation of James Baldwin." *Journal of Human Relations* 12: 30-33.

Coles, Robert. "Baldwin's Burden." *Partisan Review* 31: 409-16.

Collier, Eugenia. "The Phrase Unbearably Repeated." *Phylon* 25: 288-96.

———. "Thematic Patterns in Baldwin's Essays: A Study in Chaos." *Black World* 21,viii: 28-34.

Corona, Maris. "La saggistica di James Baldwin." *Studi Americani* (Rome) 15 (1969): 433-63.

Coulibaly, Yedieti E. "Weeping Gods: A Study of Cultural Disintegration in James Baldwin's *Go Tell It on the Mountain* and Chinua Achebe's *Things Fall Apart.*" *Annales de l'Université d'Abidjan* 9D (1976): 531-42.

Cox, C. B., and Jones, A. R. "After the Tranquilized Fifties: Notes on Sylvia Plath and James Baldwin." *Critical Quarterly* 6: 107-22.

Curling, Maud. "James Baldwin y la iglesia negra norteamericana en lanovela *Go Tell It on the Mountain.*" *Revista de la Universidad de Costa Rica* 34: 87-95.

Dance, Daryl. "James Baldwin." In *Black American Writers: Bibliographical Essays II*, edited by M. Thomas Inge, Maurice Duke, and Jackson R. Beyer, pp. 73-120. New York: St. Martin's Press, 1975.

————. "You Can't Go Home Again: James Baldwin and the South." *CLA Journal* 18: 81-90.

Daniels, Mark R. "Estrangement, Betrayal and Atonement: The Political Theory of James Baldwin." *Studies in Black Literature* 7,iii: 10-13.

Eckman, Fern Marja. *The Furious Passage of James Baldwin.* New York: Popular Library, 1966.

Elkoff, Marvin. "Everybody Knows His Name." *Esquire* 62,ii: 59-64, 120-23.

Fabre, Michel. "Pères et fils dans *Go Tell It on the Mountain*, de James Baldwin." *Etudes Anglaises* 23: 47-61.

Farès, Nobile. "James Baldwin: Une interview exclusive." *Jeune Afrique* 1 (1970): 20-24.

Farrison, William Edward. "If Baldwin's Train Has Not Gone." In *James Baldwin: A Critical Evaluation*, edited by Therman B. O'Daniel, pp. 69-81. Washington, D.C.: Howard University Press, 1977.

Featherstone, J. "Blues for Mr. Baldwin." *New Republic*, November 27, 1965, pp. 34-46.

Ferguson, Alfred R. "Black Men, White Cities: The Quest for Humanity by Black Protagonists in James Baldwin's *Another Country* and Richard Wright's *The Outsider.*" *Ball State University Forum* 18,ii: 51-58.

Finn, James. "The Identity of James Baldwin." *Commonweal* 77: 113-16.

————. "James Baldwin's Vision." *Commonweal* 77: 447-49.

Fischer, Russell G. "James Baldwin: A Bibliography, 1947-1962." *Bulletin of Bibliography* 24: 127-30.

Fleischauer, John F. "James Baldwin's Style: A Prospectus for the Classroom." *College Composition and Communication* 26: 141-48.

Foote, Dorothy N. "James Baldwin's 'Holler Books.'" *College English Association Critic* 25,viii: 8, 11.

Ford, Nick Aaron. "The Evolution of James Baldwin." In *James Baldwin: A Critical Evaluation*, edited by Therman B. O'Daniel, pp. 85-104. Washington, D.C.: Howard University Press, 1977.

Foster, David E. " 'Cause my house fall down': The Theme of the Fall in Baldwin's Novels." *Critique: Studies in Modern Fiction* 13,iii: 50-62.

Franzbecker, Rolf. "James Baldwin: *Go Tell It on the Mountain* (1953)." In *Der Roman in Englischunterricht der Sekundarstufe, II: Theorie und Praxis.* (Informationen zur Sprach—und Literaturdidaktik II.), edited by Peter Freese and Liesel Hermes, pp. 223-39. Paderborn: Shöningh, 1977.

Freese, Peter. "James Baldwin: *Blues for Mister Charlie.*" In *Theater und Drama in Amerika: Aspekte und Interpretionen*, edited by Edgar Lohner and Rudolph Hass, pp. 328-52. Berlin: Schmidt, 1977.

_____. "James Baldwin: 'Going to Meet the Man' (1965)." In *The Black American Short Story in the Twentieth Century: A Collection of Critical Essays*, edited by Peter Bruck, pp. 171-85. Amsterdam: Grüner, 1977.

_____. "James Baldwin und das Syndrom des Identitätsverlustes: 'Previous Condition' im Lichte des Gesamtwerkes." *Literatur in Wissenschaft und Unterricht* (Kiel) 4: 73-98.

Friedman, Neil. "James Baldwin and Psychotherapy." *Psychotherapy* 3: 177-83.

Gayle, Addison, Jr. "A Defense of James Baldwin." *CLA Journal* 10: 201-8.

_____. "The Dialectic of 'The Fire Next Time.'" *Negro History Bulletin* 30: 15-16.

Gérard, Albert. "James Baldwin et la Religiosité Noire." *Revue nouvelle* 33: 177-86.

Gibson, Donald B. "James Baldwin: The Political Anatomy of Space." In *James Baldwin: A Critical Evaluation*, edited by Therman B. O'Daniel, pp. 3-18. Washington, D.C.: Howard University Press, 1977.

_____. "Ralph Ellison and James Baldwin." In *The Politics of Twentieth-Century Novelists*, edited by George A. Panichas, pp. 307-20. New York: Hawthorne Books, 1971.

Golden, Harry. "A Comment on James Baldwin's Letter." *Crisis* 70: 145-46.

Goldman, Suzy B. "James Baldwin's 'Sonny's Blues': A Message in Music." *Negro American Literature Forum* 8: 231-32.

Gounard, J. F. "L'Avenir de James Baldwin." *Europe* 578-79: 186-97.

————. "La carrière singulière de James Baldwin: 1924-1970." *Revue de l'Université d'Ottawa* 44: 507-18.

Graves, Wallace. "The Question of Moral Energy in James Baldwin's *Go Tell It on the Mountain*." *CLA Journal* 8: 215-23.

Gross, Barry. "The 'Uninhabitable Darkness' of Baldwin's *Another Country*: Image and Theme." *Negro American Literature Forum* 6: 113-21.

Gross, Theodore. "The World of James Baldwin." *Critique* 7: 139-49.

Hagopian, John V. "James Baldwin: The Black and the Red-White-and-Blue." *CLA Journal* 7: 133-40.

Harris, Trudier. "The Eye as Weapon in *If Beale Street Could Talk*." *MELUS* 5,iii: 54-66.

Hassan, Ihab. "The Novel of Outrage: A Minority Voice in Postwar American Fiction." *American Scholar* 34: 239-53.

————. *Radical Innocence*. Princeton: Princeton University Press, 1961.

Hernton, Calvin C. "Blood of the Lamb and a Fiery Baptism: The Ordeal of James Baldwin." *Amistad* 1: 183-225.

Howe, Irving. "James Baldwin: At Ease in Apocalypse." *Harper's Magazine* 237 (September): 92-100.

Inge, M. Thomas. "James Baldwin's Blues." *Notes on Contemporary Literature* 2,iv: 8-11.

Jacobson, Dan. "James Baldwin As Spokesman." *Commentary* 32: 497-502.

Jacoby, Bruce Jay. "The Music Is the Massage: Teaching Baldwin's 'Sonny's Blues.' " *English Record* 29,iv: 2-4.

Jarrett, Hobart. "From a Region in My Mind: The Essays of James Baldwin." In *James Baldwin: A Critical Evaluation*, edited by Therman B. O'Daniel, pp. 105-25. Washington, D.C.: Howard University Press, 1977.

Jay, Salim. "Une Rencontre avec James Baldwin." *L'Afrique Littéraire et Artistique* (Senegal) 38 (1975): 51-54.

Jones, A. R., and Cox, C. B. "After the Tranquilized Fifties: Notes on Sylvia Plath and James Baldwin." *Critical Quarterly* 6: 107-22.

Jones, B. B. "James Baldwin: The Struggle for Identity." *British Journal of Sociology* 17: 107-21.

Jones, Harry L. "Style, Form and Content in the Short Fiction of James Baldwin." In *James Baldwin: A Critical Evaluation*, edited by

Therman B. O'Daniel, pp. 143-50. Washington, D.C.: Howard University Press, 1977.

Kazin, Alfred. "The Essays of James Baldwin." In *Contemporaries*, pp. 254-56. Boston: Little, Brown, 1962.

Kent, George. "Baldwin and the Problem of Being." *CLA Journal* 7: 202-14.

Kindt, Kathleen A. "James Baldwin: A Checklist, 1947-1962." *Bulletin of Bibliography* 24: 123-26.

Kinnamon, Keneth, ed. *James Baldwin: A Collection of Critical Essays*. Englewood Cliffs, N.J.: Prentice-Hall, 1973.

Klein, Marcus. "James Baldwin." *After Alienation*. Cleveland: World Publishing, 1964.

Küster, Dieter. "James Baldwin: *Tell Me How Long the Train's Been Gone*." In *Amerikanische Erzählliteratur 1950-1970*, edited by Frieder Busch and Renate Schmidt-von Bardeleben, pp. 142-54. Munich: Fink, 1974.

Lash, John S. "Baldwin Beside Himself: A Study in Modern Phallicism." *CLA Journal* 8: 132-40.

Leaks, Sylvester. "I Know His Name." *Freedomways* 3: 102-5.

Lee, Robert A. "James Baldwin and Matthew Arnold: Thoughts on 'Relevance.' " *CLA Journal* 14: 324-30.

Levin, David. "Baldwin's Autobiographical Essays: The Problem of Negro Identity." *Massachusetts Review* 5: 239-47.

Long, Robert. "Love and Wrath in the Fiction of James Baldwin." *English Record* 19: 50-57.

Lottman, Herbert R. "It's Hard to Be James Baldwin: An Interview." *Intellectual Digest* 2: 67-68.

Macebuh, Stanley. *James Baldwin: A Critical Study*. New York: Third Press, 1973.

MacInnes, Colin. "Dark Angel: The Writings of James Baldwin." *Encounter* 21: 22-33.

Matata, Godwin. "James Baldwin, the Renowned Black-American Novelist, Talks to Godwin Matata." *Africa: International Business, Economics, and Political Monthly* 37: 68-69.

Mayfield, Julian. "And Then Came Baldwin." *Freedomways* 3 (Spring): 143-55.

Meriwether, L. M. "*The Amen Corner*." *Negro Digest* 14 (January 1965): 40-47.

————. "James Baldwin: Fiery Voice of the Negro Revolt." *Negro Digest* 12 (August 1963): 3-7.

Milligan, Arthemia Bates. "Fire as the Symbol of a Leadening Existence in 'Going to Meet the Man.'" In *James Baldwin: A Critical Evaluation*, edited by Therman B. O'Daniel, pp. 170-80. Washington, D.C.: Howard University Press, 1977.

Mitra, B. K. "The Wright-Baldwin Controversy." *Indian Journal of American Studies* 1: 101-5.

Miura, Mitsuyo. "Fonny's Inner Change." *Kyushu American Literature* (Fukuoka, Japan) 17: 25-28.

Modette, Carlton W. "James Baldwin as a Playwright." In *James Baldwin: A Critical Evaluation*, edited by Therman B. O'Daniel, pp. 183-88. Washington, D.C.: Howard University Press, 1977.

Moore, John Rees. "An Embarrassment of Riches: Baldwin's *Going to Meet the Man.*" *Hollins Critic* 2,v: 1-12.

Mowe, Gregory, and Nobles, W. Scott. "James Baldwin's Message for White America." *Quarterly Journal of Speech* 58: 142-51.

Murry, Donald C. "James Baldwin's 'Sonny's Blues': Complicated and Simple." *Studies in Short Fiction* 14: 353-57.

Neal, Laurence P. "The Black Writer's Role: James Baldwin." *Liberator* 5 (April 1966): 10-11, 18.

Neverson, Yvonne. "The Artist Has Always Been a Disturber of the Peace." *Africa: International Business, Economics, and Political Monthly* 80: 109, 111-12.

Newman, Charles. "The Lesson of the Master: Henry James and James Baldwin." *Yale Review* 56: 45-59.

O'Daniel, Therman B. "James Baldwin: A Classified Bibliography." In *James Baldwin: A Critical Evaluation*, edited by Therman B. O'Daniel, pp. 56-68. Washington, D.C.: Howard University Press, 1977.

––––––. "James Baldwin: An Interpretive Study." *CLA Journal* 7: 37-47.

––––––, ed. *James Baldwin: A Critical Evaluation*. Washington, D.C.: Howard University Press, 1977.

Ogutu, Martin. "James Baldwin on Christianity." *Kucha* (Nairobi) 1,i (1977): 25-28.

Orsagh, Jaqueline E. "Baldwin's Female Characters: A Step Forward?" In *James Baldwin: A Critical Evaluation*, edited by Therman B. O'Daniel, pp. 56-68. Washington, D.C.: Howard University Press, 1977.

Ostendorf, Bernhard. "James Baldwin, 'Sonny's Blues' (1957)." In *Die Amerikanische Short Story der Gegenwart: Interpretationen*, edited by Peter Freese, pp. 194-204. Berlin: Schmidt, 1975.

Paliwal, G. D. "African Consciousness in Modern American Fiction: A Note on Novels by Wright, Ellison, and Baldwin." *Rajasthan University Studies in English* 10 (1977): 62-70.

Patterson, H. Orlando. "The Essays of James Baldwin." *New Left Review* 26 (Summer): 31-38.

Perry, Patsy Brewington. "One Day When I Was Lost: Baldwin's Unfulfilled Obligation." In *James Baldwin: A Critical Evaluation*, edited by Therman B. O'Daniel, pp. 213-27. Washington, D.C.: Howard University Press, 1977.

Peterson, Fred. "James Baldwin and Eduardo Mallea: Two Essayists' Search for Identity." *Discourse* 10: 97-107.

Phillips, Louis. "The Novelist as Playwright: Baldwin, McCullers, and Bellow." *Modern American Drama: Essays in Criticism*. Deland, Fla.: Everett/Edwards, 1968.

Podhoretz, Norman. "In Defense of James Baldwin." In *Doings and Undoings*. New York: Farrar, Straus and Co., 1964.

Popkin, Michael, ed. *Modern Black Writers*. Library of Literary Criticism. New York: Ungar, 1977.

Potter, Vilma. "Baldwin and Odets: The High Cost of 'Crossing.' " *California English Journal* 1,iii: 37-41.

Prasad, Thakur Guru. "*Another Country*: The Tensions of Dream and Nightmare in the American Psyche." In *Indian Studies in American Fiction*, edited by M. K. Naik et al., pp. 296-310. Dharwar: Karnatak University (Delhi: Macmillan India, 1974).

Pratt, Louis H. "James Baldwin and 'the Literary Ghetto.' " *CLA Journal* 20: 262-72.

Reilly, John M. " 'Sonny's Blues': James Baldwin's Image of Black Community." *Negro American Literature Forum* 4: 56-60.

Sayre, Robert F. "James Baldwin's Other Country." In *Contemporary American Novelists*, edited by Harry T. Moore. Carbondale: Southern Illinois University Press, 1964.

Schrero, Eliot M. "*Another Country* and the Sense of Self." *Black Academy Review* 2,i-ii: 91-100.

Schroth, Raymond A., S.J. "James Baldwin's Search." *Catholic World* 148: 288-94.

Schwank, Klaus. "James Baldwin: Blues for Mr. Charlie." In *Das amerikanische Drama der Gegenwart*, edited by Paul Goetsch, pp. 169-84. Kronberg: Athenäum, 1976.

Simmons, Harvey G. "James Baldwin and the Negro Conundrum." *Antioch Review* 23: 250-55.

Spender, Stephen. "James Baldwin: Voice of a Revolution." *Partisan Review* 30: 256-60.

Standley, Fred L. *"Another Country,* Another Time." *Studies in the Novel* (North Texas State University) 4: 504-12.

———. "James Baldwin: The Artist as Incorrigible Disturber of the Peace." *Southern Humanities Review* 4: 18-30.

———. "James Baldwin: A Checklist, 1963-1967." *Bulletin of Bibliography* 25: 135-37, 160.

———. "James Baldwin: The Crucial Situation." *South Atlantic Quarterly* 65: 371-81.

Strong, Augusta. "Notes on James Baldwin." *Freedomways* 2: 167-71.

Strout, Cushing. *"Uncle Tom's Cabin* and the Portent of Millennium." *Yale Review* 57: 375-85.

Tedesco, John L. "Blues for Mister Charlie: The Rhetorical Dimension." *Players* 50: 20-23.

Turner, Darwin T. "James Baldwin in the Dilemma of the Black Dramatist." In *James Baldwin: A Critical Evaluation,* edited by Therman B. O'Daniel, pp. 189-94. Washington, D.C.: Howard University Press, 1977.

Virágos, Zsolt. "James Baldwin: Stereotype vs. Counterstereotype." *Hungarian Studies in English* 11 (1977): 131-41.

Watson, Edward A. "The Novels of James Baldwin: Case-Book of a 'Lover's War' with the United States." *Queens Quarterly* 72: 385-402.

Weixlmann, Joe. "Staged Segregation: Baldwin's *Blues for Mister Charlie* and O'Neill's *All God's Chillun Got Wings." Black American Literature Forum* 11: 35-36.

Wills, Antony A. "The Use of Coincidence in 'Notes of a Native Son.' " *Negro American Literature Forum* 8: 234-35.

Zahorski, Kenneth J. "James Baldwin: Portrait of a Black Exile." In *James Baldwin: A Critical Evaluation,* edited by Therman B. O'Daniel, pp. 199-204. Washington, D.C.: Howard University Press, 1977.

JEAN TOOMER

Ackley, Donald G. "Theme and Vision in Jean Toomer's *Cane." Studies in Black Literature* 1,i: 45-60.

Bell, Bernard W. "A Key to the Poems in *Cane.*" *CLA Journal* 14: 251-58.

_____. "Portrait of the Artist as High Priest of Soul: Jean Toomer's *Cane.*" *Black World* 23,xi: 4-19, 92-97.

Blackwell, Louise. "Jean Toomer's *Cane* and Biblical Myth." *CLA Journal* 17: 535-42.

Blake, Susan. "The Spectatorial Artist and the Structure of *Cane.*" *CLA Journal* 17: 516-34.

Bontemps, Arna. Introduction to *Cane.* New York: Harper & Row (Perennial Classic), 1969.

Caneel, Rafael A. "Male and Female Interrelationship in Toomer's *Cane.*" *Negro American Literature Forum* 5: 25-31.

Chase, Patricia. "The Women in *Cane.*" *CLA Journal* 14: 259-73.

Christ, Jack M. "Jean Toomer's 'Bona and Paul': The Innocence and Artifice of Words." *Negro American Literature Forum* 9: 44-46.

Davis, Charles T. "Jean Toomer and the South: Region and Race as Elements within a Literary Imagination." *Studies in the Literary Imagination* (Georgia State College) 7,ii: 23-37.

Dillard, Mabel M. "Jean Toomer: The Veil Replaced." *CLA Journal* 17: 468-73.

Du Bois, W. E. B., and Locke, Alain. "The Younger Literary Movement." *Crisis* 27: 161-63.

Duncan, Bowie. "Jean Toomer's *Cane*: A Modern Black Oracle." *CLA Journal* 15: 323-33.

Durham, Frank. "Jean Toomer's Vision of the Southern Negro." *Southern Humanities Review* 6: 13-22.

_____, ed. *Studies in "Cane."* Columbus, Ohio: Charles E. Merrill, 1970.

Farrison, W. Edward. "Jean Toomer's *Cane* Again." *CLA Journal* 15: 295-302.

Faulkner, Howard. "The Buried Life: Jean Toomer's *Cane.*" *Studies in Black Literature* 7,i: 1-5.

Fischer, William C. "The Aggregate Man in Jean Toomer's *Cane.*" *Studies in the Novel* (North Texas State University) 3: 190-215.

Fisher, Alice P. "The Influence of Ouspensky's *Tertium Organum* upon Jean Toomer's *Cane.*" *CLA Journal* 17: 504-15.

Fullinwider, S. P. "Jean Toomer, Lost Generation, or Negro Renaissance?" *Phylon* 28: 396-403.

Grant, Sister M. Kathryn. "Images of Celebration in *Cane.*" *Negro American Literature Forum* 5: 32-34, 36.

Griffin, John C. "A Chat with Marjorie Content Toomer." *Pembroke Magazine* (Pembroke, N.C.) 5: 15-27.

————. "Jean Toomer: A Bibliography." *South Carolina Review* 7,ii: 61-64.

Gysin, Fritz. *The Grotesque in American Negro Fiction: Jean Toomer, Richard Wright, and Ralph Ellison.* Cooper Monograph 22. Bern: Francke, 1975.

Holmes, Eugene. "Jean Toomer, Apostle of Beauty." *Opportunity* 3: 252-54, 260.

Howell, Elmo. "Jean Toomer's Hamlet: A Note on *Cane. Interpretations* 9: 70-73.

Ianes, Catherine L. "The Unity of Jean Toomer's *Cane.*" *CLA Journal* 15: 306-22.

Jackson, Blyden. "Jean Toomer's *Cane*: An Issue of Genre." In *The Twenties: Fiction, Poetry, Drama,* edited by Warren French, pp. 317-33. Deland, Fla.: Everett/Edwards, 1974.

Jung, Udo. "Jean Toomer: 'Fern' (1922)." In *The Black American Short Story in the Twentieth Century: A Collection of Critical Essays,* edited by Peter Bruck, pp. 53-69. Amsterdam: Grüner, 1977.

————. " 'Nora' Is 'Calling Jesus': A Nineteenth-Century European Dilemma in Afro-American Garb." *CLA Journal* 21: 251-55.

————. " 'Spirit-Torsos of Exquisite Strength': The Theme of Individual Weakness vs. Collective Strength in Two of Toomer's Poems." *CLA Journal* 19: 261-67.

Kerman, Cynthia E. "Jean Toomer? Enigma." *Indian Journal of American Studies* 7,i: 67-78.

Kopf, George. "The Tensions in Jean Toomer's 'Theater.' " *CLA Journal* 17: 498-503.

Kraft, James. "Jean Toomer's *Cane.*" *Markham Review* 2 (1970): 61-63.

Krasny, Michael. "The Aesthetic Structure of Jean Toomer's *Cane.*" *Negro American Literature Forum* 9: 42-43.

————. "Jean Toomer's Life Prior to *Cane*: A Brief Sketch of the Emergence of a Black Writer." *Negro American Literature Forum* 9: 40-41.

————. "Design in Jean Toomer's *Bale.*" *Negro American Literature Forum* 7: 103-4.

Kramer, Victor G. "The 'Mid-Kingdom' of Crane's 'Black Tambourine' and Toomer's *Cane.*" *CLA Journal* 17: 486-97.

McCarthy, Daniel P. " 'Just Americans': A Note on Jean Toomer's Marriage to Margery Latimer." *CLA Journal* 17: 474-79.

MacKethan, Lucinda H. "Jean Toomer's *Cane*: A Pastoral Problem." *Mississippi Quarterly* 28: 423-34.

Martin, Odette C. "*Cane*: Method and Myth." *Obsidian* 2,i: 5-20.

Mason, Clifford. "Jean Toomer's Black Authenticity." *Black World* 20,i: 70-76.

Matthews, George C. "Toomer's *Cane*: The Artist and His World." *CLA Journal* 17: 543-59.

Munson, Gorham B. "The Significance of Jean Toomer." *Opportunity* 10,viii: 252.

Quirk, Tom, and Fleming, Robert E. "Jean Toomer's Contributions to the New Mexico Sentinel." *CLA Journal* 19: 524-32.

Rankin, William. "Ineffability in the Fiction of Jean Toomer and Katherine Mansfield." In *Renaissance and Modern: Essays in Honor of Edwin M. Moseley*, edited by Murray J. Levitt, pp. 160-71. Saratoga Springs, N.Y.: Skidmore College, 1975. [Available from Syracuse University Press.]

Reilly, John M. "Jean Toomer: An Annotated Checklist of Criticism." *Resources for American Literary Studies* 4: 27-56.

_____. "The Search for Black Redemption: Jean Toomer's *Cane*." *Studies in the Novel* (North Texas State University) 2 (1970): 312-24.

Richmond, Merle. "Jean Toomer and Margery Latimer." *CLA Journal* 18: 300.

Riley, Roberta. "Search for Identity and Artistry." *CLA Journal* 17: 480-85.

Rosenfeld, Paul. "Jean Toomer." *Men Seen*. New York: Dial, 1925.

Scruggs, Charles W. "Jean Toomer: Fugitive." *American Literature* 47: 84-96.

_____. "The Mark of Cain and the Redemption of Art: A Study in Theme and Structure of Jean Toomer's *Cane*." *American Literature* 44: 276-91.

Solard, Alain. "The Impossible Unity: Jean Toomer's 'Kabnis.' " *Myth and Ideology in American Culture*. (Cahiers Américains 1) Villeneuve d'Ascq: Université de Lille III, 1975, pp. 175-94.

Spoffurd, William K. "The Unity of Part One of Jean Toomer's *Cane*." *Markham Review* 3: 58-60.

Stein, Marian L. "The Poet Observer and Form in Jean Toomer's *Cane*." *Markham Review* 2: 64-65.

Taylor, Clyde. "The Second Coming of Jean Toomer." *Obsidian* 1,iii: 37-57.

Thompson, Larry E. "Jean Toomer: As Modern Man." *Renaissance* 2: 7-10.

Turner, Darwin T. Introduction to *Cane*. New York: Liveright, 1975. .

———. "An Intersection of Paths: Correspondence between Jean Toomer and Sherwood Anderson." *CLA Journal* 17: 455-67..

———. *In a Minor Chord: Three Afro-American Writers and Their Search for Identity*. Carbondale: Southern Illinois University Press, 1971.

Twombly, Robert C. "A Disciple's Odyssey: Jean Toomer's Gurdjieffian Career." *Prospects: An Annual Journal of American Cultural Studies* 2: 437-62.

Van Mel, Kay R. "Primitivism and Intellect in Toomer's *Cane* and McKay's *Banana Bottom*: The Need for an Integrated Black Consciousness." *Negro American Literature Forum* 10: 48-52.

Waldron, Edward E. "The Search for Identity in Jean Toomer's 'Esther.' " *CLA Journal* 14: 274-76.

Watkins, Patricia. "Is There a Unifying Theme in *Cane*?" *CLA Journal* 15: 303-5.

Westerfield, Hargis. "Jean Toomer's 'Fern': A Mythical Dimension." *CLA Journal* 14: 274-76.

Withrow, Dolly. "Cutting through Shade." *CLA Journal* 21: 98-99.

CHARLES W. CHESNUTT

Andrews, William L. " 'Baxter's Procrustes': Some More Light on the Biographical Connection." *Black American Literature Forum* 11: 75-78.

———. "Chesnutt's Patesville: The Presence and Influence of the Past in *The House behind the Cedars*." *CLA Journal* 15: 284-94.

———. "The Significance of Charles W. Chesnutt's 'Conjure Stories.' " *Southern Literary Journal* 7,i: 78-99.

———. "The Works of Charles W. Chesnutt: A Checklist." *Bulletin of Bibliography* 33: 45-47, 52.

———. "A Reconsideration of Charles Waddell Chesnutt: Pioneer of the Color Line." *CLA Journal* 19: 136-51.

———. "Charles Waddell Chesnutt: An Essay in Bibliography." *Resources for American Literary Study* 6: 3-22.

Baldwin, Richard E. "The Art of *The Conjure Woman*." *American Literature* 43: 385-98.

Britt, David D. "Chesnutt's Conjure Tales: What You See Is What You Get." *CLA Journal* 15: 269-83.

Cunningham, Joan. "Secondary Studies on the Fiction of Charles W. Chesnutt." *Bulletin of Bibliography* 33: 48-52.

———. "The Uncollected Short Stories of Charles Waddell Chesnutt."
    Negro American Literature Forum 9: 57-58.
Dixon, Melvin. "The Teller as Folk Trickster in Chesnutt's *The Conjure
    Woman*." *CLA Journal* 18: 186-97.
Elder, Arlene A. "Chesnutt on Washington: An Essential Ambivalence."
    Phylon 38: 1-8.
Ellison, Carter W., and Metcalf, E. W., Jr. *Charles W. Chesnutt: A
    Reference Guide*. Boston: G. K. Hall, 1972.
Farnsworth, Robert M. "Charles Chesnutt and the Color Line." In *Minor
    American Novelists*, edited by Charles A. Hoyt, pp. 28-40. Carbon-
    dale: Southern Illinois University Press, 1971.
———, ed. Introduction to *The Conjure Woman* by Charles W. Chesnutt.
    Ann Arbor: University of Michigan Press, 1969.
Flusche, Michael. "On the Color Line: Charles Waddell Chesnutt." *North
    Carolina Historical Review* 53: 1-24.
Giles, James R. "Chesnutt's Primus and Annie: A Contemporary View of
    The Conjure Woman." *Markham Review* 3: 46-49.
Heermance, J. Noel. *Charles W. Chesnutt: America's First Great Black
    Novelist*. Hamden, Conn.: Archon, 1973.
Hemenway, Robert. "The Functions of Folklore in Charles Chesnutt's *The
    Conjure Woman*." *Journal of the Folklore Institute* 13: 283-309.
———. " 'Baxter's Procrustes': Irony and Protest." *CLA Journal* 18:
    172-85.
———. "Gothic Sociology: Charles Chesnutt and the Gothic Mode."
    Studies in the Literary Imagination (Georgia State College) 7,i:
    101-19.
Hovet, Theodore R. "Chesnutt's 'The Goophered Grapevine' as Social
    Criticism." *Negro American Literature Forum* 7: 86-88.
Jackson, Wendell. "Charles W. Chesnutt's Outrageous Fortune." *CLA
    Journal* 20: 195-204.
Lee, A. Robert. " 'The Desired State of Feeling': Charles Waddell Ches-
    nutt and Afro-American Literary Tradition." *Durham University
    Journal* 35: 163-70.
Mixon, Wayne. "The Unfulfilled Dream: Charles W. Chesnutt and the
    New South Movement." *Southern Humanities Review* 9: 23-33.
Muhlenfeld, Elisabeth. "Charles Waddell Chesnutt." *American Literary
    Realism* 8: 220-22.
Oden, Gloria C. "Chesnutt's Conjure as African Survival." *MELUS* 5,i:
    38-48.
Ogunyemi, Chikwenye Okonjo. "The Africanness of *The Conjure Woman*

and *Feather Woman of the Jungle." Ariel: A Review of International English Literature* 8,ii: 17-30.

Reilly, John M. "The Dilemma in Chesnutt's *The Marrow of Tradition." Phylon* 32: 31-38.

Render, Sylvia L., ed. *The Short Fiction of Charles W. Chesnutt.* Washington, D.C.: Howard University Press, 1973.

Sedlack, Robert P. "The Evolution of Charles Chesnutt's *The House behind the Cedars." CLA Journal* 19: 123-35.

Selke, Hartmut K. "Charles Waddell Chesnutt: 'The Sheriff's Children' (1889)." In *The Black American Short Story in the Twentieth Century: A Collection of Critical Essays*, edited by Peter Bruck, pp. 21-38. Amsterdam: Grüner, 1977.

Smith, Robert A. "A Pioneer Black Writer and the Problems of Discrimination and Miscegenation." *Costerus* 9: 181-85.

Taxel, Joel. "Charles Waddell Chesnutt's Sambo: Myth and Reality." *Negro American Literature Forum* 9: 105-8.

Terry, Eugene. "Charles W. Chesnutt: A Victim of the Color Line." *Contributions to Black Studies* (Amherst) 1 (1977): 13-44.

Turner, Darwin. Introduction to C. W. Chesnutt, *The House behind the Cedars.* New York: Collier, 1970.

Walcott, Ronald. "Chesnutt's 'The Sheriff's Children' as Parable." *Negro American Literature Forum* 7: 83-85.

Wintz, Cary D. "Race and Realism in the Fiction of Charles W. Chesnutt." *Ohio History* 81: 122-30.

Index

Note: **Boldface** page numbers indicate the location of the major discussion of a work.

About the Author

Donald B. Gibson is Professor of English at Rutgers College, Rutgers University. His critical works include *The Fiction of Stephen Crane* and articles in many journals. He edited the well-known *Five Black Writers: Essays on Wright, Ellison, Baldwin, Hughes, and LeRoi Jones* and *Modern Black Poets: A Collection of Critical Essays.*